"Living in a house without utilities is not too different from living in a cave. The requirements for surviving a storm in a stranded car are the same as those for weathering a cold blast in the back-woods. The human necessities for a family living in a Chicago suburb are the same as those for an Alaskan Eskimo or a vagrant on the streets of San Francisco. Wherever we go...the veneer that separates modern civilization from the wilderness of our ancestors is very thin. All of us have experienced moments when the lights flicker and we are plunged into the darkness of the past. In those moments we have only our own resources. We become islands. And without our accustomed connections, some of us survive and some of us perish."

—TOM BROWN, JR.

Also available in this Series:

Tom Brown's Field Guide to Wilderness Survival

Tom Brown's Field Guide to Nature Observation and Tracking

Tom Brown's Field Guide to Living with the Earth

Tom Brown's Guide to Wild Edible and Medicinal Plants

Tom Brown's Field Guide to the Forgotten Wilderness

Tom Brown's Field Guide to Nature and Survival for Children

TOM BROWN'S FIELD GUIDE TO CITY AND SUBURBAN SURVIVAL

ABOUT THE AUTHOR

At the age of eight, Tom Brown, Jr., began to learn tracking and hunting from Stalking Wolf, a displaced Apache Indian. Today Brown is an experienced woodsman whose extraordinary skill has saved many lives, including his own. He manages and teaches one of the largest wilderness and survival schools in the U.S. and has instructed many law enforcement agencies and rescue teams.

TOM BROWN'S FIELD GUIDE TO CITY AND SUBURBAN SURVIVAL

Tom Brown, Jr., with Brandt Morgan

Illustrated by Heather Bolyn

BERKLEY BOOKS, NEW YORK

32 00658

THE BERKLEY PUBLISHING GROUP
Published by the Penguin Group
Penguin Group (USA) Inc.
375 Hudson Street, New York, New York 10014, USA
Penguin Group (Canada), 90 Eglinton Avenue East, Suite 700, Toronto, Ontario M4P 2Y3, Canada
(a division of Pearson Penguin Canada Inc.)
Penguin Books Ltd., 80 Strand, London WC2R 0RL, England
Penguin Group Ireland, 25 St. Stephen's Green, Dublin 2, Ireland (a division of Penguin Books Ltd.)
Penguin Group (Australia), 250 Camberwell Road, Camberwell, Victoria 3124, Australia
(a division of Pearson Australia Group Pty. Ltd.)
Penguin Books India Pvt. Ltd., 11 Community Centre, Panchsheel Park, New Delhi—110 017, India
Penguin Group (NZ), 67 Apollo Drive, Rosedale, North Shore 0632, New Zealand
(a division of Pearson New Zealand Ltd.)
Penguin Books (South Africa) (Pty.) Ltd., 24 Sturdee Avenue, Rosebank, Johannesburg 2196,
South Africa

Penguin Books Ltd., Registered Offices: 80 Strand, London WC2R 0RL, England

A Berkley Book / published by arrangement with the author

This Field Guide contains material, knowledge of which could be invaluable in dealing with a sudden emergency—an unexpected "survival situation" when knowledge of fundamental survival techniques could be life-saving.

Neither the publisher nor the author claim that all techniques in this Guide will ensure survival in all situations. Some of the techniques and instructions described in the Guide may be inappropriate for persons suffering from certain physical conditions or handicaps. Misuse of any of the techniques described in the Guide could cause serious personal injury or property damage, for which the publisher and author disclaim any liability.

Chart on pages 23 and 24 reprinted with permission from *Journal of Psychosomatic Research*, volume II, Drs. T. H. Holmes and R. H. Rahe, "The Social Readjustment Rating Scale," copyright 1967, Pergamon Press, Ltd.

TOM BROWN'S FIELD GUIDE TO CITY AND SUBURBAN SURVIVAL

PRINTING HISTORY
Berkley trade paperback edition / May 1984

ISBN: 978-0-425-09172-2

PRINTED IN THE UNITED STATES OF AMERICA

30   29   28   27   26   25   24   23   22   21   20   19

TOM BROWN'S DEDICATION:
To Frank and Karen Sherwood
For their dedication to the greater vision.

BRANDT MORGAN'S DEDICATION:
To Cindy Lewis, for contributions both in print and between the lines.

A SPECIAL THANKS TO:
John Bierlein, Dave Boyd, Rusty Brennan, Jim Brown, Tom Brown, Sr.,
Jon Clark, Phil Cogan, Mike Donahoe, Sid Drell, Loren Foss, Jean
Gruver, Petra Illig, Charlie and Judy Herring, Charlie Johnson, John
Lewis, Randy Matthews, Dick and Vicki Mills, Arthur and Ruth Morgan,
Laurie Schultz, Jim Shedd, Frank and Karen Sherwood, Bob Smith,
Billie Wiliamson, and Wanda Wonosowicz. Wayne and Linda Blais,
Randy and Paulla Miller, Jim Spina, and to Eric E. Herline for technical
drawings.

CONTENTS

TOM BROWN'S FIELD GUIDE TO CITY AND SUBURBAN SURVIVAL

INTRODUCTION

Many residents of cities and suburbs think they are safe from the ravages of weather and immune to the environmental emergencies that affect people in more isolated areas. Yet every year, cities and towns undergo the same batterings that affect the farther reaches. Rainstorms, floods, blizzards, cold, heat, hurricanes, tornadoes, earthquakes, and tidal waves remind us that no place, no matter how civilized, is immune to the grand violence of nature.

Nor are we immune to the failures of technology. When the electricity goes off, we feel strangely cut off and alone. Gone in an instant are accustomed sources of heat, light, communication, entertainment, and many other fragile strands that connect us with the web of life and the world at large. When our cars run out of gas, we feel stranded not only physically but emotionally. Momentarily we are forced to deal with distance and time in a completely unaccustomed way. At times like this, we more fully realize our human frailties and how heavy a price we pay for our comforts.

An unseen part of that price is our inner security. While embracing the wonders of modern technology, few of us stop to acknowledge the personal strengths we so willingly leave behind. Of what value are self-confidence, resourcefulness, adaptability, and physical and mental health? They are beyond price. Without them, life in the modern world offers only a false sense of security—a veneer of easy living so thin it rips apart at the slightest tug.

Personally, I have never lived in a city or suburb. I was brought up on the outskirts of Toms River, New Jersey (a town of 4,000 people then), and I spent most of my boyhood and youth in the maze of wild sand trails, swamps, and scrub trees known as the Pine Barrens. My primary occupation since 1978 has been the teaching of nature observation and wilderness survival skills. However, I have also spent a considerable amount of time in most of the major cities of the United States, and wherever I go I habitually ask myself what I would do if I were to find myself in a survival situation.

Some of the answers come from the practicality I absorbed from my parents. Others come from applications of wilderness survival techniques taught to me by Stalking Wolf, an Apache Indian elder and scout. Still others come from unlikely but enterprising people I have met in my travels—people who by choice or necessity have adapted to environments very different from the ones I am used to and who have their own wisdom to pass on.

Of course, there are important differences between wilderness and city survival. In the wilds we may be completely isolated, while in the city we are more likely to have the support of family and friends. In the woods we may have little more than a knife and the provisions on our backs, while in the city we may have access to an array of tools and survival resources.

There are other differences, too. But the commonalities are much more striking. The requirements for survival while living in a house without utilities are not too different from those while living in a cave. The requirements for surviving a storm in a stranded car are similar to those for weathering a cold blast in the backwoods. The necessities for a family in a Chicago suburb are the same as those for an Alaskan Eskimo or a vagrant on the streets of San Francisco. Wherever we go, survival is basically the same.

However, survival preparedness and response are much less natural for urban people. Shelter, water, fire, and food are so easily acquired in the city and suburbs that we rarely see them as necessities until they are no longer available. Our urban shelters are equipped with a maze of wires, pipes, and dimly-understood mechanisms that provide for every want and need. The flick of a switch gives heat. The turn of a faucet gives water. The ring of a cash register gives food. We forget that these switches and buttons are tiny parts of complicated systems. And we don't always know how to provide for ourselves when such systems break down.

How should we prepare for a hurricane or snowstorm? What should we do during a gas shortage or a trucker's strike? How can we stay warm when the heat goes off? Where would we find food and water if stranded in a remote area in our cars? How would we cope in the aftermath of a major disaster? Most of us don't know the answers to these questions because we have forgotten to ask them. To our ancestors every day was an uncertain struggle. Survival was a way of life. Today our instincts are dulled and our survival knowledge has trailed off like the vapors from a steam engine. Most of us have traded our natural heritage for comfort and convenience.

I do not mean to belittle the advantages of modern technology. I appreciate them as much as anyone. My point is that while living in a largely human-made world, we should never forget our origins or the origins of all that we depend on. Survival knowledge may seem obsolete, but it is still the basis of our existence. The city is tied to the country through a complicated system of highways and skyways, each providing food, water, or power like so many life-support lines attached to an astronaut on a foreign planet. For the most part, our machines are fueled on ancient life. Our lives are linked to blades of grass. We cannot push a button or turn a key without leverage from our roots in the earth.

People often speak of security today as though it could be bought

by anyone who had enough money. However, I have yet to hear of anyone who has bought his or her way out of a survival situation. Survival respects no social status. No matter how rich we are, we cannot buy a cup of water on a desert. On the other hand, if we know how to find water, we will not fear going thirsty. No amount of insurance can guarantee that we won't lose our homes or jobs, but if we know how to fend for ourselves, we will be able to enjoy our lives whatever the outward circumstances. Money, insurance, and social status cannot bring us inner peace or compensate for what we lack in our hearts and minds. True security can only be found within.

The veneer that separates modern civilization from the wilderness of our ancestors is very thin. All of us have experienced moments when the lights flicker and we are temporarily plunged into the darkness of the past. In these moments we have only our own resources. We become islands. And without our accustomed connections, some of us survive and some of us perish. All too often, though, I hear of urban tragedies that could have been avoided through an application of common sense and simple survival skills.

This book is in large part an explanation of the principles of survival and how to adapt them to life in and around the city. One of my hopes is that the survival techniques explained here will help to prevent some of the hundreds of deaths that occur in city environments each year for lack of knowledge, judgment and understanding. I also hope that by learning how to cope with emergency situations, many people will gain more respect for their own resourcefulness and adaptability, thereby better enabling themselves to cope with problems and discomforts that arise in daily living.

However, the last thing I want to do is dwell unnecessarily on disasters and discomforts. The city is a complex and fascinating place. In its own way it is as full of excitement and wonder as the wilderness. Many would argue that it is even more exciting and wonderful. Like the wilderness, it should never be seen by those who live there as a place to be feared, tolerated, or endured, but rather as a place to live fully and joyfully.

For this reason, I have not limited the discussions in this book to emergencies and disasters. I have put just as much (if not more) emphasis on understanding the city environment, living frugally and thoughtfully, knowing how things work, gaining confidence and control in one's life, and becoming familiar with the machines and systems that are so much a part of it. This, too, is a logical extension of the survival philosophy. For survivalists do not feel like victims or cogs in a machine. They feel at home in their environment, wherever it might be. They are not apathetic or fatalistic about life, but actively and optimistically involved in it. And above all, they have a strong conviction that their involvement can make a difference, both to their own well-being and to the well-being of others.

Today there are endless opportunities for the expression of the survival philosophy. The world is crying for wisdom, leadership, and active concern. Never before has there been such an urgent need for the social involvement of individual citizens. Planet Earth today is more than ever a global village where individual thoughts and actions expand like ripples, ultimately washing up on distant shores and permeating the lives of others. There is no limit to the effect an individual can have. For this reason, it is all the more important for city people to have a sense of purpose and fulfillment in their lives. We must remember that our individual lives are not separate from our collective life as a species, or from the fate of the earth as a whole.

Organization of This Book

This book is divided into eight chapters, roughly organized into the areas of primary concern for city and suburban emergencies.

Chapter 1 talks about the all-important survival attitude and how to stay mentally and physically prepared for all kinds of crises. It also tells how to use the survival attitude to create a healthier environment, reduce stress, deal more effectively with others, and get more out of daily living.

Chapter 2 tells how to make a variety of survival shelters in the home, at work, on the street, and in the car. It includes the basic principles common to all shelters, plus discussions of hypothermia, insulation, clothing, and many commonsense tips that could help to keep a person warm and dry or even save a life.

Chapter 3 briefly explains the organization of urban water systems and what to do if they break down. Included are tips on how to collect emergency water from reservoirs in the home, from rooftops, from dew on the ground, and through a variety of simple distillation methods. This chapter also explains how to treat questionable water and store it safely for long periods of time.

Chapter 4 deals with the critical subject of heat and light. It explains the magical workings of electricity, outlines the usual ways we provide heat and light in our cities, and offers some simple suggestions for cutting down on energy costs in the home. It also discusses ways of starting fires without matches and offers many heating and lighting alternatives, from makeshift lanterns to hot rocks and wood stoves.

Chapter 5 talks about food. Among other things, it discusses buying, storing, cleaning, growing, dehydrating, raising, gathering, hunting, and trapping. Also included is a section on unconventional food sources that should be remembered in a survival situation.

Chapter 6 deals with urban crime and what to do about it. It focuses on commonsense methods of crime prevention that can be employed in the home, at work, on the street, and in the car. It explains differences between various kinds of criminals, from burglars and pickpockets to muggers and rapists, including how to avoid them and what to do if confronted by them. It also tells how to keep your children from becoming crime victims.

Chapter 7 talks about the weather. As a prelude to the natural disasters described in Chapter 8, it briefly explains our global weather system, how to see more signs in the skies, how to predict the weather through personal observation, and how the weather is affected by the city itself.

Chapter 8 deals with a wide variety of mostly natural disasters, from hurricanes and floods to earthquakes and tidal waves. It briefly explains the origins of each problem, how to be prepared for the problems, and how to cope with them. This final chapter also includes a short section on the ever-present threat of nuclear war. Since this is the one potential disaster for which we would be entirely responsible and from which there might be no recovery, all the emphasis is placed on prevention rather than on preparation and survival.

How to Use This Book

As with the other volumes in this series, I suggest you use this book as a working manual. First read it clear through to get an overview of the subject. Then study and discuss it with friends and family. As you read, pay special attention to the survival attitude and the things that particularly apply to you and your area. But don't treat this book as the answer to all your survival problems. Use it as a stimulus for further study. Read other books. Take courses in first aid, auto mechanics, and other subjects that will add to your storehouse of survival knowledge.

And practice, practice, practice. The information in this book can help you only if you make it a part of your life. Do whatever is necessary to prepare for the most likely emergencies in your area. Shore up the house, fix the car, find the safest evacuation route, set aside emergency supplies. Discuss with others what you'd do in the event of an earthquake, a flood, a power outage, or a theft. Better yet, set up survival scenarios and act them out. Try living for several days without electricity. Try evacuating the house in three hours. Try subsisting on survival rations. In the end, the practical applications you dream up and carry out will be worth more than all the survival reading you'll ever do. This is as it should be, because in the end survival depends entirely on you.

1
BODY AND MIND

Two days after I had begun jotting down notes and ideas for this book, the Central Atlantic states (New York, New Jersey, Pennsylvania, and Delaware) were hit with the biggest snowstorm in fifty years. I was out on the Jersey coast when I heard the announcement of an impending storm, and late that evening I went into the Pine Barrens to feel the storm's pulse. The radio had forecast only a few inches of snow, but there was no doubt it was going to be a big one. In spite of twinkling stars in a clear midnight sky, the wind brought messages of brewing turmoil. Sensing what was to come, the animals had gone into a frenzy of feeding and preparation, shoring up their energies for a major snowfall.

By contrast, life in the cities went on as before. It was a Thursday night, and most people continued with only slightly altered plans for the last workday of the week and the two-day vacation ahead. The snow started about 5 a.m. Friday, with a light flurry that caused no great alarm. Commuters went to work as usual, assuming the storm would cause no great inconvenience. As the day wore on, though, the storm became spectacular. It was laced with thunder and lightning and fueled by winds up to forty-five miles per hour. It did not stop for more than thirty hours.

Long before it was over, the storm had immobilized the greater part of four states. Snow fell at rates up to three inches an hour, leaving a blanket up to twenty-four inches thick and drifts up to nine feet deep in places. In major cities such as Philadelphia, Newark, and New York, there were limited power and water outages. Most transportation was brought to a complete standstill. Thousands of motorists were stranded on state highways. Hundreds were stuck in bus and subway terminals. La Guardia, Kennedy, and Newark airports were shut down for three days, leaving thousands more stranded in plane terminals without hotel accommodations. The National Guard and emergency services frantically battled the storm with snowplows, to little avail.

The Blizzard of '83, as it was called, was not a disaster by any stretch of the imagination. But it was a widespread emergency, and it is rather typical of the kinds of situations that every year immobilize cities and present urban dwellers with serious challenges to comfort, security, and even survival.

During the storm, it was particularly interesting to see how varied were people's reactions. Human emotions ran the gamut. Some people felt isolated and unsure, while others celebrated and cheered. Some motorists abandoned their cars, while others anxiously waited for help.

17

Some people fumed, while others were patient and understanding. Insults and blaring horns mixed with reassurances and acts of kindness. Some people pitched in to help and others became opportunists. Gangs broke into stores and robbed stranded motorists. Opportunists asked (and got) outrageous prices for shoveling snow and wiping windshields. And through it all, children threw snowballs and sledded right alongside the snowplows.

The reasons for these different reactions are as varied as the reactions themselves. However, there are some common denominators worth noting. One is that society continued much as before, but with all of its strengths and weaknesses greatly magnified. This is typical of emergency and survival situations. Heroes and villains appear in equal numbers. Another observation is that most of those who were able to help others had first taken care of their own needs. But by far the most important observation is that most reactions to the storm were determined by attitude. And attitude is governed by choice, not chance.

Preparedness

The choice of how we will react to an emergency or survival situation is determined long before the occurrence of a threatening event. In fact, our reaction is in large part the sum total of the choices and decisions we have made all our lives, from basic decisions about where to live to the choices that determine our knowledge, physical condition, and character.

Good Health

One of the first requirements for success in a survival or other stress situation is a healthy body and mind. This lesson is very clear in nature, for any wild animal that is unable to provide for itself quickly weakens and becomes prey for other animals. Fortunately "survival of the fittest" does not apply so starkly to human societies. We try to care for those who are unable to provide for their own needs. But most of us can control our fitness, and for many of us it is not what it should be.

Physical Fitness. Through apathy and easy living, tens of thousands of people in modern society have let their bodies go. Thousands more are not even aware of their physical capabilities. Under normal circumstances, flabbiness is all that is required. But survival and stress situations make heavy demands. Many people who found themselves stranded in their cars in the Blizzard of '83 did not risk walking even short distances to safety because they were not sure their legs could take them that far. During and after the storm, approximately a dozen people died of heart attacks while shoveling snow.

It is important to know our limits, and it is just as important to keep ourselves in good shape. In our not-too-distant past, we naturally maintained our bodies through the demanding activities of hunting, gathering, farming, and foot travel. Physical exercise was built into our daily routines. Today, in largely urbanized, sedentary environments, most of us need some form of sport or regular exercise to maintain a good biological balance.

There are many ways modern people can stay in shape. The opportunities for healthful exercise are almost as vast and varied as the choices in a modern supermarket. People who like fast, strenuous action can take up racquet sports such as handball, squash, or tennis. Those who like solitude and fresh air can try walking, hiking, or jogging. Weight lifting and bike riding have become particularly popular in recent years, as have a wide variety of martial arts such as judo, karate, and kung fu. Another demanding but vastly healthful exercise is aerobics. Whatever your frame of body and mind, regular exercise will improve it.

There are also many things we can do around our homes and offices to improve our fitness. For one, we can stop trying to make things easier. We can use hand can openers instead of electric ones. We can mix batter with spoons instead of egg beaters. We can walk up stairs instead of taking elevators. We can take frequent breaks for relaxation and stretching. We can walk or ride bicycles on short errands instead of driving cars.

While I'm on the subject, I would like to put in a special word for walking. Walking is one of the best all-around exercises there is, and it is especially healthful if it's done right. But most of us have become sloppy about walking. No longer do we have to worry about tripping over rocks and roots, so we don't lift and place our feet with as much care as our ancestors did. Many of us don't even look where we're going.

Stand on a street corner and watch people walking sometime. In the city, most people lurch and clomp along the sidewalk with their heads down at a forty-five degree angle and their feet splayed out like ducks. They come down heel first, throwing their bodies forward with each step. This leaves them constantly off balance as one foot tries to catch up with the other. I call this gait the city shuffle, and it is the root of many evils. Among them are bad posture, aching backs, flabby thighs, baggy buttocks, fallen arches, weak ankles, and aching feet.

You can cure many of these ills by returning to a more natural walk—or, as I call it, the fox walk. To imitate the artful fox, hold your head high and look straight ahead. This automatically straightens the back and shoulders. Walk not just with the calves, but with the thighs and buttocks, lifting the feet instead of swinging them. Instead of walking duckfooted, keep the feet parallel. Rather than coming down on the heel, come down on the outside of the foot and roll to the inside. Keep each step balanced and controlled. You should be able to stop at any time without falling over.

It is no coincidence that most professional athletes, including dancers and martial arts experts, use the fox walk. It strengthens the feet, straightens the back, gives added stability, and promotes quiet, confident movement. It may seem a little awkward at first, especially on a city sidewalk, but it's worth practicing. In time, you'll develop a healthful rhythm and flow down the street more comfortably than ever. You'll also be much more aware of what's going on around you, which can also be of great benefit to your health (see "Crime," page 159).

Preventive Medicine. Another thing we can do for our health is to take more responsibility for it. Certainly it is important to consult a doctor for regular checkups and body maintenance, but many of us put far too much reliance on cures and "quick fixes" and far too little on preventive medicine. Every year we consume mountains of tranquilizers, pain killers, and pep pills, not realizing that the source of many of our discomforts is in ourselves. In the short run, it may seem easier to take a pill than to change our life-styles and easier to rely on authorities than our own good sense. But the dividends we receive in taking responsibility for our health (or anything else) are all out of proportion to the effort expended.

For example, every year American surgeons perform about five hundred thousand coronary bypass operations. The need for most of these could have been prevented with regular exercise. In fact, recent studies have shown that even half an hour of vigorous exercise three or four times a week can improve cardiovascular fitness up to one hundred percent.

Most people pay little attention to such things until the situation becomes critical, but even then there is hope. I know a woman whose doctor told her she had a terminal heart condition and would probably not live more than a few more years. The woman sold her car and began a regular walking program. She has been walking several hours a day now for over twenty years and is still going strong. In addition to improving her health, she has added a new dimension of independence to her life. Largely through positive visualization techniques, another woman I know cured herself of "incurable" cancer. Her life was so transformed in the process that she decided to write a book about her journey back to health. She plans to call it "Cancer Saved My Life."

There are many good books that can help us take more responsibility for our health and reduce our doctor bills in the process. One useful reference is *The Well Body Book*, an easy-to-read manual of preventive medicine and commonsense remedies to minor ailments, by Hal Bennett and Michael Samuels. Another, which deals primarily with the healing power of the mind, is *Getting Well Again*, by Carl Simonton. Health books abound, and I heartily recommend a trip to your local library or bookstore to explore the possibilities. One word of warning, though: be skeptical of fad diets and other instant solutions to long-term problems. There is no shortcut to good health. It must be made an integral part of your life.

Good Nutrition. Physical and mental health are also closely related to what we eat. An animal in the wilderness instinctively knows what foods it needs to maintain its health. We have these instincts, too, but often they are clouded by habit, convenience, and the incessant urgings of advertisers. A general commonsense rule is to get plenty of fresh fruit, nuts, greens, lean meat, fish, and milk products and to stay away from anything that has more than three ingredients you can't pronounce. (If you are a vegetarian, you will have to plan carefully to make sure you're getting enough protein, and this may not be possible in a serious survival situation.) It is also a good idea to know where your food comes from, what pesticides or additives have been used in its production, and what foods you can eat with minimal danger of long-term effects.

In the wilderness one of the first rules of survival is not to eat anything you cannot positively identify. It often strikes me as ironic that in the city we ignore this rule almost every day. To a great extent, we have to simply trust that those who have grown, prepared, and packaged our food have some concern for our health—and by law they must. But ultimately we are responsible for our own safety. We should be aware that the greater the distance our food has traveled from its origins and the more processes it has gone through, the less nutritive value it is likely to contain and the more danger there may be in eating it. To these cautions I would only add, "Eat to live, don't live to eat." That way you'll be ready for a survival situation whenever it comes up. (For specific information on survival nutrition, see "Food," page 127.)

Dealing with Stress. Mental health, too, is something to consider when preparing for emergencies, and dealing with stress in particular is something worth practicing. Fortunately or unfortunately, most of us have ample opportunity to do so. Modern life is a veritable testing and proving ground for stress management, and both the experts and the general public are learning more about it every year.

Stress is an unavoidable part of life. We face it in our homes, at work, and even at play. We have to cope with it at every stage of our lives, from childhood and adolescence to adulthood and old age. If managed well, stress can be a great boon that spurs us on to achieve our goals and to live more fully. If poorly managed, though, it can cause a host of problems, from chronic anxiety to ulcers and mental breakdowns.

Stress itself is not necessarily unhealthy; it is our reactions to it that cause the problems. A stressful situation for one person may be a stimulating experience for another. One person may enjoy loud rock music while another can hardly stand it. One person may get the jitters thinking about giving a speech while another sees speechmaking as an exciting opportunity. Even positive experiences cause stress.

In large part our reactions to stress depend on what we're used to. A new job may be unusually stressful at first because of the unaccustomed demands it places on us. But with time we may get a feeling for what to do and find it very stimulating and satisfying. It is the same thing with survival. A person who has been through an emergency situation, or even rehearsed for it, will react more positively to survival stress than a person who hasn't.

Stress management is a popular term in cities today. To alleviate the things that go wrong with our bodies and minds, we try everything from aspirin and tranquilizers to biofeedback machines and psychiatrists. All of these things have their places, and I don't mean to make light of the good they can do if wisely used. But again, as with so many other aspects of life, we often look outside ourselves for the answers to our problems. Most often the real answers lie within.

Stress management begins with a sensitivity to our own minds and bodies. It begins by standing aside and looking at our situation and asking ourselves, "Why am I reacting this way?" and "What can I do about it?" In some cases, it may mean simply getting used to an unfamiliar situation. In others it may mean cutting out some activities so that we can effectively deal with more important things.

One of the most interesting discoveries researchers have made regarding stress is that those who have a feeling of control in their lives experience far fewer stressful effects. People who have chosen to work in noisy offices and who know they can leave at any time do not get nearly as upset as those who feel they must simply endure the discomfort. Similarly, people tend to accept stressful situations much more gracefully if they feel there is a purpose to them. The pain and shock of a necessary and carefully planned surgery is far less stressful than an equal amount of pain and shock caused by a sudden accident.

One of the greatest tools in stress management is advance planning. This can be done quite deliberately, simply by monitoring the number and type of changes in our lives. In a study first published in the *Journal of Psychosomatic Research* in 1967, Drs. T.H. Holmes and R.H. Rahe discovered that people who experienced many life changes over a short period of time were much more likely to get seriously ill or injured than those who experienced very few changes. Surprisingly, it made little difference whether those changes were positive or negative. A marriage was as stressful as a broken leg. A business promotion was as emotionally difficult as dealing with bothersome in-laws.

As part of their study, these doctors developed a Social Readjustment Rating Scale so that people could assess changes in their lives and plan ahead to minimize illness. Take a look at the chart below and add up your own stress points for changes that have occurred in your life over the last year. You start with a ten-percent chance of serious illness, whether you have any points or not (just through virtue of being alive). If your total is less than 150, you have about a 33-percent chance of winding up in the hospital during the next two years. If your total is between 150 and 300, your chances of serious illness or injury increase to 50 percent. If your total is more than 300, your chances of a serious health problem over the next two years rise to as much as 90 percent.

Life Event	Points
1. Death of spouse	100
2. Divorce	73
3. Marital separation	65
4. Jail term	63
5. Death of close family member	63
6. Personal injury or illness	53
7. Marriage	50
8. Fired from job	47
9. Marital reconciliation	45
10. Retirement	45
11. Change in health of family member	44
12. Pregnancy	40
13. Sex difficulties	39
14. Gain of new family member	39
15. Business readjustment	39
16. Change in financial state	38
17. Death of close friend	37
18. Change to different line of work	36
19. Change in arguments with spouse	35
20. Mortgage or loan for major purchase (home, etc.)	31
21. Foreclosure of mortgage or loan	30
22. Change in work responsibilities	29
23. Son or daughter leaving home	29
24. Trouble with in-laws	29
25. Outstanding personal achievement	28

Aside from rationing changes in our lives, there are many other things we can do to minimize the effects of stress. Exercise is a wonderful antidote. Simply walking for fifteen minutes can relieve tremendous amounts of pent-up energy. So can working in the yard or doing relaxation exercises.

Relaxation. One such exercise is the tension release. First lie or sit in a comfortable position (preferably with loose-fitting clothing) and allow the mind to drift. Then, beginning with the feet, systematically tense and release each muscle in the body. Concentrate on feet, calves, thighs, buttocks, abdomen, back, arms, chest, neck, and face, one muscle group at a time. Then tense the entire body for a few seconds and relax completely. Let yourself sink into the chair or melt into the ground. Feel the tension draining away.

If you find this exercise helpful, try a variation in which you imagine each muscle group becoming very heavy. Repeat in your mind for twenty or thirty seconds, "My right foot is heavy . . . My right foot is heavy," while imagining it sinking into the floor. Then do the same with the other parts of your body. In time you will find you can control your feelings to a remarkable degree. The reason for this is that to a great extent we act as we think. The body follows the lead of the mind. If the mind is agitated and troubled, the body is nervous and tense. If the mind is quiet and calm, the body is also tranquil. (Invariably I run into skeptics who discount this body-mind connection, and when I do, I ask them to vividly imagine cutting and squeezing a ripe, juicy lemon. Within seconds most of them are salivating.)

Many of our stress reactions are habitual, and with practice we can short-circuit them. One way of doing this is through breath control. Under stress our breathing often becomes very short and shallow, which deprives the body of needed oxygen. When you feel stress coming on, take a deep breath, then concentrate on breathing slowly and rhythmically. Listen to the air entering your nostrils and lungs. Breathe "into the stomach," letting it expand and contract naturally. Feel the life-giving oxygen cleansing your body. With each exhalation, imagine the tension being released. With each inhalation, let your body fill with new life and energy.

Solitude is another vital necessity that seems to be in short supply in modern society. Many of us spend so much of our lives in the company of others or engaged in various forms of activity and entertainment that we fear spending time alone. Yet through solitude we can get to know our deeper selves, get in touch with the roots of our problems, and chart the course toward our higher aspirations. An Olympic ski jumper, when asked what was the most important aspect of his training, said simply, "The ability to be alone with myself." Take time out to consult with your inner voice. It is a reservoir of strength, peace, and wisdom like no other.

Relaxation and solitude are important pathways to good health.

Meditation. One of the best ways to tap this hidden reservoir is through meditation. There is nothing magical about meditation (unless, like I do, you consider life itself a rather magical experience). Today it is used not just by Eastern mystics, but by millions of people all over the world to achieve deeper states of calm, awareness, and spiritual strength. It is simply "going within" to make contact with the source of our being.

Meditation begins with relaxation. As the mind and body slow down, we begin to drift into a new frame of mind. We let go of worries, preoccupations, and surging thoughts. Once we are relaxed, the next step is concentration. Focusing on the breath is one useful approach. Another useful point of focus is the repetition of a calming word such as "relax," "quiet," "peaceful," or "deeper." As you silently repeat the word, really try to feel its meaning. Allow yourself to embody the concept you're concentrating on. If stray thoughts or impulses interrupt you, just notice them and let them dissolve. Gently nudge your mind back to your point of focus and continue as before.

A third technique is to concentrate on a pleasing object such as a candle, a leaf, or a flower. Whatever your point of focus, stay with it for at least fifteen minutes, and do it daily. During the first few sessions you may experience quite a bit of frustration as you discover how hard it is to concentrate. But if you persevere, before long you will feel waves of peace and joy emanating from within. This is a sign that you are beginning to make contact with your own personal sanctuary, or "center." This center is the source of all innate wisdom, instincts, and creativity. It is also a reservoir of power and healing that few people ever tap to its full potential. When we do, though, we gradually discover that love and happiness do not depend on outward circumstances, and that we need not work so hard to find them.

Meditation is a vast and varied subject. It deserves a much more detailed study than this book allows, and I highly recommend that you spend some time pursuing it. There are many good books that explain the art in more detail. One that is especially helpful for beginners is *How To Meditate: A Guide to Self-Discovery,* by Lawrence LeShan. Another is *The Relaxation Response,* by Herbert Benson. A third book that gives a particularly Western perspective is *Active Meditation: The Western Tradition,* by Robert R. Leichtman and Carl Japiske. For related reading, I would also recommend *Silva Mind Control,* by Jose Silva. But don't be satisfied just to read about meditation and relaxation. Practice them and make them a part of your daily life. Then you will have their strengths to draw on whenever you need them.

Awareness of Hazards

For survival preparedness, being aware of potential hazards is almost as important as health. In the wilderness, good survivalists are always on the lookout for storms, avalanches, falling trees, and other dangers. They make sure their shelters are located in an area that is free from winds and floods. They know the habits and whereabouts of dangerous animals. They develop keen senses and stay alert to sights and sounds. They do these things naturally because their lives depend on it.

Those of us who live in cities and suburbs would do well to emulate this example. Some of our urban areas are regularly subject to hurricanes and tornadoes. Others run a high risk of earthquake damage. Still others are especially clouded by industrial pollution or large amounts of allergens. Every city has its particular climatic cycles that bring problems associated with prolonged heat or cold. Yet few of us are even aware of the hazards of living where we do.

There is no reason to be overly concerned, but it is foolish not to be aware of potential hazards. If you live in Tampa, Florida, it only makes good sense to know that the state has a very high incidence of hurricanes and tropical storms. If you live in Houston or Fort Worth, you would take more than passing interest in the fact that more than three hundred people in Texas have been killed by tornadoes in the last twenty years. If you have heart or lung problems, it would be more healthful to live in San Jose than in Los Angeles. If you are trying to decide between jobs in Chicago or Denver, it would be worthwhile to consider relative crime rates, weather patterns, and the risks of earthquakes and air pollution. (A useful book for this purpose is Dr. Robert A. Shakman's *Where You Live May Be Hazardous to Your Health*.)

Awareness then continues as a part of daily life. A survivalist in the wilderness always asks, "What if?" questions: "What if my tent were blown away? What if I lost my food? What if I sprained an ankle or broke a leg?" Survivalists in the city should ask similar questions: What if my electricity went off? What if the house caught fire? What if I got stuck on the highway or in a subway train or an elevator?

It is not so much the asking as the answering that is important. Even a mental rehearsal is extremely valuable. It forces the mind to envision responses, to take notice of resources and imagine how they would be used, and to develop greater confidence in our survival abilities. The mind does not distinguish between a real or imagined experience. Whether we want to become better basketball players or better survivalists, mentally going through the motions works wonders. We can do this in city and suburban environments exactly as we do on an airplane while watching a flight attendant point out the emergency exits and oxygen equipment—

that is, by imagining ourselves actually carrying out the emergency procedures.

The applications of this kind of mental exercise are astounding, and a great deal has been written on them. In a book called *Psycho Cybernetics,* Dr. Maxwell Maltz contends that visualization—specifically our ability to imagine ourselves as we would like to be—is critically important in reaching personal and professional goals.

Eventually, though, awareness must also lead to action. Often we hear our subconscious voices warning us to put a quart of antifreeze in the car or to re-roof the house, but we keep putting it off. Then we are dismayed when the car won't start or the plaster is ruined. Similarly, many people hear of storm warnings or health hazards and do nothing to prepare for them until it is too late.

Part of this lack of preparedness, especially in urban areas, is based on the false assumption, "It can't happen to me," or "It can't happen here." While doing some interviews in New York, for example, I was surprised to discover that most people gave emergency situations little thought. Aside from the obvious and well-publicized peril of crime, survival was not a major concern. "This is New York," I was told. "Nothing can happen here." On the contrary, almost anything can happen in New York, and almost everything has.

Self-Reliance. Another reason that many city people are not alert to potential dangers is that they feel government agencies (the police, the fire department, the weather bureau, and others) will protect them. But this is not always possible, as illustrated by the Blizzard of '83. In that case, the weather bureau had predicted a storm but had incorrectly gauged its intensity and duration. Relying on good authority, thousands of people went about their business as though nothing serious could happen, then found themselves stranded or debilitated for lack of preparation.

Another example along these lines is the case of a friend in Hoboken who was told about an impending water shortage two days before it occurred. Because the authorities had said the shortage would only last for twelve hours, he and his wife filled a few pans with extra water and thought no more about it. The shortage actually lasted for four days. In spite of government efforts to supply city residents by tank truck, the situation was a serious survival test for my friend and for many others before their regular water supply was restored.

To really be prepared, you have to overcompensate. If the weather bureau predicts two inches of snow, prepare for ten. If the water department says twelve hours with no water, have enough for a week. Experts and authorities are not infallible. They cannot foresee every eventuality, and they cannot make everything right once it goes wrong. They usually do their jobs as best they can, but don't expect them to be your mother. They have to take care of themselves before they can tend to anyone else.

Heed Emergency Warnings. Over-reliance on authorities is one problem, but an even greater one is not relying on them enough. Even after the weather people and the news media had accurately gauged and reported the intensity and duration of the above-mentioned storm, many people still did not take it seriously. Repeatedly, thousands of people scoff at warnings to evacuate before hurricanes, tornadoes, and tidal waves. Most of us have quick access to the very latest information affecting our safety and welfare, but for various reasons some of us choose to ignore it.

One reason for this is sheer laziness and complacency. But an even more common one is a false sense of security. To most of us, home is the ultimate safe haven, and we would rather not think about its being damaged or destroyed. So some of us fall into the denial syndrome, rationalizing that everything will be all right.

Many people have drowned because they preferred to believe that nothing could happen to their homes. Many others have been injured or killed because they refused to take approved routes to safety or to follow other carefully planned emergency procedures. Unsettling as it may be, our homes are not impregnable, and we should have no hesitation in leaving them if our lives are threatened. Unless we have carefully planned our own emergency procedures, we should not assume we know more than the authorities.

Above all, we should never underestimate nature's power. In 1981, shortly after the eruption of Mount St. Helens, someone wrote on a coffee-house wall in Seattle: "Nuke Mount St. Helen's—teach Mother Nature a lesson." It was a humorous reminder both of our arrogance and our ultimate frailty in the face of nature. Nothing can plug a volcano. Nothing can keep back the tide. Yet sometimes we like to think we have ultimate control over our planet, and many of us either resent nature's interruptions or think that our machines will always get us around the problems nature puts in our paths.

Arrogance, ignorance, and lack of awareness only lead to disappointment. The only insurance is preparation. If you're in an area that is prone to earthquakes, learn how earthquakes work, what damage they can cause, what dangers they pose, and what you can do to lessen those dangers. If you're living in a storm center, know the difference between a hurricane and a tropical storm. Choose living and working places that offer the greatest strategic and structural safety. Familiarize yourself with the expected times and frequencies of such emergencies. And know just how to minimize their effects on your family and property.

It is also wise to be aware of non-natural health threats in your area: to understand the long-term effects of such things as air and water pollution, hazardous wastes, food additives, and nuclear fallout; to know what to do in the event of a fire, a poisoning, or a person choking on food; and to know what things will help to keep you and your family safe from such urban hazards as automobile accidents and crime. In the game of survival, knowledge is power, and the best insurance is foresight.

The various chapters of this book list many things you can do to become better prepared for specific emergencies and survival situations. But don't be satisfied just to read about these dangers. Study them in detail and rehearse with your family just what you would do so you'll be ready for action when the time comes. Also consult other books. Regardless of where you live, take a first-aid course, including cardiopulmonary resuscitation (CPR). Know where to get help. Jot down emergency phone numbers in several spots for easy access. Be aware of the emergency frequencies on your radio. Know the layout of your home, yard, neighborhood, and city and understand how they fit into the meteorologic and geologic trends throughout the country. With this knowledge, you'll have a solid foundation for survival.

Know How Things Work

Another critical aspect of preparedness is to know how things work. In a time when we were closer to the earth, we had the skills to forge our own metal, make our own tools, grow and preserve our own food, and raise our own livestock. These skills were especially important in times of crisis because we did not have technology and emergency services to fall back on. Nor could we always count on nearby neighbors coming to our aid. In a survival situation our homes were islands, and in order to get along, we had to be generalists, knowing a little of everything.

Today we are specialists. Modern transportation and communication have pushed us away from the soil and catapulted us into the cities and even into outer space. Many of us spend our professional lives in bureaucratic and technological niches that would have astounded our forefathers, and the effects spill over into our personal lives. A corporate executive may understand the complexities of the stock market and not know how to tune up his car. A housewife may know how to manage the family finances but not know how to fix a leaky faucet or change a tire. Profession, status, sex, and other modern roles often keep us from developing the kind of self-sufficiency that would give us inner security. Yet we can challenge these roles and break out of them if we try.

There is an old saying that we work so that we can hire others to do the things we don't have time to do because we work. There is some truth to this. Much of our money goes to pay others to do things we could do ourselves. We are fortunate that specialization allows us to do more of the things we really want to do. But what happens if our car has a breakdown and there is no mechanic nearby? Or if the water goes off and there is no plumber?

It's fine to hire specialists to do the things we would rather not do ourselves, but it is also good to know that we could do them ourselves if we had to. Last year I bought most of my firewood because I didn't have the time to cut and split it myself. But it was nice to know that I could have. I also paid someone to come in and fix the oven because I didn't want to be bothered with it. But it was good to be able to explain the problem to the repair person and to know that, if necessary, I could have bought the parts and done the wiring and soldering myself. It's all a matter of self-confidence. No amount of money can buy the peace of mind that it brings. Nothing can substitute for its security.

Personally, I can't stand not knowing how things work. Every time I pick up a tape recorder or punch a computer key or get into a car or plane, I want to have at least a vague idea of what's going on. One of the reasons for this is that I don't always like to put out money to pay for something I can do myself. Another reason is curiosity. Machines are almost as intriguing as nature. To understand the workings of a piston is almost as satisfying as knowing what makes the wind blow or why a weasel went down a rabbit hole. Most of all, I have a burning desire to feel a connection to things.

Everything is part of the earth in one form or another. Everything is connected. Even the cogs in a machine are earth fragments melted and amalgamated to suit some human purpose. The more we understand this relatedness, the more secure and satisfying our lives will be. And the more we act with this knowledge, the better we will be as stewards of the earth.

Learning how things work saves money whether or not you actually "do it yourself." If you go into a camera store and say the shutter spring needs replacing, you're much less likely to be overcharged than if you have no idea what's wrong. If you know about automobile suspension systems, you're not going to be taken in by someone who tries to sell you an old set of shock absorbers when all you want is a new muffler. If you get a bill for $180 and you know the cost of parts was only $60, you're going to be more likely to ask the repair person to justify the extra expense. Most of us put more trust in sales and repair people than we do in ourselves, but it doesn't have to be that way.

Learning how things work doesn't take much time, either. The library is full of instructional books, and a quick onceover may be all you'll need to try fixing or making something yourself. It can also be immensely rewarding to take control of your life in this way. Far from being a burden or a chore, many people find home repair a very creative and therapeutic experience—especially when they find that technological mysteries are actually well within their realm of understanding.

Crisis Response

Now that we have reviewed the basic approaches to survival preparedness, let's look more closely at what happens in an actual emergency.

There comes a moment in all crises when we realize that something is seriously wrong. In the wilderness this may be the moment we become lost, injured, or separated from our companions or provisions. At home it may be the realization that a toddler is playing at the top of a stairwell, or that there is a grease fire in the kitchen. On a dark street it may be the sudden knowledge that someone is following us. For many in the Blizzard of '83, it was the moment people found themselves stuck on the highway with no one to turn to. The realization takes many forms, but its message is always loud and clear: "Danger—do something!"

Don't Panic

In situations that demand split-second decisions, we usually react without thinking. We reflexively pull our hands away from a hot burner, slap a choking baby on the back, or jump out of the way of an oncoming car. It all happens so fast that we do not experience real fear and concern until later. But in situations that allow time for thought, our first reaction is often fright.

Fear is the body's instinctive way of calling on physical and mental strengths that we don't have under normal circumstances. The heart speeds up. Adrenalin surges into the bloodstream. The brain and muscles are instantly charged for action.

The mind and body are capable of heroic and sometimes astounding feats in survival situations—if they are kept under control. But if we have no reservoir of survival knowledge or experience, fear can quickly lead to poor judgment and even to unreasoning terror. It is critically important to keep a rein on the emotions at times like this. If you know what to do, by all means do it. But if panic begins to well up, stop and think before you act. Reassure yourself and try to calm down. Even if you have no survival experience, quickly assess the situation and think about your priorities so that your energies will be well directed.

Survival Priorities

The survival priorities, in their usual order of importance, are (1) air, (2) shelter, (3) water, (4) fire, and (5) food. This list is not unalterable, for there are times when the body may have an urgent need for a "lesser" priority item. But in general that is the order, whether in the wilderness or in the city. The list is short and easy to remember. Giving it some quick thought can save a great deal of time and energy—and maybe even a life.

It is often said that we can live about four minutes without air, four days without water, and forty days without food. Any situation involving loss of air must be tended to immediately, which again points out the importance of knowing first aid and CPR. Quick and sure response is also necessary for heart stoppage and severe bleeding, and to a lesser extent poisoning. But beyond these pressing emergencies, the survival priorities become more difficult to determine, and in crisis situations many people choose the wrong ones.

All animals need shelter. Whether they carry it on their backs in the form of a shell or a coat or whether they seek it out in a tree stump or condominium, it serves the same primary functions: warmth and protection. Human beings are especially susceptible to the effects of cold, wind, and rain. Even a minor drop in body temperature can so adversely affect the brain that it no longer functions well enough to make survival decisions. Without adequate shelter in the form of warm clothes and/or a protective place away from the elements, humans can get hypothermia (a dangerous lowering of the body's core temperature) and die within hours. This is why shelter is so important. (See also "Hypothermia," page 43.)

Water and fire are often interchangeable as survival priorities. In a situation where cold threatens debilitation or death, fire is obviously of greater importance. But some of the functions of fire, such as cooking and light, are geared more toward comfort and keeping up the spirit than toward physical survival. Water, on the other hand, is part of our lifeblood and must be replenished daily in order for us to maintain health and strength.

Most people are especially concerned about lack of food during an emergency. This misconception springs largely from our life-styles. In fact, food is the least important of the survival priorities. The pangs between breakfast and lunch that most people associate with starvation are primarily pangs of habit. Food can be very important as a means of staving off hypothermia and keeping up vital body energies, but it is much more important to keep the body warm and well protected than to have the larder stocked with steak and instant pudding. Because of our conviction that we must have three square meals a day, we may have to remind ourselves in a survival situation that we can get along without food for much longer than we think.

Think—Then Act

In any situation where you don't have to act immediately, remind yourself of the above necessities and ask yourself which ones are most important. If you are caught in a storm, your first priority will probably be a safe shelter. If you are in a home without power, warm clothes and a fire may be your most urgent needs. Decide what your immediate needs are, then choose a logical course of action to provide them.

Once you have decided what to do, go ahead and do it without delay. Don't vacillate wondering whether you have made the right decision. Don't fret and fume or allow yourself to be overcome by despair. No matter how hopeless the situation may seem, act! Through action you will gain strength. If you should discover that one course of action is the wrong one, change to another, but always keep your mind on the goal and think positively.

And don't be afraid to act boldly. Unusual circumstances call for unusual action. In the face of overpowering necessity, caution, modesty, status, and all the other trappings of civilization must be thrown to the wind. Anything that will not help must be forgotten. Many people have died in fires because they were too modest to leave the house without their clothes. I know a woman who, during the Blizzard of '83, was offered safe hotel accommodations in New York but who spent the night stranded in the Lincoln Tunnel because she felt uneasy about spending the night in a strange place! Do the safest thing, even if it seems a little scary.

Dealing with Adversity

Aside from outright panic, nothing can debilitate us faster in a survival situation than getting upset. Often, once our initial survival needs are taken care of and we have more time to think, our reaction is one of anger, blame, impatience, or disappointment. Things did not turn out the way they were supposed to. Why did this happen to us? We may feel angry at having to change our plans or expend unusual effort to help ourselves.

True, the world does not always give us just what we want, but often we feel that it should. And that's where we get into trouble. We blame others when there is really nobody to blame. Many of the people who were caught in the Lincoln Tunnel during the blizzard had expected to drive right through and found that it took more than three hours even to reach the tunnel entrance from the New York side. Once inside the tunnel itself, they discovered there was no escaping for the better part of the night.

To be trapped in a dark, fume-filled corridor beneath the Hudson River is decidedly an unwanted and uncomfortable situation. But many people made the situation worse by getting upset about it. They leaned on their horns, cursed the drivers in front of them, and acted like spoiled children. In situations like this, we should slow down, take stock of the situation, and ask ourselves, "Am I alive?" "Do I have everything I need at the moment, even though I may not have everything I want?" If so, we should stop complaining and try to do something to help others.

Blame, anger, worry, and other upsets are common reactions to many problems. They are especially popular because they all place the responsibility for our problems somewhere else. Somebody else did it. It was beyond our control. It was nature's fault. Convenient as these excuses are, they are also crippling because they assume we can't do anything to help ourselves. It's like kicking the television set because it doesn't work.

Survival Is Work. Keep in mind that survival and emergencies are hard work. Many people avoid problems and take a defeatist attitude through sheer laziness. Let's face it—life in urban America is pretty easy for most people. Many of us have become so addicted to comfort and convenience that we complain about having to take out the garbage and avoid walking two blocks to the grocery store. Urban survival demands unusual efforts and energies. Under normal circumstances we may be able to get by with laziness, but in a survival situation it can kill.

Harmony. Our efforts must also be well directed. We should not try to resist the situation. Fighting doesn't work. The best approach is to be like the grass, to bend and flow with the circumstances. In the wilderness, a person who is caught in an avalanche cannot expect to survive by trying to stop the snow. That person must use his or her energies to stay on top and "swim" to the side. The same is true in city survival. You cannot expect to survive by boarding up your house or sweeping the water out of the basement. Your chances will be much better if you go to high ground or perch yourself on something that will float.

Helping Others. Once we have taken care of ourselves, we will be in a better position to help others. Then we can let our actions fit the situation. In a flood we might help load and place sandbags. In a storm we might help shovel snow or supply those who are cut off. During the Blizzard of '83, I heard of one man who left a stranded bus and came back an hour later with pound cake and coffee for everyone.

The thoughtful action of one person can often turn a situation completely around. What appears to be a miserable predicament can be transformed into an experience so special that in retrospect we would not have missed it for anything. As one man noted in a newspaper interview during the blizzard, "It's wonderful, it's really amazing. To think that it takes a disaster like this to bring people together!" There are hidden blessings in hard times—especially when we try to make meaningful contact with others.

Be Patient. If we can slow down enough, we sometimes discover that the temporary collapse of technology can be a real boon. For some it is a chance to get to know and share with those around them. For others it is a chance to catch up on reading or some other leisure project. For still others it is the chance to relax and reconnoiter. We don't need a crisis for these things. Wherever we are, there is always room for a smile and a kind word. Whether we are stuck in a long checkout line or adjusting to a debilitating storm, we can practice patience every day of our lives.

Say "Yes!" to Life. I am reminded of a modern day monk who, when talking about the meaning of faith, replied that faith is not so much believing as it is trusting. He described it as the capacity to say "Yes!" to whatever life offers. This is partly the ability to take the bad with the good, but it is also the ability to embrace discomforts and to find hidden blessings in difficult trials.

Some of the best examples of the power of the human spirit are given by those who survived in concentration camps during World War II. Most city survival situations pale in comparison. Yet there were those who took even these experiences as a challenge, and who among the debris of their ruined lives, managed to maintain a spark of hope and a reason to go on living.

It takes courage and character to take a blow as a challenge but that is what emergencies and survival situations ask of us. They challenge us to be wise, active, strong, and understanding—to be the best of what we are. That is the common denominator we all share regardless of age or social standing.

Let Go of Status. In most crises there are people who think that their money or influence will get them anything they want. These people are often dismayed to find that no amount of money will fulfill their desires, and that their status means nothing in a survival situation. The laws of creation do not discriminate. Nature does not care whether we are paupers, criminals, or kings. When a storm hits an unprotected coastline, it wipes out the mansions along with the shacks. When the stock market crashes, the rich discover they can be as vulnerable as the poor.

Some people with an overblown sense of importance have threatened to sue the airlines during a storm if they don't get to their destinations on time. They might as well sue the Creator for all the good their ranting will do. We must simply accept the fact that some things are beyond our control. This was a major lesson for many people during the gasoline crisis of 1973-74, when lines of cars wound all the way around the block and gas was only sold for a few hours each day. Many people pulled up to the pump and were horrified to discover that gas was not only more expensive, but that in some cases it couldn't be bought at any price.

Possessions Are Not Important. Most people quickly discover that knowledge and character are the only valuable currency in a survival situation. However, possessions can be major stumbling blocks to survival for other reasons. This is particularly true in emergencies such as fires, in which a person may be torn between running to safety and trying to retrieve some precious article from the blaze. Let go of possessions. They can be reacquired soon enough. It does no good to give up your life to save your house.

One Moment At a Time. Some survival situations are so dismal that if we stop to consider all that is left to endure, we will be overwhelmed by despair. I heard of a woman who was trapped in the rubble of an earthquake for twenty hours. If she had thought of how long it would take, she might easily have given up. But throughout the rescue she thought only of making it through the next hour, and she came through just fine. Another woman, caught in a massive avalanche, lived for five days beneath the snow on little more than willpower. Had she thought it would take five days to be rescued, she almost certainly would have died. Instead, she provided for her immediate needs as best she could and waited. And her rescue finally came.

The only way to get through a survival situation is one moment at a time. Indeed, the only way to get through life is one moment at a time. If we are all right in the moment, that is all we need. Aside from constructive planning, it does no good to think about what might happen in the future because we cannot predict it. If we imagine future pain and discomfort, we only compound our problems and weaken our resolve.

Unfortunately, many of us haven't had much practice with "now" living. We spend most of our waking moments living in the past or the future. We feel bad about a conversation we had yesterday and spoil the one we're having today. We sit down in the dentist's chair and feel the pain before the drilling has even begun. We imagine all the things that could go wrong at tomorrow's meeting, rehearsing confrontations and catastrophes. All week long we look forward to a party on the weekend and then are disappointed when it turns out to be less than we had hoped. Or worse, we say, "Things will be better when I get to be head nurse, or vice president of the company, or when I have a higher salary." By not living in the moment, we sap our strength and set ourselves up for frustration and disappointment.

It is important to set goals, but it is a mistake to live within them.

In doing so, we lose out on many valuable experiences. I remember passing a beautiful campsite when I was a boy and repeatedly promising myself that someday I would camp there. By the time I got around to it, the place had been bulldozed away and made into a dump. Since then I pay more heed to the old saying, "Happiness is found along the way, not at the end of the trail." Live from moment to moment, even in a crisis. That way, the difficult times will be easier to endure, and the good times will be enjoyed to the full.

A Child's View. Children are excellent teachers of this attitude. Throughout the Blizzard of '83 I saw children sledding, laughing, and throwing snowballs. Granted, most disasters and emergencies are not opportunities for play. It's also true that most children's needs are taken care of by their parents. But there is a lesson to be learned in their carefree attitudes. Children are flexible to change. They have an uncanny ability to find the unusual in the commonplace, and they can somehow accept the disruption of life's routines as perfectly normal. Many adults, on the other hand, complain of the inconvenience of a snowstorm during the week and then pray for snow on the weekend so they can go skiing and become children again.

There is no reason we cannot all take time out from our adult worries and preoccupations to laugh and play. Even in the middle of stressful situations we can look for opportunities to take life in a more lighthearted way. Often the only requirement is to drop our stodgy adult masks and to look at things through the eyes of a child.

Detachment. Negative emotions can greatly distort a survival challenge. For this reason, it often helps to dissociate yourself from the situation. If you find yourself getting overly concerned, mentally back out of the situation and pretend you're seeing it on a movie screen or reading about it in a book. Pretend you're a fly on the wall, watching your own reactions. Then ask yourself whether they're really constructive or whether you're getting upset over nothing. In such a dissociated state, it is often much easier to come up with logical solutions.

Humor. If you try this detached view, you may even discover you can laugh at your problems. A friend of mine with cancer had every good reason for despair. She had lost part of her hip and was in terrible pain, with no guarantee that she would recover. But when asked how she was, instead of complaining, she laughed good-naturedly and said, "Well, I'm not going to die this week."

Humor is a powerful tonic. It has the power to put our problems into perspective, and it has tremendous healing power, too. Norman Cousins, the longtime editor of *Saturday Review*, cured himself of a supposedly fatal disease largely through the application of large doses of humor. His amazing account is detailed in his best-selling book, *Anatomy of An Illness*. Finding reasons to laugh and make light of a bad situation always makes adversity easier to bear because it sets us apart from our suffering.

The Survival Instinct. Essentially, we have a simple choice in facing a problem of any kind. Either we can take it as a burden or we can take it as a challenge. The temptation to feel burdened can be strong, especially if we are unprepared. But regardless of our knowledge and resources, all of us have survival instincts. Somewhere deep down in each of us there is a tremendous will to live and to triumph over bad situations.

It is good to remind ourselves that we have this will, just by virtue of our humanity. It is also good to remind ourselves that our attitude can turn a crisis either way. Sometimes a simple declaration is enough to summon our innate survival instincts. When you feel yourself getting irritated or upset or despairing, that is the time to say, "I'm not going to let this problem get me down. I'm not going to become debilitated. I'm going to get myself through this no matter what happens." With this attitude, you probably will.

2
SHELTER

At first glance, a chapter on shelter in the city might seem unnecessary. Why should we worry about shelter in our own homes? Aren't they secure enough? Isn't the city filled with buildings that can keep us warm and protected in the event of an emergency?

The answer is both yes and no. Most of the time, our homes are excellent shelters. Most of the time the buildings that pepper our neighborhoods and rise on our skylines are as safe and sound as can be. But they are not fortresses. Take away their internal heating systems and they are little better than caves. Hit them with a flood and they are no more secure than crab pots. Shake their foundations with an earthquake or batter them with high winds and they can crumble like tinkertoys. All these things have happened to unsuspecting city people.

It's also sobering to remember that much of the time we're not even in our homes and workplaces. What if something should force us to stay put in an unfamiliar building for a night or a day or longer? What if we weren't even near a building? What if we were stranded in a subway, bus, or train? What if we were stuck in a car on a deserted highway or an isolated backroad? We would simply have to do the best we could.

That's why it's so important to prepare your home for potential emergencies before they occur (see "Disasters," page 197), and to know how to make a shelter anytime and anywhere. As you'll see, the principles of good shelter construction are the same, whether you're in the backwoods, in a stranded car, or in the corner of a freezing bedroom. Once you know how to provide a warm, cozy nook in your own home, you'll be able to apply your survival knowledge to almost any situation.

Basic Principles of Shelters

The main functions of any survival shelter are to provide warmth, protection, and security—even without an internal fire, warm clothing, or a sleeping bag. With this in mind, there are several important guidelines to follow.

(1) **Make It Safe.** A survival shelter should be located in a high, dry area that is free from flooding and away from natural drainages. It should be on a firm foundation, protected from hazards such as wind, rain, snow, fire, falling obstacles, and dangerous animals (including humans).

(2) **Make It Convenient.** A survival shelter should be located as near as possible to available construction materials and other vital neces-

sities such as water, fire, and food. Survival situations put unusual burdens on our energies. Wise placement of the shelter will help to assure maximum efficiency and conservation of energy.

(3) **Make It Warm.** Shelter warmth can be provided in one or more of three ways: through an internal heating source such as a furnace or fire (see "Heat and Light," page 87); through sunlight; or through insulation. Since sources of fire and fuel are not always available, I urge my survival students to concentrate on the last two heating methods first. Whenever possible, face the opening of your shelter toward the morning sun. (In the North American summer, the sun rises in the east and sets in the west. During the winter months, it rises in the southeast and sets in the southwest. For this reason, I always build my wilderness shelters with entrances facing east or southeast.) And make sure they are literally packed with insulation (see "Insulation: The Key to Warmth," page 45).

(4) **Make It Small.** The size of a shelter depends mostly on whether or not it has an internal heat source. If you have an unlimited amount of oil, gas, or electric heat, you can warm a "shelter" the size of a castle. If you have enough fuel, a firestarter, and a fireplace, you can heat an entire room. But in many survival situations we have to rely on our own body heat. There is no way for the human body to warm up a whole room, much less an entire house. The conclusion is simple: If it's cold and you have no additional heat source, make a small shelter—the smaller the better.

(5) **Make It Sturdy.** If your shelter is located inside a building, its main purpose will be for warmth rather than protection. In such cases, sturdiness is not so important. But if the shelter is located outside, it must be able to withstand the batterings of the elements and your own movements. In such cases, take extra care to provide a strong foundation or protective "skeletal" structure before adding the insulation.

Universal Principles

For an illustration of just how widespread these basic principles of shelter construction are, let's consider the usual shelters of two common animals, a gray squirrel and his neighbor, Mr. Jones. Different as Mr. Jones's life-style may be in his suburban home, his biological needs for shelter, water, and food are almost identical to those of the gray squirrel that lives in the adjoining park.

The squirrel locates its shelter high up in a fir tree, where it is well protected from predators, yet conveniently close to water and a variety of food sources such as nuts, fruits, and greens. In fact, it can find everything it needs within a radius of two hundred yards of its home tree, including the materials to build its nest. In this case, its nest is made with a sturdy foundation of sticks overlaid with a large, protective pile of grasses and leaves, with a thick layer of cedar bark strips, soft grasses, and feathers on the inside. In the fall, when the days grow colder, the squirrel adds on to its shelter, forming a large dome above the entrance that is impermeable to wind and rain. Though bulky on the outside, the interior of the nest is hardly larger than the squirrel's body—just roomy enough for it to curl up and encircle itself with its bushy tail. To the squirrel, this humble shelter is all that is needed or wanted.

Mr. Jones's arrangement is somewhat more complicated. He has bought a two-bedroom house at $10,000 down, with a mortgage of $69,000 and monthly payments in excess of $500. However, like the squirrel, it is important to Mr. Jones to keep his shelter safe and secure. Before he bought it, he made sure the roof and basement weren't leaking and that all the gutters and downspouts were clear. Though he had little fear of most animal predators, he installed deadbolt locks and a burglar alarm. He also made sure that his house was close to a major shopping center, where he could conveniently pick up his favorite foods and drinks.

If we disregard the obvious disparity in life-styles, the biggest difference between these two shelters is that Mr. Jones's has an internal heating system. While the squirrel's shelter is warmed only by its own body, Mr. Jones's is warmed by natural gas. It is primarily for this reason (and not his income) that Mr. Jones can afford a relatively large shelter.

But when the heat mysteriously goes off on a subzero winter's night, Mr. Jones begins to think much more like a squirrel. He wakes up shivering and wonders what's wrong. Not wanting to get up, he curls up in a ball and gathers the covers more tightly around him (not unlike the squirrel fluffing up its nest and encircling itself with its tail). When this doesn't work, he gets up and checks the thermostat and the furnace. He can't fix it, and it's too late to call the gas company. So he puts on long underwear and a wool cap, and piles more covers on the bed. Though Mr. Jones probably couldn't explain it much better than the squirrel, he warms up enough to fall asleep. And the next day, the gas company restores his heating system.

Hypothermia: Killer of the Unprepared

If the gas company hadn't come to the rescue, Mr. Jones would probably have been in a survival situation. If he had been any more exposed to the weather, he might even have begun to suffer from hypothermia, or exposure. Hypothermia is by far the most common cause of death in survival situations. In simple terms, it is a lowering of the body's core temperature to the point where vital organs no longer function adequately. Unfortunately, the brain is one of the first organs to be affected.

Happiness is knowing how to insulate.

This makes it increasingly difficult to recognize the symptoms as the cold progresses.

Actually, we've all experienced mild degrees of hypothermia. Shivering is one of the first symptoms. That's the body's way of warning us that our core temperature is going down. The action of the vibrating muscles helps to restore our heat balance. If this isn't enough, we can generate more warmth by moving or exercising. But these activities all drain our heat reserves. If we're really cold and the body is not warmed by some external source—ideally with hot, nourishing drinks and warm, dry clothing—the brain may be affected and we may soon lose our ability to make rational decisions. In later stages of hypothermia we may experience stumbling, slurred speech, violent shivering, deep fatigue, and finally unconsciousness and even death.

It is important to recognize the symptoms of hypothermia (both in ourselves and others) and to do something about them as soon as possible. Don't wait to treat someone you think may be suffering from it. Replace cold, wet clothes with warm, dry ones. Give hot, sugared drinks such as tea or cocoa to replenish dwindling energies. Better yet, serve nourishing soups that will maintain energies for a long time. If the situation is serious, take off the victim's clothing and have someone lie with him or her, skin to skin, inside a warm bed or sleeping bag.

Better yet, keep yourself and others from getting cold in the first place. Some of the most common ways we lose heat are through sweating, contact with cold water and cold wind, and contact with cold objects such as concrete and steel. Lack of food can contribute to hypothermia by reducing the body's fuel reserves. Our susceptibility to cold also depends to a great degree on our general level of fitness, our mental state, and what clothing we wear.

Insulation: The Key to Warmth

If there is one principle of shelter construction that everyone should know about, it's insulation. Insulation is the key to warmth. We use it unwittingly every day of our lives, but most of us are unaware of how it works.

In its most general sense, insulation is a layer of nonconductive material that is placed between two conductive materials to prevent the transfer of electricity, sound, or heat. For example, rubber is a good electrical insulator because it doesn't conduct electricity. Wood is a fairly good sound insulator because sound waves tend to bounce off it instead of passing through it. Wool and styrofoam are good heat insulators because they tend to slow down the transfer of heat and cold.

Good heat insulators that keep warm air in and cold air out are made of materials that contain a lot of dead air space that can trap and hold the heat. Down feathers are excellent insulators (as long as they don't get wet) because their soft projections form millions of little air pockets. Animal fur is also a good insulator because air is trapped between (and sometimes inside) the overlapping hairs. More solid materials such as iron, concrete, and wood are poor heat insulators because they lack air pockets and conduct heat and cold very quickly. In general, the denser and heavier the material, the worse the insulation; the softer and fluffier, the better.

You can also make good insulation from materials that may not seem very promising. Paper, for example, is not a particularly good insulator when it's flat. But when crumpled or put down in layers, its insulating qualities increase dramatically. The same is true of other thin materials. Reshape or layer them so they trap more air space, and they hold more warmth. The thicker the insulation, the better the heat retention. Dark colors also absorb and retain heat better than light ones. These basic principles can be used with all kinds of shelters.

Types of Shelters

Clothing: Our Most Personal Shelter

Now let's look at some ways we can apply the principles of shelter in everyday life. One way is with clothing. One of the best clothing materials for survival situations is wool. Wool maintains its thickness and insulating capacity even when wet. While materials such as cotton tend to absorb moisture and quickly become sopping wet, wool garments resist water and even regain much of their original heating capacity after they are wrung out. (You can compare the absorptive capacities of cotton and wool by suspending wool and cotton socks in a pan of water and watching how fast they soak up water.)

Goosedown, which is an excellent insulator under dry conditions, becomes useless when wet because the feathers lose their "loft." For this reason, many people who live in wet, cold areas today prefer to use synthetic insulators such as Dacron, even though they are heavier. Taking a tip from the deer, some of these fibers are now manufactured with microscopic air shafts, which increases their insulating capacity even more. Most expeditions to the Himalayas these days use some form of Dacron for sleeping bags. Even when wet, it retains its loft and heating capacity so well that climbers can slip into their bags with wet clothing on at night and it will be dry by morning.

Like anything else in survival, clothing is mainly a matter of preparedness. If you live in a wet or cold climate, have plenty of warm clothes on hand no matter where you go. Don't go to work on a threatening day wearing only a meager suit and dress shoes. Or if you do, make sure you have other things, too. It doesn't take a lot of effort to put a sweater, a wool hat, a pair of boots, and a raincoat in the car before a trip. You'll thank yourself for it if you ever have to change a tire on the highway in foul weather. If you're stuck for a longer period of time, it may even save your life.

You can also keep an extra sweater, warm socks, and other important shelter items in a handy drawer or locker at your workplace. Don't be afraid to wear or carry long woolen underwear. I almost always carry extra clothing items in my attache case when I travel because I know from experience that nature is changeable and I want to be ready for it.

Dress in Layers. The best way to dress for warmth is by using the "layer principle." For example, if it's cold and wet out, you might want to start by wearing a T-shirt, a cotton shirt, a wool shirt, a sweater, and a waterproof garment over the top. This way, dead air space is caught not only inside the material, but also between each layer. If you're going to be inactive, you'll probably keep all these layers on. If you get too warm, you can always take off a layer of clothing to stay within your personal "comfort zone." If you're in a situation where exertion or changeable weather causes repeated heating and cooling, it's best to wear shirts and sweaters that button or zip down the front rather than turtlenecks and pullovers that are more difficult to take off.

**The layer principle: many thin layers are warmer and
more convenient than one or two thick ones.**

**Emergency wind
and rain protection
using cardboard and
plastic bag (Fashion
means nothing in
a survival situation).**

If you're not ready when the weather turns bad, improvise. If you're caught in a storm without a raincoat, buy a newspaper and drape it over your head. Or use a cardboard box as a makeshift hat. If you're in a serious windstorm or downpour with no bodily protection, a large plastic garbage bag can be used as a makeshift raincoat or windbreaker, cutting holes for your head and arms.

If you're embarrassed to be seen in such a contraption, put it on underneath your outer layer of clothing. But if you're seriously threatened, never worry about what other people will think. At a football game once, it started to pour and very few people had brought raincoats. I went to a nearby grocery store, bought a box of plastic garbage bags, and made myself a garbage bag raincoat. At first people looked a little incredulous. But when they realized how well it worked, it wasn't long before I was passing out plastic bags. Fashion means nothing in a survival situation, and it only takes one person to start a new style trend.

The same is true in especially cold or windy weather. If your clothes aren't warm enough, improvise some insulation. If you're wearing a fur coat, turn the coat inside out (the fur side is warmer). Anyone can buy a newspaper and surreptitiously slip a few flattened pages inside a meager jacket (front and back) to create a weather break and keep the vital body parts warm. This is the same principle used by people who sleep on park benches. A newspaper spread over the body serves amazingly like a blanket. In a really bad situation, you can crumple up individual pages and stuff them inside your clothing. Many times in the woods I have stuffed my clothing with some light, airy material like leaves or cattail down to add to its insulating qualities. Even such unlikely materials as fir sprigs can have a tremendous warming effect if you tie off your cuffs to keep the stuffing in.

These materials don't even have to be dry. The important thing is the dead air space. You can even make your own naturally insulated clothing. When I was a boy, I often made insulated vests by sewing two old shirts together and stuffing them with leaves or cattail down. Using different materials, you can do the same in the city.

**Crumpled newspaper stuffed inside clothing
helps create dead air space and more warmth.**

Keep the Head Warm. The most important parts of the body to keep warm are the head and trunk, since they contain the most vital organs. The brain in particular receives a heavy flow of blood and loses a disproportionate amount of heat. In cold weather, for example, you can lose up to forty percent of your body heat through your head. If you cover it with a wool cap, most of that heat is retained and recirculated through the body. In fact, when the extremities get cold, it's often a sign of heat loss through the head. If your feet are cold, put a hat on.

Cold Feet. At home and work, I recommend taking the shoes off and wearing socks. This increases circulation and warmth at the same time. If your feet are cold because the floor is cold, you can remedy this by putting a pillow under your feet or by wrapping them with a towel or other article of clothing.

For outside environments, warm socks and durable footwear are the most obvious answers. Like extra sweaters and pants, these can be kept in the car or at work for emergency use. But if you don't have them, you can improvise. One emergency answer to cold feet is to put a layer of newspaper in the soles of your shoes. Better yet are makeshift insoles cut from a packing box like those given away at grocery stores. The added thickness gives more insulation, at least until the cardboard is matted down. Best of all are thick wool inserts slipped inside the shoes.

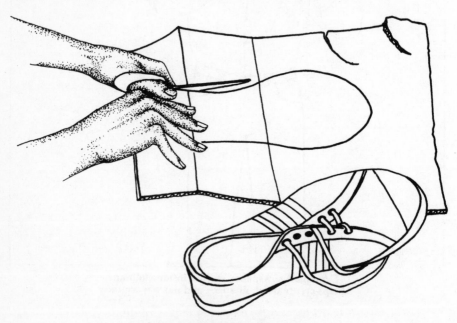

Insulating insoles cut from cardboard
help keep the feet warm.

Another effective approach is to use plastic bags as "vapor barriers" between two pairs of socks. This way, heat-containing moisture is absorbed by the inner sock but held inside the plastic bag. The outer sock provides another insulating layer to slow down heat loss through radiation. Even if you have only a single layer of clothing, this method works wonders. And like many survival principles, it works equally well for any part or all of the body. In their first-aid and survival kits, most experienced outdoorspeople carry a lightweight, body-sized plastic bag, or "survival shelter," they can quickly crawl into. Even a simple garbage bag can be a great help in a crunch.

Cold Hands. Mittens are best for the hands because they allow the fingers to warm each other by direct skin contact. If you need to use your hands outside, get a pair of pigskin leather gloves. If your hands are sweaty in cold weather, never grab any metal because your hands will stick to it. If you have to take care of delicate business that requires a lot of dexterity, you can wear silk or nylon gloves beneath a pair of mittens. This allows you to touch and manipulate cold objects without exposing your hands. Alternatively, you can use mittens with fingers cut off at the ends. Then, when your work is done, you can quickly slip these back into a pair of warm mittens. Another thing you can do is sew two wool insert pockets on the insides of your overcoat and stick your hands in there on really cold days.

Shelters in the Home

If it gets too cold in your house and you have no source of heat other than your body, you can increase your comfort by making a "shelter within a shelter," using the same survival principles that are used in the wilderness. In the woods one of the most effective survival shelters is the "debris hut." It is built much like a squirrel's nest. It is small (conforming inside to the shape of the body), sturdy (made with stick "ribs" propped along both sides of a strong ridgepole), and well insulated (with two to four feet of light, forest debris over the ribbing and a cocoon-like stuffing of leaves, grasses, or pine boughs on the inside).

Following the basic survival principles listed above (see page 41), pick the smallest room in the house that is safe, dry, convenient, and least exposed to the cold. For maximum protection, pick a room without windows, or with windows facing the sun. Pick a room with doors that can be periodically opened for adequate ventilation, but closed and blocked off to keep down the draft.

Then gather up all the insulating materials you can find—mattresses, pillows, blankets, towels, diapers, and clothing. In extreme cases, you might even consider using draperies and carpeting. Unless the tem-

Construction of wilderness "debris hut"

perature is extremely cold, it's likely you can keep the entire family warm without even constructing much of a shelter. Just use the insulating material in the way that seems most logical. First insulate the floor, since it's likely to be much colder than the walls. Then make sure everyone is well bundled up. If everyone huddles together, you can increase your warmth manyfold. Like logs on a fire, there is nothing like two or more closely packed human bodies for generating warmth and family togetherness. If this isn't enough, there are a number of shelters you can make with home furnishings in very short order.

The Mattress Cocoon. If you're alone, you can make a cocoon-like shelter simply by wrapping up in several layers of insulating material such as blankets, draperies, or carpeting (warm side in). If you have several small, thin mattresses such as those used in bunkhouses, you can lay them side by side, as shown, lie down crosswise at one end, and curl the other ends over the top of your body. You can then stuff the inside with pillows and other good insulating material, cover your head, and drift off to a pleasant sleep.

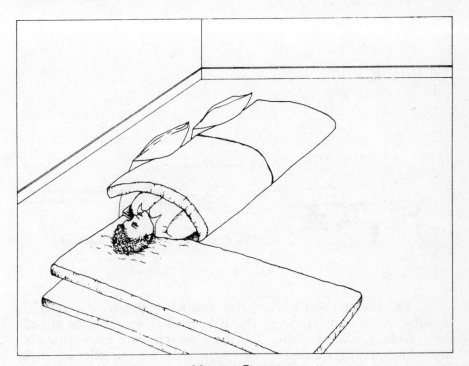

Mattress Cocoon

The Mattress Sandwich. A variation on this theme is to sandwich yourself between two mattresses with stuffing around the sides. This is especially useful for those with standard to king-sized beds and mattresses. It is also a more practical way of sheltering two or more people at once. Just take the mattress off the box spring and pad the box spring with clothing or blankets. Then place a thick border of pillows, wadded blankets, clothing, and cushions around three sides of the box spring, leaving one end open. Finally, put the mattress on top and crawl in. Again, you can stuff more insulation into any cold spots and control the snugness of the fit by adding or subtracting the "sandwich" material.

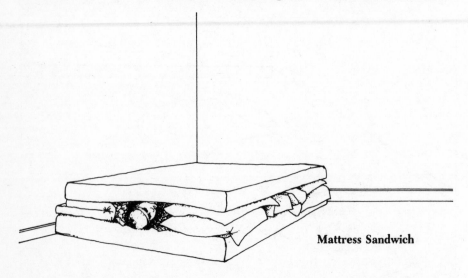

Mattress Sandwich

The Mattress Shack. For larger numbers of people, a roomier alternative is the mattress shack. This is an internal shelter made of bedding, clothing, and furniture. There are several ways to construct it, depending on what's available. One is to make a rectangular box with mattresses. In a corner of the room, place two box spring mattresses upright and parallel to each other. Put the first mattress against a wall with one end in the corner and the second parallel to it, a few feet away. The second mattress can be supported by any number of things, sturdy pieces of furniture being the best. Then roof the shelter in with a lighter mattress or several thicknesses of blankets. Fill the interior of the "shack" with insulating pillows and cushions and drape a quilt or blanket over the entryway.

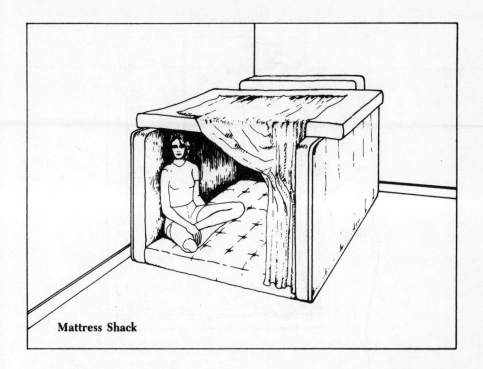

Mattress Shack

The more insulation you use and the closer everyone huddles, the warmer it will be. And don't forget the dead air space principle. Ten sheets laid flat on the floor provide very little insulation. Many times better is one sheet flat on the floor and one sheet on top, with eight sheets wadded up in between. Most important, don't feel limited to the materials mentioned here. Look around. Anything in your house should be considered fair game when your life is on the line.

Final Protection. Once your shelter is made, confine most of your activities to that area. This conserves energy and prevents unnecessary drafts. To cut down on drafts even further, shut all doors and windows in the house. Insulate drafty windows by tacking up fabric and filling the window area with crumpled newspaper or clothing. Seal off drafty doors with cushions, pillows, newspaper, or clothing items. But remove these and open the doors periodically to make sure you get plenty of fresh air. Be especially careful about ventilation if there are lots of people in one small area or if you're using candles in the room, as people and flames consume lots of oxygen. Above all, don't bring flames of any kind into the shelter itself.

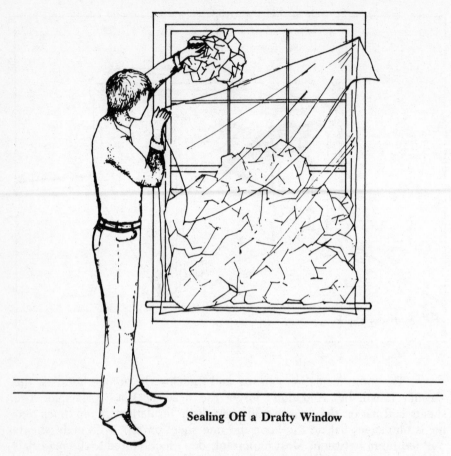

Sealing Off a Drafty Window

Inside the shelter, take off your shoes and wear two or more pairs of warm socks instead. Shoes restrict the blood flow to the feet. Also, never go into the shelter wearing wet clothes. Water saps body warmth faster than almost anything. For maximum warmth, stay close together. Watch infants and older people carefully to make sure they are always warm enough. If you detect symptoms of hypothermia, you may be able to warm the person up in a car. If this isn't possible, follow the standard procedure for treating hypothermia (see page 43).

Shelters in Other Buildings

Regardless of location, the principles of shelter construction are the same. At work, you may not have access to the same materials you have at home, but you can use other things. Paper, cardboard, packing materials, carpeting, office furniture, and file cabinets are excellent shelter materials.

Furniture padding can be cut out and used for clothing insulation. Solid furniture such as desks and chairs can be used for the structural parts of improvised shelters. Carpeting and draperies can be cut with a knife and used for many insulating jobs, from roofing to shelter entrances. (If you're hesitant to destroy expensive home furnishings in a survival situation, ask yourself what your life is worth and how much it would cost to replace it.)

What kind of shelters can you make? Almost anything you want. For example, you can turn three desks on their sides to form three walls, using them as the basis for an office mattress shack. You can lay down two or more filing cabinets (leaving the files inside for insulation) and roof it in with a desk top. You can use books and bookcases. Whatever suits your purposes is fine. Just remember to keep the shelter relatively small and fill it with plenty of insulating material. Beyond that, improvisation is the name of the game.

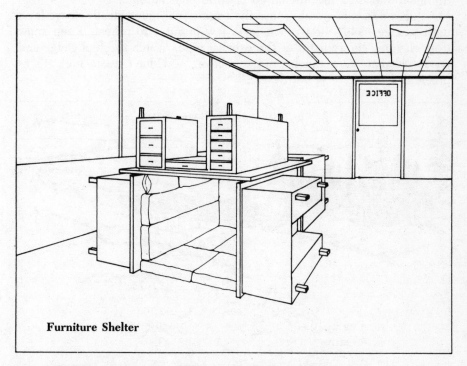

Furniture Shelter

Car Shelters (see also "Blizzards," page 199)

If you're stranded in an automobile you will have to consider many factors. The most important of these are distance to safety and weather. If the weather is fine and the distance not far, you may decide to walk to safety. If the roadway is well traveled, you may decide to flag down a car, telephone for help, or wait until someone comes along. However, unless you can easily walk to a shelter, stay close to your car until you can get a ride or help comes. In bad weather, conserve heat and energy by staying inside your car as much as possible.

If you're stranded, don't panic. The car is a shelter on wheels, and there is very little you need to do to make it livable. If you can maneuver the car, park it in a well protected place with an eastern or southeastern exposure. If you have a car with a catalytic converter, don't park on dry grass or other combustible materials, as the converter gets very hot and could start a fire.

Unless it's very cold, turn off the engine, lights, and radio to save the battery. Use lights only for signaling when there is a good chance of making contact with someone (especially the police). If the car is piled with snow or debris, make sure that rescuers will be able to spot you. Lift the hood and tie a bright-colored cloth to your antenna.

Even in cold weather, use the engine sparingly. Ideally, leave it off until you get cold, then run it for a few minutes to reheat. Keep snow from clogging the radiator or the exhaust pipe. Watch the fuel gauge and try to calculate how much time you have. And don't waste fuel; it's as precious as water on a hot desert.

The Car: A Shelter on Wheels.

Most important, provide adequate ventilation. If you leave the car idling, open the window at least a finger's width on the lee side—even in chilling cold. Keep the exhaust pipe free of snow. Such measures will allow fresh air to circulate and prevent noxious gases from accumulating in the passenger area. If you sleep in the car, turn off the engine and make sure you always have a good source of fresh air. Never go to sleep in a car with all the windows rolled up.

In cold weather with no alternative heating, first bundle up. Use blankets, coats, and other insulating material to maximum advantage. If you're sitting on an upholstered seat, use the seat to warm your back and a blanket to warm your front. Use all the insulating material you can find. If necessary, cut the upholstery and stuff the insulation into your clothing. Keep your shelter small. If you have an extra blanket, partition the unused parts of the car to provide more warmth in your "living space." Don't get out of the car unless absolutely necessary, as it will chill quickly.

Long-Term Car Shelter. Most often you'll be rescued long before your gas runs out. If not, prepare a good car shelter using the basic survival principles listed on page 41. If you don't have adequate insulating material in the car itself, look for it outside. Even on parkways and freeways you can collect quantities of grasses, leaves, and fir boughs. Such natural insulation can be used to cut down on drafts, to line a cold floor, and to provide a warm, soft bed. In extreme conditions you can even make the car into a giant sleeping bag by literally stuffing it with insulation. Spare no effort if it means your life. And take care of these preparations when you're still warm.

Outdoor Shelters

Wherever you are, anything you find should be considered in light of its survival utility and used in the most effective way possible. This is especially true if you're caught out on the street—a not infrequent situation with people whose homes are destroyed by earthquakes, floods, and storms. Outside, your first concern is to protect yourself from wind and rain by getting in under something solid.

First look for open public buildings. Many county and municipal buildings are either open all night or have guards posted who will probably let you in. Bus and train stations and airports are excellent shelter areas. They are both warm and safe, and many offer food and hot drinks as well.

If you can't find an open public building, look next for a phone booth. There, you may be able to call a taxi or a friend. If this is not possible, search for an abandoned or unused building. If it's open, so much the better. If not, and your life is at stake, don't hesitate to break in through a weak door or window. As long as you don't endanger yourself or anyone else, you'll be forgiven for not following society's usual standards. Once inside the building, use your knowledge and ingenuity to make the most appropriate shelter.

If you can't get into any building, find a warm, protected spot around a closed building. The walls of brick buildings radiate heat long after the sun has set. Without putting yourself in danger (see "Crime," page 159), pick an area that has recently been exposed to the sun and look for protective enclaves, subway vents, and door wells where warm air comes out or where artificial light provides extra warmth. Some of these areas also have hot water pipes you can huddle up to.

Protective Enclave on City Street

Use these areas to set up a makeshift shelter. Even a phone booth will do in a pinch. These enclaves will protect you from the buffeting of high winds and take the bite out of the cold rain. Bundle up as best you can, pulling your clothing tight around your torso, neck, and head. If even these measures aren't enough, search out additional items for emergency shelter.

If you have to get through a rainstorm in such a situation, simply take a cardboard box (found in almost any garbage dumpster), crush it and spread it flat, and hold it over your head like a miniature roof. Don't allow yourself to get wet if you can help it.

Many other useful shelter items can be found in dumpsters and alleyways. Boxes, packing crates, plastic sheeting, and other untainted debris can be used in much the same way as furniture and household items to form a protective shelter like those suggested for the home and car. Don't forget insulation, especially on the ground. A good rule of thumb outside is to use twice as much insulation underneath as on top.

Scenes of Destruction (see also "Disasters," page 197). If you're caught in a situation where your own house or other buildings have been destroyed and help hasn't come yet, don't despair. You'll probably have a tremendous assortment of materials to choose from. Short of looting, don't hesitate to use whatever you can find. First, pay special attention to hazards such as fire, broken gas and electrical lines, and falling objects. As long as there's no danger of further collapse or falling debris, you can use foundation walls as the basis for a sturdy "debris hut." Beams, wood, furniture, and other such materials can be used to complete the framework. You can then stuff the shelter with insulating materials in much the same way as suggested for the mattress shack (see page 56). However, be sure to avoid any burned or chemically lined materials that may have become toxic.

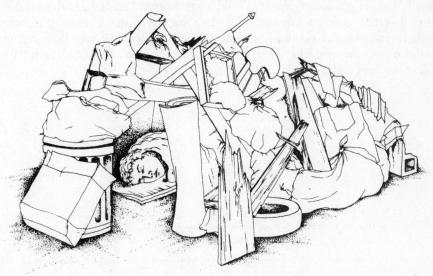

Disaster Shelter: Use Anything You Can Find.

Group Shelters Outside. In an open, exposed area just after a disaster, it may be necessary to construct a group shelter. For two to three people, you can make a variation on the mattress shack, with the opening toward a barrel fire that has a good reflector (see "Makeshift Heaters and Stoves," page 119). For a large group, one of the best approaches is to make a circular wall around a central fire pit or barrel. This can be done by stacking furniture in a circle, laying beams and other materials against the outside at an angle that is steep enough to shed the rain, and covering these with a good thickness of insulating debris. This is a variation on the "debris hut" I suggest for my survival students.

Depending on the weather, the debris layer should be from two to four feet thick. The shelter's angled wall then forms a semi-enclosed sleeping space for as many people as necessary. The warmth from the central fire radiates off the walls of the shelter just as it would from the semicircular stone, wood, or dirt reflector of a wilderness campfire. This way everyone stays warm and cozy and has the added psychological advantage of feeling part of a community.

Stay Put. Though it may be tempting, I wouldn't recommend walking out of the city to find shelter. The energy expense just isn't worth it. Besides, with most disasters, outside help in the form of civil defense and national guard personnel usually arrives within one to three days with food, water, and extra clothing. One of the first rules of survival is to make your shelter as close as possible to water, fire, food, and building materials. Unless you're an expert at wilderness survival and can find a promising spot that offers a safe and abundant supply of these necessities, stay where you are and do the best you can with what you have. (For further information on wilderness shelters, see *Tom Brown's Field Guide to Wilderness Survival.*)

3
WATER

On the outskirts of Seattle's Pioneer Square area, there is a little park called Waterfall Gardens. It is hardly bigger than a residential backyard, bordered on two sides by iron grating and on the other two by red brick and concrete. The inside of the park is landscaped with rhododendron and vine maple, and it includes a central patio furnished with wire mesh chairs and small, circular, white-topped tables.

If this were all, the place would probably seem ordinary and uninspiring. But there is also water here—flowing water. From the tops of two adjoining walls, a sparkling cataract rushes and tumbles over an array of boulders with such joyful spume and spray that it seems as though it might have been transplanted from the heart of the Cascade mountains. In one place the water drops in a thick, rushing torrent. In another, it churns downward in delightful, foaming confusion. In still another place, it forms a thin sheet that falls as lightly as a veil. Around the periphery, droplets jump and crash, ooze along rock surfaces, and seep into mossy nooks and crannies.

Many people come to relax in this little patio, as they do beside fountains and falls all over the world. They read, talk, smoke, eat, and watch the water. A few of them take their shoes off to feel the sun and the spray and the cool air. Others walk around the edge of the patio, gazing at the cataract and the pools below. Some drop pennies and dimes to see them glint in the sun as they fall to the bottom. For a few moments the rush of water washes out the sounds of the city, and people let go of their worries and cares.

Waterfall Gardens is like waterfalls everywhere. It reminds us of other water sounds: the crash of the sea; the rush of a storm; the trickle of a downspout; the drip of a faucet; the splatter of a shower. It reminds us of steam, rain, streams, seas, lakes, spigots, spouts, and a thousand other watery forms. Water is wild wherever we find it, and we are drawn to it instinctively, whether or not we realize how vital a part it plays in our lives.

In many ways, water is our lifeblood. We walk with footsteps powered partly by flowing water. We think, feel, hear, smell, and taste with water-based brains and nerves. We see the world through liquid-filled eyes. We drive in water-cooled cars through streets above water-filled pipes. We live and work in water-supplied homes and buildings. From thousands of miles of pipeline networks, we draw water for drinking, washing, heating, air conditioning, bathing, firefighting, cleaning, sprinkling, swimming, industry, and waste removal. We rely on water for electricity, transporation, commerce, and all forms of food, from fish and algae to meat and potatoes. All the metabolic processes inside our bodies are dependent on water. Wherever we live, water is the foundation of our existence.

Water: The Earth's Lifeblood

Water Systems and How They Work

Realizing the importance of water in our lives, we should take a little time to remember its wild origins, to give thanks for it, and to understand the systems that supply it. Especially in urban areas, many of us grow up with the mistaken notion that water comes from a spout when we turn a faucet. We don't often realize the connection between our tap water and the rushing stream in the mountains or the great oceans that separate the continents. But the connection is there, in a beautiful and never-ending process known as the water cycle.

The Water Cycle. The water cycle is the world's circulatory system. In this process, water evaporates from the surface of oceans, lakes, and streams; travels invisibly on the wind from continent to continent; condenses and falls as rain and snow; flows from mountains to valleys; collects in natural and manmade reservoirs; seeps through the systems of all living things; and once more evaporates and purifies itself to begin the cycle all over again. This natural water system runs the biosphere, and it in turn is run by the energy of the sun and the force of gravity. It does not depend on pipes or pumps, and it cannot be contained or controlled. Most important, what happens to the water in one part of the system may eventually affect another part of the system and ultimately the life within it.

In most wilderness areas, animals get their water directly from rivers, creeks, seeps, springs, lakes, and other natural catches and leave

WATER CYCLE

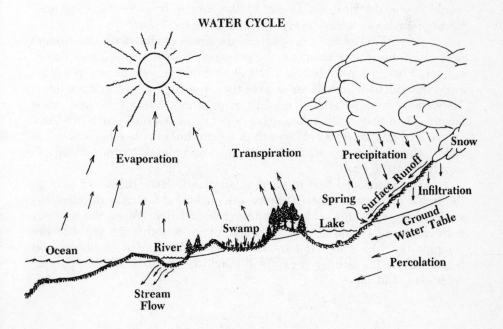

their wastes almost anywhere with little danger of seriously polluting the water supply. There was a time when humans could do this, too, but no longer. Our numbers are too great, and the pollutants we pour into our waters are too widespread.

In modern society, we spray our forests with herbicides. We spread our farmlands with fertilizers and pesticides. We seed the skies with clouds of sulfur dioxide and flush tons of industrial waste into our rivers and oceans. We litter the land with mountains of trash and toxic chemicals. We often try to convince ourselves that there is no danger in doing these things. But nature does not care what we think, and has its own way. As the water cycle continues its journey, many of these pollutants are washed into our streams, rivers, lakes, and reservoirs. The wastes come back to haunt us—and, if we are not careful, to poison us.

Today only about three percent of the earth's water is considered pure enough to drink without treatment. Even our wilderness lakes and rivers are afflicted with chemical and bacterial pollutants, and it's getting worse. In human communities, then, we must not only have a fresh water source, but also a safe way of getting rid of poisonous wastes and of purifying polluted water.

City Water Systems. Most municipal water systems require a tremendous amount of thought and calculation. Imagine trying to provide water for a million people. Where would you find it? How would you supply it? How would you make sure it's safe to drink? How would you use the water to flush out the city's wastes? And not least of all, how would you make sure it's on tap at the proper pressure for everyone, twenty-four hours a day, every day of the year?

As with all of life's necessities, the answers start with the wilderness. And, more often than not, the principal water source is a major river system. Figuring from 100 to 150 gallons of water per person per day, engineers calculate how large an area they're going to have to draw from. They figure average annual rainfall, evaporation, absorption, and other factors. Then they build a dam, or series of dams, each of which produces an artificial lake or series of lakes to catch and hold the needed amount of water. These reservoirs are fitted with pipes and pumps to draw water and supply it to the city.

The pipes lead first to purification plants. Here the water may go through a number of different processes, including filtering, disinfection, stabilization, softening, chlorination, and fluoridation. When the water is both clean and palatable, it is then sent on its way through pipes to the community. And finally the treated water is distributed to homes and businesses at the proper pressure through a system of smaller pumps, reservoirs, and pipes.

CITY WATER SYSTEM

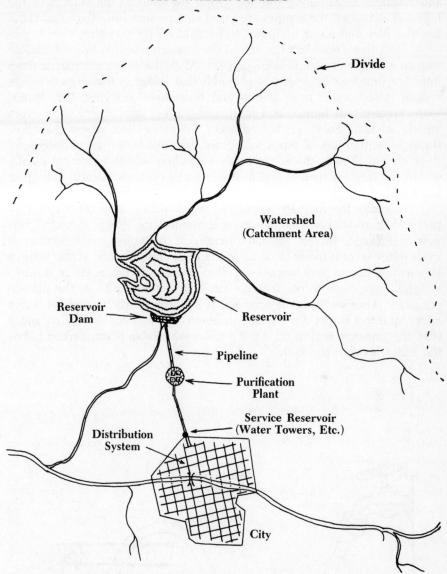

Most of these pipes are laid underground just beneath the city's streets. Some, such as those that supply water for fighting fires, connect with hydrants that are conveniently spaced to safeguard the buildings on each block. Others branch into smaller pipes that feed individual homes and businesses. All along the way, from the dam to the spigots in the tallest skyscrapers, these pipes are fitted with meters and valves that regulate the flow and allow the pipes to be shut off for servicing.

But that's only half the story. The kitchen faucet is just the middle step in a long and complicated process. After the water is used, it flows into a separate set of pipes and channels that make up the city's drainage system. Used water from homes and businesses (carrying dirt, paper, soap, grease, and human and industrial wastes) joins storm water from streets, gardens, roofs, yards, and parks. Together these wastewaters flow through another set of pipes and drainages, much like an underground river system. Finally the sewer pipes work their way to treatment plants, where the waste is treated and flushed into lakes, bays, oceans, and other large bodies of water.

Usually the drainage system is kept separate from the water supply, and there is almost no danger of contamination except through overflow or leakage. In fact, in non-emergency situations, contamination of fresh water is most likely to occur at the midpoint—that is, at the fixtures in our own homes and businesses. That is the only place where the two systems come close to connecting—or "cross-connecting," as the plumbers put it. One way this may happen is if a sink overflows and the water backs up into a faucet. Or if a garden hose is left in a bucket of dirty water after the pressure is shut off. Or if a toilet inlet valve is submerged below the water level in the tank.

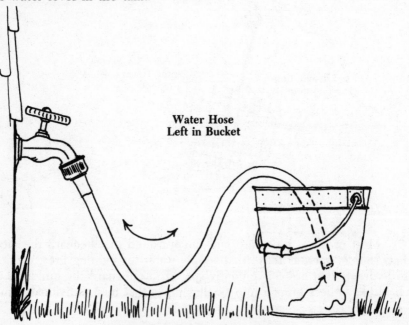

**Water Hose
Left in Bucket**

**"Cross Connections" Like this Can
Contaminate the Water Supply.**

Water is supplied to homes and workplaces by a network of underground pipes running parallel to the streets. On the outskirts of the city, supply pipes branch off from central "feeder" pipes and run parallel to arterial roadways. In the more congested parts of the city, central feeders supply gridiron patterns of pipes that correspond to individual city streets. Sometimes there is only one pipe, or main, per street; most often there are two for added insurance. Double mains are usually buried beneath the sidewalks.

In each block, there are shutoff valves for the main pipes so they can be serviced. The mains are also connected to fire hydrants, and normally the whole system is kept under constant pressure. Some parts of the city, because of their location, may have to be supplied by separate pumps that draw on the main system and boost the water to higher elevations. Modern fire trucks have their own pumps that can increase water pressure from the hydrants when needed. And large buildings and industrial plants often have separate storage tanks and pumps to assure a constant supply of water at adequate pressures.

Building Systems. For each building or dwelling within this system, a branch pipe comes off the street main and leads first to the water

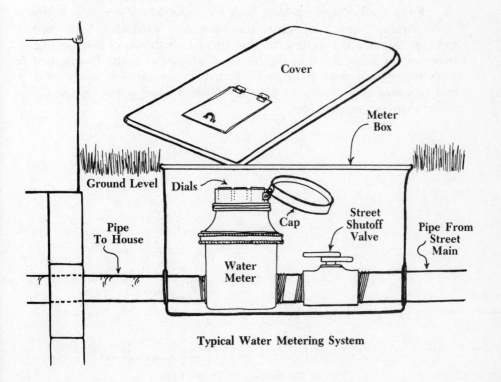

Typical Water Metering System

meter. This meter is usually contained underground in a box with a heavy metal lid, located near the sidewalk. If the meter isn't covered with dirt, you can see that one pipe leads from the street to the meter, and another leads from the meter to each house or building. As water flows through the meter, it turns dials that measure the flow so that city officials can calculate how much water you use. There is also a shutoff valve between the main street pipe and the meter.

After you've located your water meter, look from the meter to your home and you'll see the most logical point of entry for the supply pipe: the nearest wall. Just imagine a ditch from the meter to your home and that's where the pipe probably runs. Then go into the basement (or the main floor if you have no basement) and look for the main shutoff valve on that wall. This is the valve that controls all the water that comes to your house.

Now follow the pipes from the main shutoff valve. You'll probably find that they lead first to the water heater. Here, the single supply pipe branches into two pipes that separate the hot and cold water systems. One branch enters the heater cold and comes out another pipe hot, while the second branch continues carrying cold water. If you're in doubt, feel the pipes for a difference in temperature. (Also notice the separate shutoff valves for the hot water heater and other water treatment equipment.)

From the hot water heater, both hot and cold water pipes usually run in parallel pairs. They serve the downstairs appliances first, then reach up through the ceiling to the kitchen, bathrooms, and outside faucets on the other floors of the house. Each pair of vertically-oriented supply pipes has branch pipes, each with their own shutoff valves, that serve different appliances and fixtures. These branch pipes are usually smaller than the supply pipes.

Home Water Supply System

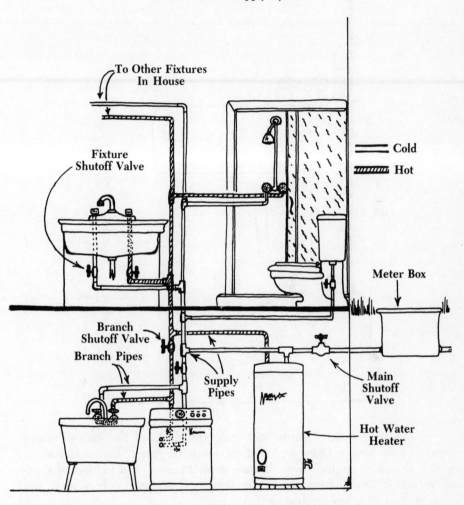

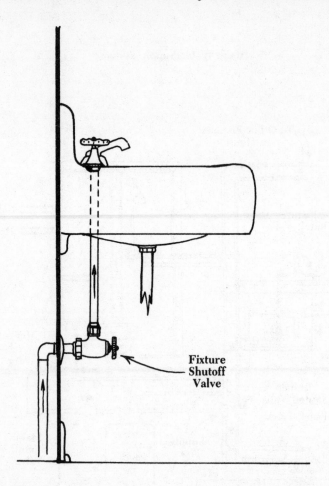

Fixture
Shutoff
Valve

    See if you can identify and trace the paths of the various water
pipes in your house. Draw a plan of the house on paper. Locate the water
meter, the main shutoff valve, branch shutoff valves, and individual shutoff valves. This will help you understand your water supply system and
how to deal with any problems that arise.

    Drainage Systems. In a survival situation, it's also important to
have an understanding of your building's drainage system. In general,
drainage pipes are quite a bit thicker than water pipes because they have
to carry more than just liquids. For this reason they are easily recognized.
In most buildings they run either vertically or slope slightly downward
along the walls. They are also attached to a system of pipes that serve as
air vents to the outside. These vents connect to all plumbing fixtures, for
several reasons. They carry off gases, allow wastes to flow more freely, and

provide needed air pressure to keep water inside fixture traps—for example, the curving pipes beneath most sinks. This in turn prevents gases and germs from coming back up the pipes into the house. Drainage pipes are also fitted with "cleanouts," or plugged openings, for clearing the drains if they become clogged. All of the drainage pipes (from sinks, toilets, bathtubs, and appliances) connect to a single large drainage pipe in the basement that leaves the house and eventually enters the public sewer system.

Home Drainage System

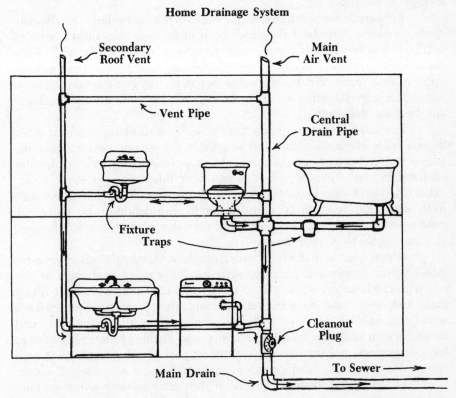

Once you get an overview of your city's water supply and drainage networks, you will see that they are simple and logical connections of pipes, valves, and fixtures. When plumbing problems come up, you may be more tempted to see if you can solve them yourself. If you have to call a plumber, you may be interested enough to watch the work so that next time you will know how to do it yourself. More important, your knowledge will help you get safe, clean water when the city system can no longer supply it.

Water in Emergencies

Most of our urban and suburban problems with water are very minor. On an everyday level, these are such things as leaks and clogged pipes that we can usually solve, either by ourselves or with a telephone call and a checkbook. But on another level, there are problems that nobody can immediately solve. These are usually caused either by mechanical failure in the pumping systems, or by storms, floods, and earthquakes that cause "cross-connections" and pollution of the fresh water through leakage or overflow.

Preparedness. Sometimes preventive measures help to alleviate these problems. The best insurance is to make sure you always have an auxiliary supply of fresh water—at least several days' worth, and better yet a week's supply. Under average conditions, most people need a minimum of one quart of drinking water per day. But don't ration drinking water in a survival situation. Your health will deteriorate very quickly if you become dehydrated.

For safety's sake, set aside a gallon a day of drinking water (or other liquids such as canned fruit and vegetable juices) per person. In areas where water shortages are common, keep an emergency supply of water on hand in plastic gallon jugs. You can pour this water out every week, using it to water your houseplants or garden, and refill the containers with fresh water. Or you can keep the water fresh indefinitely by filling the containers no more than seven-eighths full (water expands when it freezes) and storing them in your freezer.

If you hear of a storm or other problem that might affect your region's power supply and pumping systems, fill as many containers as you can with fresh water. Always have plenty of gallon jugs with tight-fitting caps, and have some extra buckets on hand, too. Draw a supply of fresh water that will last for several days or more. Then fill up the sinks and bathtubs with water for washing, bathing, and flushing toilets. If you're in for a long siege and you have a swimming pool or other such giant container, fill it up with unchlorinated water and cover it to keep it clean.

Draining the System. Finally, if the water in your home goes off and you don't have an extra supply, remember how water systems work. Just because water doesn't run out of the spigot anymore doesn't mean there isn't any left. Even after the water pressure is shut off, the pipes in your home are probably still filled with water, and you can get it by using the same forces that cause liquid to flow in a pop can or a mountain stream.

As soon as possible after the water pressure goes off (and better yet, just before), close the main shutoff valve inside your house. This will trap the water in your pipes and make sure it doesn't drain back into the street pipes. To drain the water from your pipes, first turn off all water treatment systems, including heaters. Then, beginning at the highest floor and working down, open all hot and cold water faucets and drain them into containers. Very little, if any, water will come out of the top drains. But on the next floor down or in the basement, you should get quite a bit of water draining from the pipes above. (This is especially important to remember in apartments and tall buildings.)

With each successive floor, keep the faucets open to provide air pressure, like an extra hole in a pop can. Drain the water and store it in closed containers so that it can be used for drinking, cooking, or washing. And don't forget to open the drain valves on the hot water heater. It contains from twenty to eighty gallons—and much more in large buildings.

As you might guess, you can use this same procedure to drain the water system for repairs. In this case, though, you'll also want to flush all the toilets. If you're draining the system to prevent freezing, be sure to pour antifreeze into all the drains and toilet bowls.

If you don't have enough containers to store all the water, take what you can use and come back for more when you need it. As long as the water supply is kept separate from the sewage system, it should stay fresh and safe for at least a week. Most of the bacteria that normally grow in pipes do not present a health hazard unless they reach astronomical numbers. However, if you have any doubts, be sure to treat the water before drinking it (see "Treating Water," page 83).

Water in Buildings. Most buildings have water systems much like those in individual homes. In addition, booster pumps are often installed in the basement to insure that the water reaches the highest levels of the building, and auxiliary water reservoirs are often located on the tops of buildings and on intermittent floors. If these booster pumps go out for any reason, you can get emergency water through the same procedures listed above. You may also be able to get water by locating and tapping any one of several auxiliary tanks. The only caution I would add is not to get water from pipes below the first floor. When the water pressure is reduced in a large building, there is more danger of backups and cross-connections that could pollute the fresh supply.

Most buildings also have some kind of pressurized water system in case of fire. Almost invariably this water is treated drinking water. You can get access to it by studying the building's piping system. You can also get access to a great many drains (both inside and out) simply by carrying a "water wrench," a small faucet-shaped handle sold at hardware stores. This wrench fits on most standard water valves. Such valves (with square fittings and sometimes a screw hole) are commonly installed for cleaning and other purposes in public bathrooms and on the outsides of buildings. If you don't have a water wrench, you can turn these valves with a wrench, pliers, or other instrument that provides enough leverage.

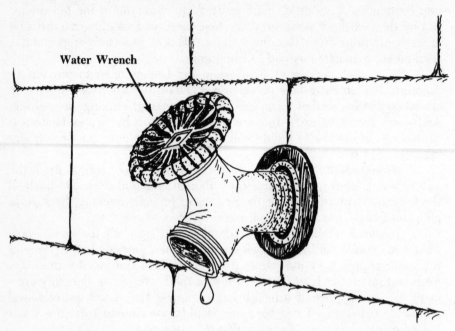

Water Wrench

Water on the Street. If you're really up against it and there's no water left in the pipes, remember the water cycle. Millions of rural people all over the world take their water directly from lakes, streams, and other natural catches. So can you—but only if you know the source is relatively clean and you remember to treat it before drinking (see "Treating Water," page 83).

Most cities have water reservoirs to periodically relieve the pressure on the system. These should not be used except in a dire emergency, but you should know where they are. Nor do I recommend fire hydrants as a water source, as they are very difficult to open without specialized equipment and would probably not be functioning if the pressure was off, anyway. Under no circumstances should you take water from a sewer system. Even with treatment, the risk of infection isn't worth it.

There are many other urban water catches, but in general I would recommend using them only as a last resort. These include storm waters in drainage ditches, creeks, puddles, lakes, and other places where the water may have flowed over a lot of dirty ground to get there. By the time the water has worked its way into such catches, it has probably picked up a host of bacterial and chemical contaminants, and there's no telling whether you'll be able to purify it adequately with primitive methods. If you have no choice but to use this water, treat it regardless of whether you think it's safe to drink. It's probably not.

Rainwater. The cleanest water is found closest to the sky. In the wilderness, this means high up in the mountains in fast-flowing streams. In the city it means fresh-fallen rainwater. If you're in an area where it rains frequently, you can collect the water that flows off your roof. Simply place a clean barrel or garbage can directly beneath the rainspouts. (Line it with a plastic garbage bag if you're not sure it's clean.) Then filter and purify the water before drinking.

Another way of collecting rainwater is to spread a clean tarp or sheet of plastic over a tree branch or other such support and arrange it so that it funnels the water into a waiting container. Or you can press the center of the tarp into a hole in the ground and elevate the four corners so that the rain collects in the pit. With a good rain and the right location, you can collect tremendous amounts of water this way. (The key is to spread the tarp as widely as possible.) This method is also safer than collecting rain off the roof, since it's less likely to pick up pollutants.

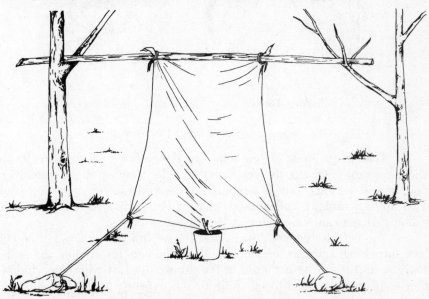

Collecting Dew. Even if it doesn't rain, you can often collect amazing amounts of water right off the ground in the form of dew. Get out early in a backyard or city park before the moisture has had a chance to evaporate from the grass and foliage and wipe a sponge, towel, or even a

T-shirt across the landscape. Then wring it out into a container. Look for grassy areas and lush spots where water droplets have condensed on leaves, bushes, and trees during the night. This is nature's invisible rain, and it falls daily, even in some of the hottest places on earth.

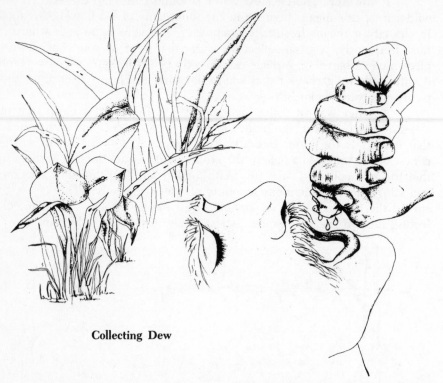

Collecting Dew

The effectiveness of dew collection depends a great deal on climate and topography. Obviously, you won't be able to collect great amounts of dew in arid regions, but in temperate areas you can be very successful. Two survival students collecting dew at my farm managed to fill a twenty-gallon garbage can with water in less than two hours.

You can also collect dew inside. House and car windows often collect surprising amounts of moisture from human respiration and other sources, and it can be gathered in the same way. Just wipe the windows thoroughly with a clean towel, wait for the moisture to collect, and soak up the freshly condensed water as you would from the ground. Another way is to simply lick it off the windows with your tongue. You won't get enough water to keep you going indefinitely, but you can take the edge off your thirst until you find a better supply.

Most dew in the wilds is as clean as rainwater. In urban and suburban areas, though, I would always recommend treating the water before drinking, as it's much more likely to pick up pollutants. Be especially careful not to use this technique in any area that's recently been sprayed or treated with fertilizers or chemicals of any kind.

Solar Still. Another useful water collection technique (and one of the most important ones I teach my survival students) is the solar distillery. This method can be used almost anywhere there's bare ground—in your own yard, in a local park, beside a backroad or highway, even on the desert. The beauty of this system is that it recreates the water cycle in miniature, and its principles can be used in many different ways. Basically, what you do is create a little cloud chamber or greenhouse to evaporate and recondense the water that has seeped into the ground. All you need is a plot of ground or patch of snow, a shovel or trowel, a sheet of clear plastic (minimum four mils thickness), a cup or pan to catch the water, and about six feet of plastic or surgical tubing.

First look for a good spot. The best areas are those with moist soil that are well exposed to the sun. Here, dig a hole about three feet deep and four feet wide. Put a container in the bottom of the hole, and run the plastic tubing from the inside of the container up and over the edge of the pit. Finally, cover the hole loosely with the clear plastic sheet and secure the sheet all around with dirt and rocks. Depress the sheet in the middle with a rock so that it forms a cone with a point no more than a few inches above the top of the container. The sheet should form about a forty-five-degree angle with the ground. As further insurance against soil bacteria, you can even drape the plastic sheeting over a length of garden hose or some other "collar" around the lip of the pit.

What you've created here is a little distillery. And what happens when you leave this contraption alone is rather amazing. As the heat of the sun shines through the clear plastic, it warms the soil and evaporates the moisture, just as in the natural water cycle. But instead of escaping, this moisture is trapped and condenses on the underside of the plastic. As more moisture collects, it forms water droplets. The droplets grow large and heavy, then roll to the bottom of the plastic and fall into the container. As long as the plastic and the container are clean, and as long as the ground contains no poisons, the liquid gathered this way will need no treatment before drinking. Simply suck up the water through the plastic tubing and you won't even have to dismantle the still when the container is full.

Since this process is slow, and since the water you get from it is relatively pure, I do not recommend using it for anything but drinking. Unless you're on a desert, water for cooking, washing, and other purposes can usually be gotten with other methods. If you want more water, you

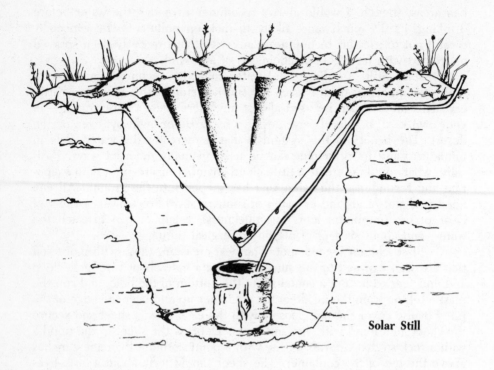

Solar Still

can build a larger still, but I would recommend making several small ones instead.

In general, the hotter the sun and the wetter the soil, the more water you'll get. Look for low, lush spots with lots of green vegetation. In particularly dry climates, you can increase the yield by adding crushed, nonpoisonous vegetation to the inside of the pit, or even by urinating in the soil around the sides of the still. Unless it rains, the still's production will probably go down after a few days. In this case, move it to another location with moist soil or add contaminated water to the pit.

Melting Snow. In areas where it's cold, you can often get water from snow. Don't eat the snow itself, as it will only cool your system and sap your energy. If possible, melt it first and drink the water lukewarm or hot (as coffee, tea, or some other nourishing drink). This can be done most efficiently by heating it in a container over a fire, or by allowing it to melt in a warm room or in direct sunlight. To hasten the melting process, use a dark-colored container. (Dark colors absorb heat, while light colors reflect it.) You can also set up any number of solar stills in the snow, with or without plastic tubing, to help augment your fresh water supply.

Treating Water

Any untreated water you pick up in the city is likely to be polluted to some degree. There's also the possibility, in the aftermath of a flood or an earthquake, that the water from your tap will have been contaminated by overflow from the drainage system. To be safe, never drink questionable water without treating it. You simply can't afford to take the chance. Even a day or two of diarrhea can put you so far out of commission that you won't be able to provide for your own needs, let alone anyone else's.

In wilderness survival situations, I recommend filtering cloudy water through wadded grasses, sand, or some other fibrous or porous material, then boiling it. In urban areas, where pollutants can be found on almost every square inch of ground, purification is even more important. If the water is dirty, first cleanse it by pouring it through a coffee filter or a clean cloth. Then boil it for fifteen to twenty minutes. Many survival manuals recommend boiling water for only three to five minutes. This is fine for most bacteria, but it doesn't always kill the spore-stage bacteria.

Quick Methods. Water can also be treated with purification tablets, two percent tincture of iodine, or a liquid chlorine bleach such as Clorox that contains hypochlorite as its only active ingredient. With iodine, use twelve drops per gallon, or about three drops per quart. With Clorox, use about eight drops per gallon, or two drops per quart. If you don't have an eye dropper, collect the liquid on the end of your finger and allow it to fall a drop at a time into the container. In both cases, wait about half an hour for the purifier to do its work before drinking. If the water is especially dirty or you want to store it for a long time, double the dosage. You can store water indefinitely in gallon jugs with a half tablespoon of Clorox.

Commercial Filters. An even quicker method is to suck or pump water through a commercial filter. Most of these contraptions combine a porous substance with a mixture of active ingredients to filter and treat the water at the same time. One inexpensive and convenient filter that's quite popular these days is the Pocket Purifier, manufactured by Calco, Ltd. This is a tube about the thickness of a finger that filters as you sip. According to Calco, it gets rid of all biological beasts and all particles larger than ten microns in diameter, and it can even purify stagnant pond water and raw municipal sewage.

An even more useful (but much more expensive) pump that's used by such groups as NATO and the Peace Corps is put out by Katadyn of Switzerland. This is a hand pump that weighs less than a pound but can be used to filter and purify relatively large amounts of water in a very short time. There are other commercial filters you can buy, too, at varying prices. If you get one, just remember that they don't filter out chemicals, they don't make freshwater out of saltwater, and you have to replace the filter mechanism when it gets clogged.

Boiling/Distilling. A slower method of purification is to put the collected water in a solar still. Purification stills can be set up in a variety of places, from backyard to kitchen sink, as long as there's a heat source to help the liquid evaporate. A few candles or a small camp stove set beneath the container will help a great deal. And a fire that brings the water to a full boil can speed the process greatly.

To get the steam to recondense, you can suspend a plastic sheet at an angle that traps it and allows the water droplets to roll down into a clean container. Even a plastic gallon jug suspended just above a tea- or coffeepot spout works for this purpose. Some of the rising steam condenses on the sides of the jug and drops into a container below. Better yet is to suspend such a jug upside-down so all the vapor condenses inside and falls into a waiting container.

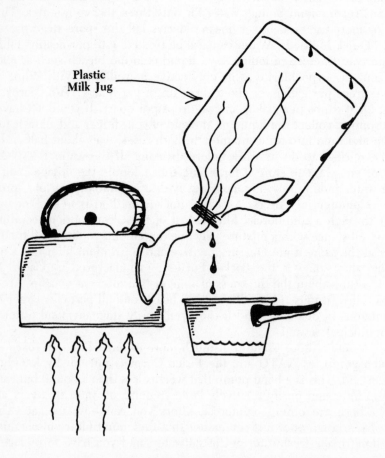

Plastic
Milk Jug

Other Distilleries. Another boiling/distilling method is to attach a U-shaped or spiraled length of copper tubing to a teapot spout so that most of the steam condenses inside the tubing and streams into a container below. For greater amounts of water, you can attach a spiraled length of copper tubing to a non-galvanized steel garbage can (burn off the galvanizing first!) and boil the water over an open fire outside. The apparatus need not be complicated. Just punch a hole in the lid of the can with a sharp instrument, spiral the tubing once or twice to make sure the vapor condenses, and keep the lid on the can while boiling the water.

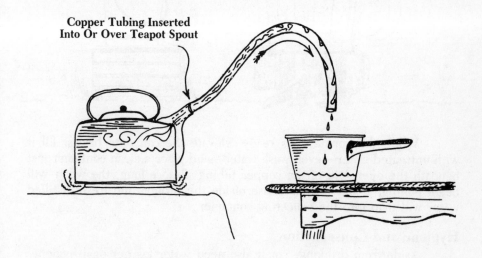

Copper Tubing Inserted Into Or Over Teapot Spout

Copper tubing can be found in the plumbing systems of nearly all buildings. Chances are, in the wake of a major disaster, it will be readily available. If not, it may be worth dismantling one or more of your home plumbing fixtures to get it (sink pipes are good). Wrap the end of the tubing with cloth or other padding material to assure a snug fit.

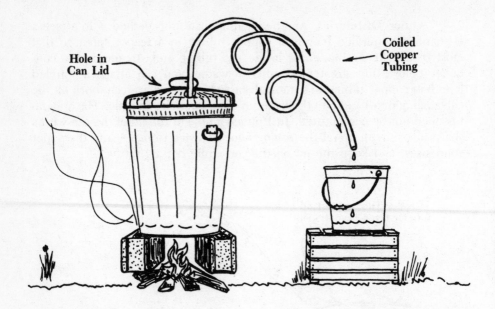

When the apparatus is ready, elevate the can onto bricks, fill it with untreated water—even wash water—and place a clean container just beneath the open end of the copper tubing. Before long, the water will begin boiling, steam will condense inside the tubing, and fresh distilled water will drip into the collecting container.

Hygiene and Conservation

Aside from drinking, you'll also need water for personal hygiene. This water should be relatively clean, but it need not be purified as long as you don't intend to swallow it. Conserve water whenever possible. If it's scarce, save most of it for drinking and ration the rest carefully. Instead of taking a bath, clean off with a sponge or wet rag. Flush toilets no more than once a day for liquid wastes, and only as necessary for solid wastes. (If the pressure is off, this can be done by pouring a gallon of water directly into the toilet bowl.)

Don't use running water for washing hands or brushing teeth. Use only as much as necessary. Recycle your water, just as Mother Nature does. Use dirty wash water for flushing wastes, and if it's really scarce, redistill your wash water for drinking. Most of all, remember how water systems work and apply the principles you've learned. If you use your head, you'll never be without an adequate supply of this most precious resource.

4
HEAT AND LIGHT

Electricity

Many thousands of years ago, we learned to make fire from smoldering coals left by lightning storms. In the centuries that followed, we learned to use fire for heating, cooking, and self-protection. Gradually, our inventive minds came up with even more sophisticated ways of controlling and using fire. We learned to box it in fireplaces and stoves, and even to harness its energy for steam power. Then, about two hundred years ago, we learned how to harness the energy of lightning itself. The discovery was an explosive one, and it is almost impossible to exaggerate the effect it has had on our civilization.

Consider Joe and Jill America's dependence on electricity in the course of a normal day. First, they wake up to an electric alarm clock. If it's dark, they flick on a bedside lamp or grope their way to a wall switch. After turning off the electric blanket, they shower with electrically heated water and brush their teeth with water supplied by electrical pumps. They put on clothes manufactured by electrical machines. If the house is cold, they turn up the thermostat, which sends an electrical impulse to ignite the fuel in their furnace.

For breakfast, Joe and Jill reach into their electric-powered refrigerator for cold milk and fruit juice. They turn on one electric stove burner for coffee, another for hot cereal, and a third for fried eggs. They drop two pieces of bread into an electric toaster. As they eat, they watch the early morning news in living color on the screen of their electrically powered television set.

As they leave for work, Jill and Joe America start their car by turning a key that sends an electrical spark to an electrical generator. If it's raining, they turn on the car's electric-powered windshield wipers. As they drive, they push a music cassette into an electrical tape deck and enjoy the sound of the New York Philharmonic as they race down the highway. Or they smoke a cigarette, which they light with the car's electric lighter. Periodically they stop at intersections, where they entrust their lives to electronically synchronized traffic lights.

If Jill and Joe are business people, they may ride up to their offices in an electric elevator. If they find the office a little stuffy, they turn on the electric air conditioning. At work they record letters on electric dictating machines, which are later copied on electric typewriters and stamped with electrical stamp machines. They make business calls on electric telephones, sending their voices instantly to New York, Denver, San Francisco, and London through a global network of electrical wires. And if they have a sophisticated electrical computer in the office, its maze of circuitry may perform scores of complicated tasks and give them instant access to whole libraries of information at the touch of an electrical button.

Back home again, Joe and Jill America have another electrically heated meal. After dinner, they do a quick load of laundry in the electric washing machine and balance their checkbooks with an electronic home computer (which also turns on the electric lights and the electric water heater when they're gone). Then they go to an electrically powered movie or relax in front of the electrical TV set once more before turning on the electric blanket for another night's sleep.

And this is only a small part of the story. If we looked at the lives of Jill and Joe more closely, we would see that nearly everything they touch and everything they depend on, from furniture, glassware, and vitamin pills to transportation, communication, and national defense systems, requires electricity either for its manufacture or operation. To put it mildly, Joe and Jill are plugged in. And since they are connected to a force they only dimly understand, they are likely to pay more for it and to have a difficult time finding substitutes for it when the power goes off.

For this reason, I would like to devote a few pages to the workings of electricity. If this seems far afield from the subject of survival, let me assure you it is not. When I live in the wilderness, my survival depends on being aware of my environment and all the important systems within it. I have to know the earth, the air, the water, and the plants and animals almost as part of myself. I have to be intimately familiar with how they "work" in order to appreciate and profit from them, and in order to live with them safely.

Electricity is one of the most important and least understood powers in the urban environment. Hundreds of people are electrocuted each year because they don't know what electricity is and how it works. Thousands of people pay great amounts of money to have specialists do simple repairs they could easily do themselves. These things alone, not to mention the mystery of electricity in itself, make it worth a little extra attention.

The Dance of Electrons

If we follow nature far enough, it always leads to the miraculous and unexplainable. Nobody can say with certainty just what electricity is. It is a vital, mysterious force that flows through nerve pathways in our bodies as regularly as through urban power lines. It permeates not only our lives, but everything around us, from oceans, whales, and foxes to forests, clouds, and mountains. Electricity is not just a convenient source of energy for humankind; it is the force that holds things together. It is the glue of the universe.

I will avoid lengthy and technical explanations, but to understand electricity, it is necessary to understand that all things are made of atoms. Each atom has a central, positively charged nucleus with one or more negatively charged electrons spinning around it. Some electrons are held close to their nuclei in tight orbits, a little like the inner planets revolving around the sun. Others are held weakly at great distances and can often be displaced by outside forces.

Through the blessing of some infinitely creative force, electrons love to dance—to spin and vibrate and streak and pulsate from one atom to another. It's as if the planets were continually jumping out of orbit to race over and circle another sun. When an electron is pushed or pulled out of orbit, it becomes a "free electron" seeking a positively charged atom to balance its charge.

Sometimes atoms become stable again by sharing electrons. When this happens, one atom "bonds" with another in an intimate electrical dance that forms groups of atoms called molecules. But in jumping from atom to atom, one electron sometimes displaces another. That electron then bumps into another atom and displaces another electron—and so on,

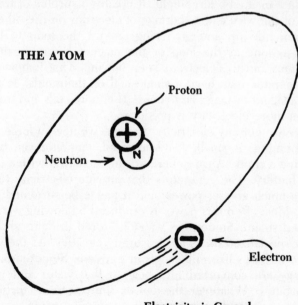

THE ATOM

Proton

Neutron →

Electron

**Electricity is Caused
by Electrons that
are "Bumped" Out of Orbit.**

in a chain reaction that goes on like an endless game of electronic musical chairs.

Now, here's the key: When a large number of free electrons all move in the same direction, they create an electrical current that flows like the impulse in a string of falling dominoes. If this current is properly harnessed, its energy can be converted into heat, light, and power to accomplish an unbelievable variety of tasks. Such is the electrical current that runs the cities of the world.

Requirements for Electricity

To get an electric current, we need several things. First is a good conductor. Copper, aluminum, and steel are good conductors because they contain lots of free electrons. For this reason, they are most often used for electrical wiring. Rubber, plastic, and wood are poor conductors because they contain very few free electrons. (For the same reason, these substances make good electrical insulators.)

Second, there has to be some kind of generator to get the electrons moving. Sometimes free electrons are generated with chemicals and stored in containers such as dry cells and flashlight batteries. But most electricity is used the instant it's produced. This is called "current electricity," and it is generated by wires and magnets.

It is an unexplainable curiosity of nature that when a loop of wire is moved inside a magnetic force field, it creates a surplus of free electrons on one side of the wire and a shortage of electrons on the other. The free electrons then pile up and go racing around the loop to balance the charge. But as long as the loop or the magnet keeps moving, the imbalance remains and the electrons keep flowing. That is how a generator works. A generator may have a single coil or thousands. It may have a single small magnet or many large ones. The more coils and the bigger the magnets, the more electricity is produced.

Before we get any electricity, though, we need a force to keep the generator spinning. A small, hand-operated generator can be run by a person turning a crank. A car generator can be started with a spark from a twelve-volt battery. The generators that provide electricity to towns and cities need a much greater power, and it has to be sustained twenty-four hours a day. Most often this power is produced by flowing water or a blast of pressurized steam. Sometimes water is stored in dams and allowed to run through specialized pipes at measured velocities. As the water flows, it spins huge turbines like millwheels in a stream. Sometimes coal, oil, or atomic energy are converted into heat to boil water and push steam-powered turbines. Whatever the power source, these turbines are attached to huge coils and magnets. As the coils spin inside the magnets (or

HOW A GENERATOR WORKS

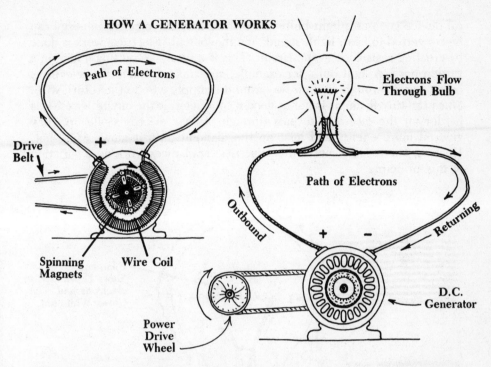

vice versa), unimaginable numbers of electrons pile up, ready to be sent racing through transmission lines to do their work.

Finally, electrons can flow only if the conducting wire makes a complete circuit. Whether the distance is only a few inches, as in a flashlight battery circuit, or thousands of miles, as in cross-country or transoceanic circuits, the electrons have to be able to flow from the generator all the way through the wire and back to the generator again. For this reason, every generator has to have two wires—one for outbound electrons and one for those that are returning. And the two wires have to be connected.

Think about this for a minute. Every time you flick on a light switch, you are connecting a circuit of wires that leads all the way back to the generating plant. The current in batteries usually travels in one direction only, so it's called direct current (DC). With most kinds of home current, the electrons reverse directions about sixty times a second. This is called alternating current (AC). The number of times the current changes direction is measured in cycles per second, or herz (Hz).

How Electricity Does Work

As long as electrons flash through a circuit unimpeded, they can't do much useful work. But once we connect the circuit wires to an electrical device such as a light bulb or a dishwasher, the electrical energy can be converted to heat, light, sound, and movement. Electrical work is done by creating resistance in the circuit. This is a little like putting a kink in a garden hose. A light bulb, for example, contains a filament that electrons have to pass through on their way from the supply wire to the return wire. Since the tiny filament is not as good a conductor as the circuit wires, it is harder for the electrons to pass through. As the electrons pile up, they give off more energy and heat up the filament until it glows white-hot. Heaters, stoves, and most other electrical appliances work on a variation of this principle.

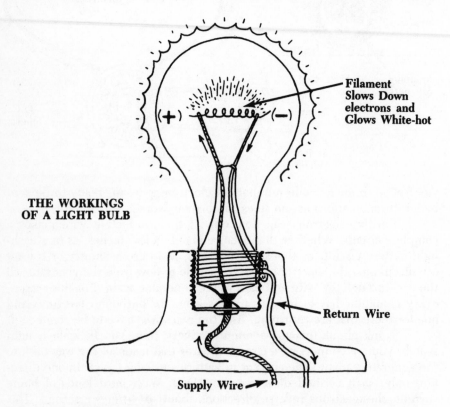

Filament
Slows Down
electrons and
Glows White-hot

THE WORKINGS
OF A LIGHT BULB

Return Wire

Supply Wire →

Electrical Measurements

Now that we have at least a vague idea of how electricity works, let's define some important but confusing electrical terms. Voltage is the amount of electrical pressure it takes to push electrons through a circuit. It can be compared to the water pressure in a hose or the suction in a vacuum cleaner. The larger the circuit and the more resistance along the way, the more pressure, or voltage, you need. A flashlight battery of one-and-a-half volts only generates enough pressure to send electrons through a very short circuit. A pressure of 120 volts can carry electricity through most home circuits. To send electricity on a cross-country circuit might take a half million volts or more.

Amps (or amperes) measure the amount of electricity (in electrons per second) that flows through a circuit. One amp is equal to 6.28 quintillion electrons. (That's 6.28 with eighteen zeroes after it!) Wires leading from large generators carry a tremendous amperage, while those that supply individual homes are geared for a much lower flow. Individual fixtures and appliances are lower still, and they are often marked with the amperage they use so you can keep from overloading the circuit (see "Service Panel," page 94).

Finally, the amount of electricity that is actually used is measured in watts. Watts are calculated by multiplying volts times amps, or pressure times rate of flow. For example, if you have a ten-amp toaster and you run it on a 120-volt line, it will use 1200 watts of electricity every second. Since a thousand watts is a kilowatt, that's 1.2 kilowatts.

The amount of work you can do with one kilowatt in one hour is called a kilowatt hour. Your monthly electric bills reflect the number of kilowatt hours you use each month. The higher the amperage on a given fixture or appliance, the more kilowatts it consumes and the more expensive it is to operate. (For tips on how to cut down on electricity and other energy costs, see pages 97 and 102.)

The Home Electric System

Now let's take a look at the overall system. Electricity is supplied to your home from a power plant through high-voltage transmission lines and a series of transformers that reduce the voltage at different stages along the way. Some of these transformers are huge substations larger than a house. The last one is usually a can-shaped contraption mounted high on a telephone pole. Its function is to reduce the high-voltage current in the power lines to 120 or 240 volts before it enters your home.

The Electric Meter. The power lines (composed of two or three wires, one each for incoming and outgoing electrons and sometimes one for safety grounding) connect to your home and go from there to an electric meter. This meter shows the power company (and you) the number of kilowatt hours of electricity you use each month. The meter is usually located outside the home inside a glass box or bulb, and it usually contains four or five dials like clock faces, each with numbers and a pointer. If you read the indicated numbers from left to right, you get the total number of kilowatt hours that register on your meter. Also look for a much larger wheel beneath the dials. Notice how slowly it turns when you only have a single light bulb burning. Then turn on an electric stove and watch it spin!

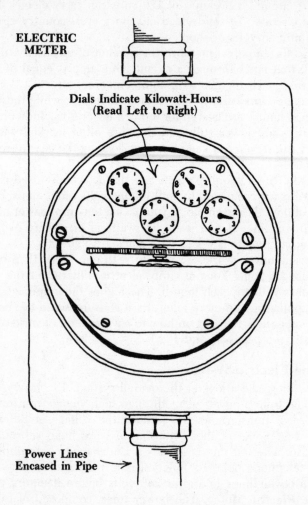

**ELECTRIC
METER**

**Dials Indicate Kilowatt-Hours
(Read Left to Right)**

**Power Lines
Encased in Pipe** ➔

Service Panel. Next, the wires run to a service panel (also called a fuse box or circuit breaker), where they connect with smaller sets of wires that serve different parts of the house. From here, one circuit of wires may lead to the kitchen, where it serves the fixtures and appliances there. Another may serve the living room, and a third the bathrooms and bedrooms. The larger the home, the more circuits it usually has.

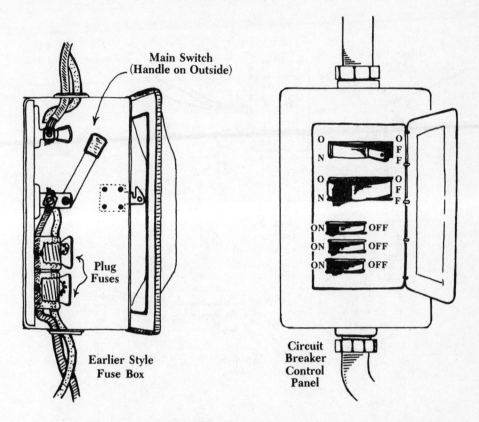

Main Switch
(Handle on Outside)

Plug
Fuses

Earlier Style
Fuse Box

Circuit
Breaker
Control
Panel

Another important function of the service panel is to protect all the electric circuits. It does this through built-in safeguards called fuses or circuit breakers. There is one fuse or levered circuit breaker attached to each circuit. If one of the circuits becomes overloaded with more electrons than it can handle and begins to heat up, the wire in the fuse melts through or the lever lifts and breaks the circuit before the wires are seriously damaged. There is also a switch or lever on the service panel that can be used to shut off all power to the house.

Switches, Outlets, and Plugs. The electrical system is completed by the individual switches, outlets, and appliance plugs in various rooms. The main function of all switches, however fancy they may be, is to open and close the circuits leading to individual outlets—that is, to turn on or shut off the flow of electrons. The function of the outlets is to provide a way of connecting the circuits to electrical devices. Like all circuits, each plug contains two wires (and sometimes a third for safety grounding). The insulation on these wires is usually color-coded: red or black for the "hot"

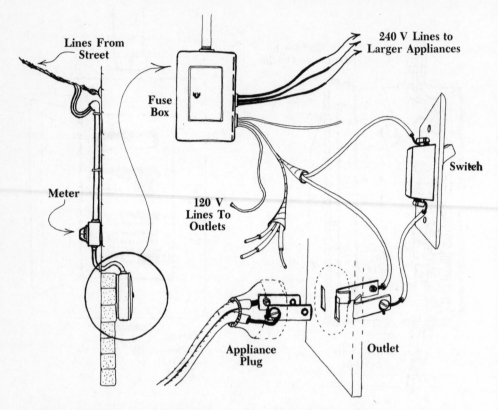

wire, and white for the "neutral" wire. Each wire is attached to a metal blade that protrudes from the end of the plug's insulation. These blades correspond to clips that are contained inside each outlet. When the blades are inserted into the clips, the circuit is completed.

As a survivor, I urge you to find out more about the electrical system in your home. Though you should always rely on an electrician when in doubt, there is no reason you can't do a lot of troubleshooting and many minor electrical repairs on your own. Short circuits, blown fuses, and simple fixture wiring are not the mysterious and impossible problems many people think they are. Most home electrical work is simple, logical, and requires no specialized tools or skills. With a little know-how, you can take care of many problems, both saving money and developing self confidence in the process.

Safety Measures. Before you start, I would only advise you to pick up a good book on home wiring. Pay particular attention to the safety section so that you never endanger yourself while doing repairs. In particular, always remember to unplug an electrical device before working on it, and always turn off the power before working on an electrical circuit.

For further protection, make sure the wires in your home are well connected and well insulated. I have already mentioned rubber and plastic as two kinds of insulation used in electrical wiring. These same materials can be used as safeguards in areas where there may be risk of shock (see also "Lightning," page 210). Rubber gloves, rubber-soled shoes, and rubber mats are especially useful when working with electrical power or appliances. You can also put plastic inserts into unused wall outlets to safeguard young children. (This has the added advantage of cutting down on drafts of cold air that often flow through such outlets.) Also stay away from water and damp places when working around anything electrical, and keep heaters and hair dryers out of the bathtub. Water is a great conductor of electricity!

In case of shock, turn off the power immediately. If this is not possible and a person can't let go of a hot wire, you can break their grip with a wooden instrument or some other poor conductor. Do not touch the person with your bare hands unless you're sure they are no longer connected to the power source. Then call an emergency ambulance as quickly as possible and administer necessary first aid until it arrives.

Watching Watts

Survival in the broadest sense is not just being able to cope with emergencies, but living deliberately and responsibly. Conserving energy is only one of many ways we can do this, but it is an increasingly important one. It is one of the most direct ways we have of both saving money and expressing our concern for the earth.

To determine the amount of electricity used by a given appliance, simply multiply the wattage of the appliance (if you can't find it, multiply amps times volts) times the number of hours you use it, then divide by 1000. This will give you kilowatt hours. Then multiply the total kilowatt hours times the rate your power company charges for electricity.

For example, let's say you want to find out what it costs to keep a 100-watt light bulb burning for 24 hours. Multiply 24 times 100 watts and you get 2400 watts. Divide by 1000 and you get 2.4 kilowatts. If your power company charges 7 cents per kilowatt-hour, that's 2.4 times 7 cents, or 16.8 cents.

Another example: Let's say your dishwasher uses 1300 watts and you want to find out what it costs to run it each month. First, estimate the amount of time you use it each day. If you use it an hour a day, that would be about 30 hours a month. Multiply 1300 times 30 and you get 39,000.

Divide 39,000 by 1000 and you get 39 kilowatts. Your dishwasher uses 39 kilowatt hours per month. At 7 cents a kilowatt-hour, that's 7 times 39, or $2.73 per month.

Finally, let's look at the water heater. If it's electric, it uses about 3500 watts, and most people use it at least 100 hours a month. That's 350,000 watts, or 350 kilowatt hours of use. If your electric rate is 7 cents per kilowatt hour, it costs you $24.50 to heat water each month. See how the kilowatts add up?

Following is a listing of the average number of watts used by various home fixtures and appliances. Using the formula above, you might want to use it to help you find out where most of your electricity is going. Knowing this, you can decide where to cut down.

Appliance	Average Watts	Appliance	Average Watts
Air Conditioner	875	Microwave Oven	650
Blanket	175	Mixer (Hand)	125
Blender	350	Oven	3500
Broiler	1500	Radio	75
Clock	2	Range Burner	
Coffee Maker		6-inch	1600
Percolator	800	8-inch	2100
Automatic	1650	Refrigerator	300
Curlers	400	Rotisserie	1300
Dehumidifier	500	Sewing Machine	100
Dishwasher	1300	Shaver	15
Dryer (Clothes)	5000	Stereo	400
Freezer	450	Television	100
Frying Pan	1200	Toaster	1100
Hair Dryer	1000	Toothbrush	5
Heater (Space)	1300	Vacuum Cleaner	600
Iron	1000	Waffle Iron	1100
Lawn Mower	1000	Washing Machine	500
Light Bulb		Waterbed	400
Incandescent	100	Water Heater	3500
Fluorescent	40		

Heating Systems

Most houses and buildings have central heating systems that are fueled by electricity, oil, natural gas, or coal. Customarily, these gifts of nature are supplied by truck, wire, or pipe from distant wells, mines, and power plants, and they often go through many complicated processes before they can be used. If anything should go wrong with the production or distribution of these things, we could be left without power. Partly for this reason, and partly because of rising energy costs, many people have turned to cheaper and more direct methods of home heating, including wood stoves and nonpolluting solar heat.

With the exception of nuclear power, virtually all the energy we use is a result of the sun's effects on our planet. Green plants capture and store the sun's energy through photosynthesis, the quiet and miraculous process that sustains all life on earth. This little electric current that cultivates the world's greenery has also produced all of our fossil fuels. Coal, oil, and natural gas are nothing more than the ancient remnants of plants and animals that have been trapped in the earth's crust for millions of years. Even most electric heat, as we have seen, is generated either by these forms of energy or through the power of flowing water whose presence is dependent on the sun's part in the water cycle.

It's a long way from a beam of sunlight to a baseboard heater, but the connection is there. Most electric heat works by passing electrons through a coil of resistance wire, which in turn warms up the air or water that releases its heat into a room. Oil and gas are ignited by a burner, often under the impulse of an electric spark from a thermostat. A natural gas burner mixes gas with air in proportions that allow it to burn with a hot flame. Oil is atomized through a nozzle before it can be mixed with air and burned efficiently. Coal, like wood, is simply dumped into a firebox or boiler and burned directly.

Whatever the fuel, it heats up quantities of air or water, which in turn are distributed to different parts of the house through air ducts, hot water pipes, or steam pipes. Hot water or steam pipes release their energy through a radiator or a tube with metal fins called a convector. Air is blown into various rooms through ducts and registers.

I cannot go into the intricacies of these systems here. But you should understand your heating system and know how to keep it in good working order. If you have an electric heater, know how to vacuum it. If you have a gas burner, know how to clean the burner pipes, light the pilot light, adjust the burner flame, and operate the manual setting in the event of a local power failure. Manual operation isn't usually possible with an oil

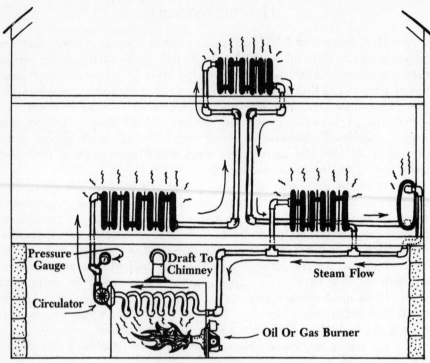

Steam Heating System

heating system because you need an electrically powered motor to vaporize the oil. Even so, you should at least know how it works so you can do some troubleshooting. You might even be interested to learn how to check, clean, and tune it up for maximum efficiency. Once you get the hang of it, it's as easy as tuning up a bike.

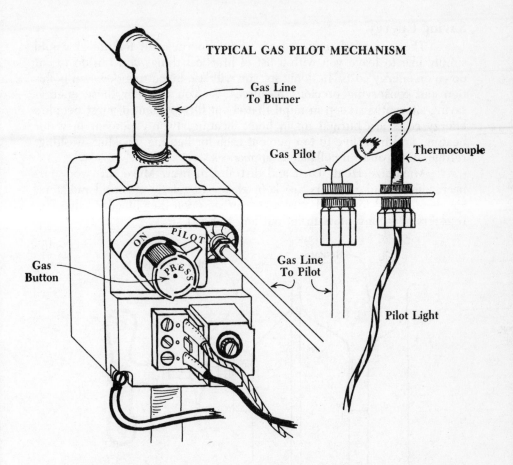

TYPICAL GAS PILOT MECHANISM

Gas Line
To Burner

Gas Pilot

Thermocouple

Gas
Button

ON PILOT

PRESS

Gas Line
To Pilot

Pilot Light

You should also know how to clean your furnace and do regular maintenance jobs on air blowers or water pumps. These things aren't difficult. You can learn volumes in short order by picking up a good book at your local library. What you learn by doing one thing may give you the confidence to go on and do other things: to service pipes, add dampers and ducts, or even to handle more technical aspects of your heating system. You may want to replace an old radiator with a new convector system. If you live in a hot climate, you may even decide to install your own air conditioning or humidifier, or to convert your oil burner to solar power. The more you learn to do for yourself, the better prepared you'll be to fix your heating system when it breaks down, or to supply heat by some alternative means if all else fails. More than that, you'll have a greater appreciation of where energy comes from, and a feeling of closer connection to the natural world that sustains all life.

Saving Energy

There is much more to say about energy. But for now I would simply like to leave you with a list of practical things you can do to cut down on energy costs. In doing so, you will also be cutting down on pollution and conserving precious resources. As you consider these energy-saving alternatives keep in mind that about fifty percent of most people's energy costs are burned up in home heating, twenty percent in water heating, and from five to ten percent each for lighting, cooking, washing, refrigeration, and miscellaneous appliances.

Maximize Heat. Dust and dirt absorb heat. Make sure your furnace, ducts, and registers are kept clean. Regularly clean all radiators, convectors, and fins. And once a year or so, open the "bleeder valves" in registers and convectors to let out any trapped air.

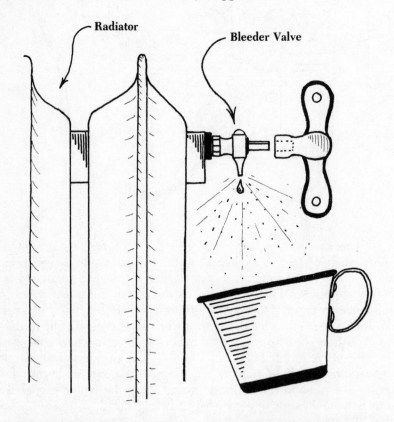

You can magnify the heat from radiators and convectors by taping heat-reflecting strips of aluminum foil behind them and by painting them a dark, non-metallic color. (Light, metallic colors don't radiate heat.) Even more effective, put insulation around pipes and ducts in cold areas of the house. And finally, adjust dampers and valves to allow a steady, even flow of air or water.

Understand Your Thermostat. The thermostat can cause lots of problems if it isn't working correctly, and very minor corrections in this little device can make a big difference in heat output. The thermostat's job is to send an electric spark to the furnace to ignite the fuel when your house temperature drops too low. It does this through the action of a small, coiled spring that expands and contracts as it gets hotter or colder. This coil is usually attached to a little vial containing a few drops of mercury. When the coil tightens up, it tips the vial just enough for the mercury to go sliding down the glass vial to complete the electrical circuit to the furnace.

The thermostat is a very delicate instrument, and several things often go wrong with it. First, it won't function well if it's placed in the wrong spot. Make sure the thermostat is on an internal wall in a place that is typical of the overall room temperature—not near a drafty door or window. A thermostat can also become jammed. Make sure the cover is put on evenly, and that the support clips don't interfere with the functioning of the spring or vial. The thermostat dial should move freely in both directions.

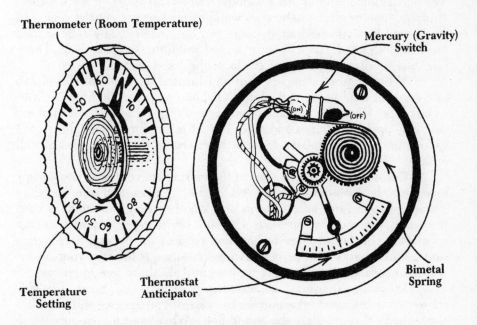

Thermometer (Room Temperature)

Mercury (Gravity) Switch

Temperature Setting

Thermostat Anticipator

Bimetal Spring

PARTS OF A THERMOSTAT

Sometimes dust and dirt can cause the coil to malfunction, too. This in turn can make the coil tip the vial at the wrong times, which in turn can cause great fluctuations in room temperature. Clean the coil periodically with a fine, soft dusting brush such as that sold in camera stores. Clean the contacts near the switch levers with a solution of vinegar and water on a cotton swab. Also make sure all wires near the coil are clean and securely connected. Always treat the coil very carefully to avoid bending it. (Also, of course, make sure the power is turned off before working on the thermostat.)

Keep the thermostat as low as you can comfortably handle. Most people think they need to keep the house at 72 degrees, when they could easily get by on 65 or lower during the day, and 55 or lower at night. It's a lot cheaper to put on a sweater and wool pants, or pajamas and extra blankets. It's also more invigorating and healthful.

Insulate. Keep precious heat in the house with well-insulated walls and ceilings. Install at least six inches of R-30 insulation in the attic and a layer of R-13-rated insulation for unheated walls and floors. ("R" is a measure of resistance to heat flow.) Good insulation can save you as much as fifty percent on your heating bills!

You can cut your heat losses by half just by installing storm windows, and you can slice off another third of the waste with caulking and weatherstripping around leaky window frames and doors. Even weatherstripping tape or clear plastic does wonders for keeping out the cold, and it's cheap. Homemade draft stoppers can be made out of a tube-shaped piece of cloth filled with a mixture of sand and little styrofoam balls. These can then be placed in front of cracks at the bases of drafty doors.

Keep fireplace dampers shut and furnace ducts unobstructed. To prevent heat from being sucked up the chimney, cover the fireplace with a glass door. Heat only as many rooms as you're going to use. If it's not too cold out, open the drapes and shades to let in the direct sunlight. Install gaskets under switch plates and plastic inserts in the receptacles of wall outlets.

Conserve Hot Water. One of the most effective money and energy savers is to heat water only when you need it. You can do this by installing a timer on your water-heater thermostat. Another thing you can do is keep the water temperature between 120 and 130 degrees, rather than the usual 140. This both conserves heat and reduces the possibility of burns. And a third energy- and money-saving precaution is to cover your heater with an insulation jacket. Some utilities provide these free of charge.

Washing. Showers take less energy than baths. Short, low-flow showers are the most economical. To make them cheaper still, install a showerhead that restricts the water flow. When washing clothes, wash with cold or warm water whenever possible, and dry clothes only as long as necessary. Wait to wash clothes and dishes until you have a full load. Rinse the dishes in cold water and dry them by hand or in the open air.

It's also smart not to pipe the heat from the clothes dryer outside in the winter. You can save the heat and catch the lint by disattaching the flexible pipe from the outside vent and attaching it to a piece of panty hose. Just make sure to replace the panty hose frequently enough so the lint buildup doesn't cut off the flow of warm air.

Kitchen Efficiency. Keep kitchen utilities working smoothly. Defrost the refrigerator when the frost gets more than a quarter-inch thick. Dust or vacuum refrigerator and freezer coils and grills. Clean the oven when it gets dirty. And make sure the door seals on cooling appliances are tight (especially on upright freezers) so the cold air doesn't escape. Check seals and gaskets by closing the door on a piece of paper. If you can easily pull the paper out, you probably need to replace the seal.

Plan your meals for maximum efficiency. When possible, use electric pans and small ovens—better yet, a microwave. If you use a conventional oven, don't preheat it unless absolutely necessary, and cook several dishes at the same time. Use a timer instead of opening the oven to check the food, and turn the oven off before the meal is done. If your timing is right, it will retain enough heat to finish the cooking.

When cooking on burners, use the smallest ones first. Match the pot or pan to the size of the burner, and keep pots covered to hasten the cooking time. Better yet, use a pressure cooker. Keep all burners, vents, and reflectors clean and free of grease.

Lighting. Lamps and lights take comparatively little electricity, but if they're allowed to burn constantly, their wattage adds up fast. Turn them off when not in use. Also, buy low wattage bulbs and look for bulbs that will give you the best illumination per watt. Fluorescent lamps give from three to five times more light than incandescent lamps. But if you're using incandescent ones, stay away from the tinted and long-life types. You can also profit from keeping lampshades clean, and from light-colored walls and ceilings that don't absorb the light.

Thermal Landscaping. There are actions you can take outside the house, too, to cut down on energy costs. When the wind picks up in cold weather, it prevents radiant heat from getting through the walls and also penetrates through cracks to cause drafts. In short, it makes your heating system work overtime. For example, it takes twice as much heat to warm a house in a twenty-mile-an-hour wind as it does when there's only a slight breeze. You can help to prevent this not only with insulation, but by planting trees and shrubs on the sides of the house that are most exposed to the prevailing weather systems.

You can also use the natural shade of trees to prevent excessive heat radiation through walls and windows in summer. Windows and walls can let in tremendous amounts of heat when exposed to direct sunlight, just as they do in a greenhouse. Trees not only provide shade for buildings and grounds, but also protect from excessive heat and cold by providing natural pockets of dead air space next to the house (see "Insulate," page 104).

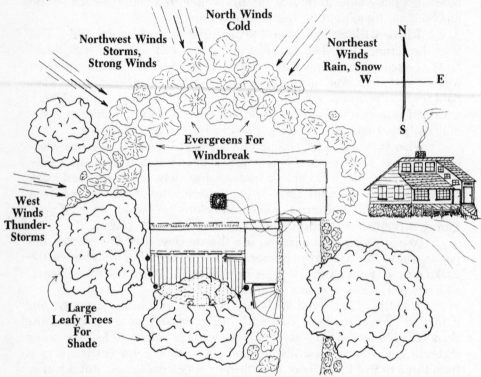

The best thermal landscaping is provided by deciduous trees. In the summer their leaves block the heat, and in the winter their bare branches let in the sunlight. Fir trees, on the other hand, are best for controlling wind, since the air has to sift through millions of tiny needles before hitting your house. They are also excellent snow blocks.

Trees are most effective as shading if planted on the east and west sides of a dwelling. You can control the extent of the shade by the number and type of trees you choose and where you plant them. They don't have to be full grown to make a big difference. You can also use trees or ground contouring to deflect the wind over or around your house in particularly chilly areas.

Fix Your Fireplace. Generally, fireplaces are pleasant but not very good heat producers. Sometimes this is because of poor design. The fireplace may be taller than it is wide and allow smoke to billow out the top instead of going up the chimney. Sometimes there's a poor draft, which can be fixed either by opening a door or window or by building on to the chimney so it's more exposed to moving air. And sometimes the chimney is full of soot. This problem can be solved either by calling a chimney sweep or by scraping the insides of the chimney yourself with a bag of gravel attached to the end of a long rope.

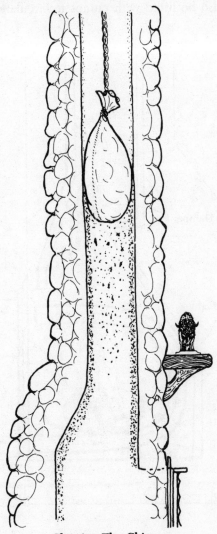

Cleaning The Chimney

One of the best ways to improve the heat output of your fireplace is with a simple fire reflector. In the woods when I'm concerned about making the most of my fire's heat, I depress the fire in a little disk-shaped hole and build a reflecting wall of wood, rocks, or dirt around one side. In the city you can install a thick iron plate in the back of your fireplace to bounce the heat into the room. In fact, you can do almost as well with a thick sheet of aluminum, or even a sheet of heavy-duty aluminum foil. A more expensive alternative is to buy a convection gate—a C-shaped set of hollow tubes that sucks in cold air at the bottom and blows hot air out the top. These can also be fitted with pumps to circulate the air.

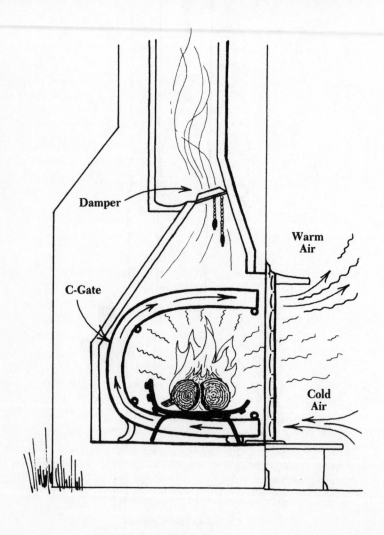

Install a Wood Stove. Until recently, wood stoves were looked on as relics of the pioneer age or artifacts of the cold north. As the price of oil and gas have spiraled, though, wood-stove heating has become more and more popular. Though it isn't likely to replace oil and gas in urban areas, it can save a considerable amount of money by supplementing central heating systems. A wood stove can even be attached to an already-existing ductwork and take over the central heating job completely. (See also "Makeshift Heaters and Stoves," page 119.)

What Kind of Wood? Whether you have a fireplace or a wood stove, you should use the best fuel you can get for a reasonable price. The best ones are those that burn the longest and with the least amount of smoke and sparks. Ideal is hard coal, which burns virtually without smoke and soot and produces a great deal of heat. Surprisingly, sawdust logs are also near the top of the list for energy output and burning time, but are quite expensive. Next come the slow- but even-burning hardwoods such as the hickories and oaks. Most of these produce from twenty-five to thirty million BTUs per cord, but most of them also have to be well seasoned. In the middle range are the medium hardwoods such as maple, birch, and fir. These produce a lot of heat (twenty to twenty-five million BTUs per cord) but burn faster with more smoke and sparks. And at the bottom of the list are the light softwoods such as cedar and pine, which make good kindling but which generally put out only between fifteen and twenty million BTUs per cord. They also burn very hot and fast, usually with lots of smoke and/or sparks.

Emergency Lighting and Heating

When the power goes off, we have to forget the frills and get back to basics. If we're well prepared, we can supply heat and light with backup systems. If not, we have to use more primitive methods.

Some Lighting Alternatives

Flashlights are indispensable in urban emergency and survival situations. They are good not only for short-term problems such as flat tires and household problems, but also for finding and organizing the things you need for long-term survival.

Flashlights come in a variety of shapes and sizes. You can find everything from tiny penlights with AA batteries to gargantuan lunchbox types that carry a half dozen or more D-cell batteries. For most household and automotive purposes, a standard-sized flashlight with two C- or D-cell batteries is adequate and convenient. I would recommend having at least two in the home and one in the car at all times. I would also recommend buying alkaline, cadmium, or some other type of long-lasting batteries. And since all batteries gradually discharge with time whether they're used or not, check them frequently and replace them every six months.

Kerosene lanterns and oil lamps also provide good emergency lighting. Furthermore, they are safer than candles, can be refueled, and often burn with adjustable flames. One of the best is the large Coleman camping lantern. I would recommend keeping at least one such lantern in the house, along with several small oil or kerosene lamps and plenty of extra fuel. With some reservation, I would also recommend kerosene

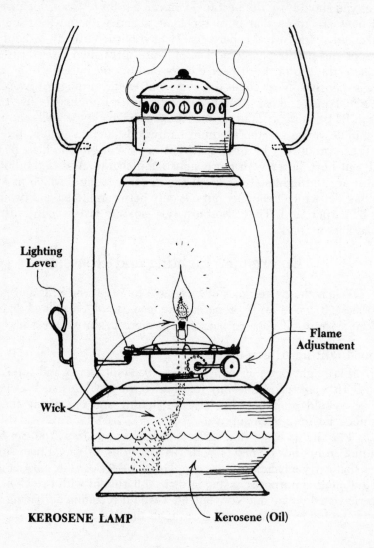

Lighting Lever

Flame Adjustment

Wick

KEROSENE LAMP   Kerosene (Oil)

heaters. They can be dangerous (they are banned in some states), but if watched while burning, they can be a godsend in an emergency.

As a final precaution, it's always smart to have a good supply of long-burning candles. These should never be used inside emergency shelters, but only in the open where there is no danger of fire. They should also be set in sturdy holders or foundations and watched from time to time. For more light and safety, you can make an emergency lantern with a candle and a tin can, as shown in the illustration. (Hint: The larger the can, the better the reflecting surface.)

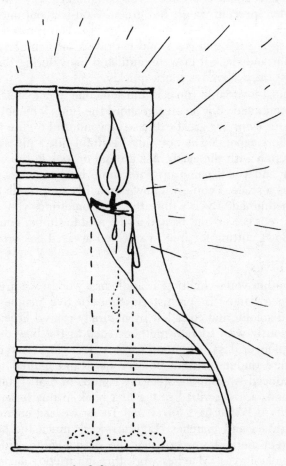

Makeshift Tin Can Lamp

The Wood Option

A wood stove or fireplace with plenty of stored fuel is always good survival insurance. In the far north, where most people rely on wood for heating and cooking, it's common practice to lay away half a dozen or more cords of wood for the winter. In the city, even if you use wood fires only for decoration and added cheer, I would recommend having at least a cord or two on hand for an emergency. Get plenty of well-seasoned wood to last you through a power outage, and some more wet wood that you can allow to season for six months or more.

A cord of wood measures four-by-four-by-eight feet, and when well dried it weighs about two tons. Even completely "dry" wood contains up to twenty-five percent water, but green wood is about one-third water by weight and reduces the efficiency of the fire. You can tell dry wood from wet because it begins to crack and is quite a bit lighter to heft. For best results, split and stack it in well-ventilated piles during the warm months when moisture evaporates more quickly.

Almost invariably you can find someone to cut, split, and deliver all the wood you need. But if you can afford the time, why not try cutting and splitting your own? It's great exercise, a wonderful excuse to get outdoors, and the effort expended is not only healthful but a pleasant reminder of our connection with the earth. Ask around or look in the want ads of your newspaper and you'll come up with some likely sources. Most sawmills have scraps for sale. People who own orchards and woodlots often want to have them thinned. Even within the city sometimes you can find people who want trees cut up and hauled away. And in timber country the Forest Service allows cutting for free in selected areas. Look around.

Starting Fires

Whether you're lighting a candle or a woodstove fire, you first have to produce a flame. In prehistoric times native peoples gathered and transported smoldering coals left by naturally caused fires or started their fires laboriously with friction methods such as the bow drill and the fire thong. In pioneer days, mountain men carried a little wad of charred cloth or other fine tinder inside a powder horn and ignited the tinder with sparks produced by rapping steel on a piece of flint. (Many of these ancient methods are described in the first book in this series, *Tom Brown's Field Guide to Wilderness Survival.*) Today we use chemical firestarters such as lighters and matches. Lighters work much the same as the old flint-and-steel methods, except that the sparks ignite a fuel-impregnated wick or a volatile gas. Matches work through friction against highly combustible dry chemicals such as phosphorus and sulfur mixed with powdered sand and glass.

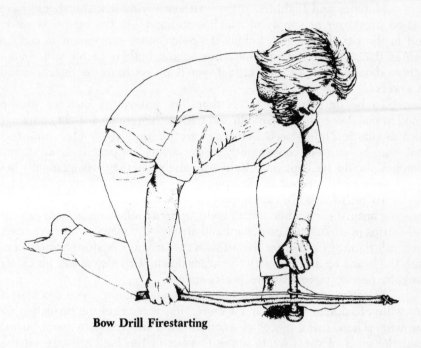

Bow Drill Firestarting

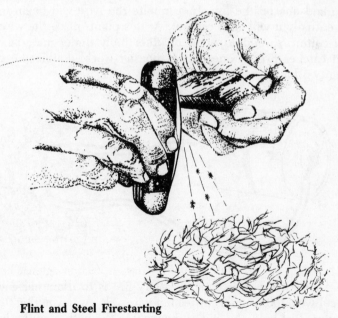

Flint and Steel Firestarting

Matches and Lighters. It goes without saying that you should have a good firestarter or supply of matches on hand—in the house, at work, and in the car. Personally, I think it's much more convenient to carry a lighter than a bunch of matches. But having both is better still. If the lighter should fail or run out of fuel, you'll always have the matches; and vice versa.

To be on the safe side, either buy waterproof matches or dip wooden matches in liquid paraffin and encase them in an airtight container such as plastic Ziploc bags. Better yet are plastic vials or film cannisters that can be carried conveniently in a variety of places. Even safety matches should be kept in airtight containers, as they will gradually acquire moisture if left out in the open.

To guard against closely-packed "strike-anywhere" matches from scraping against each other and all going up in a puff of smoke, you can cut little strips of corrugated cardboard and arrange the matches one to a hole, then roll them up and store them this way. Or you can store half of them with the heads up and half with the heads down. This also makes for closer packing; hence, more matches per container.

Batteries. If you run out of matches and lighters, you can start a fire with a flashlight battery and a short, thin wire. Peel the insulation off the wire. Then, using pieces of wood or other insulation to avoid burns, hold the ends of the wire to opposite ends of the battery—one on the bottom and one on the top. In a minute the wire will begin to heat up, and eventually it will glow red-hot. At this point, place the wire against a wad of cotton, shredded paper, or other fluffy tinder material, and blow until it catches fire. If one battery doesn't work, double the voltage by holding two batteries together.

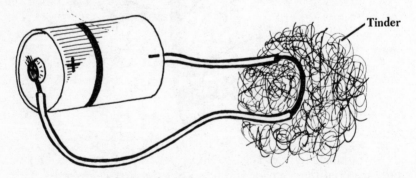

Tinder

Another way of making a battery fire is to use a half-inch strip of fine steel wool (00 or finer) instead of wire. This way you don't even need any tinder. Just hold one end of the wool to the bottom of the battery and rub the other end over the top until it sparks. When the steel wool catches a spark, simply place it in the fire and blow until it flames up.

Magnifying Lenses. On a hot day, you may be able to start a fire with a magnifying glass by focusing the rays of the sun to a tiny point on a bundle of fine tinder such as a ball of cotton. If the sun is hot enough, the tinder will start to smoke. At this point, blow gently until it bursts into flame.

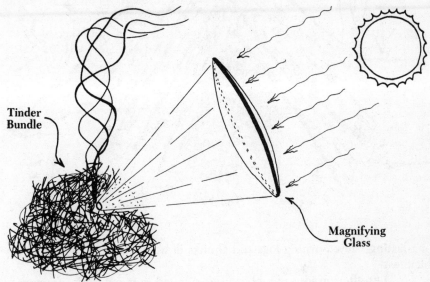

Tinder Bundle

Magnifying Glass

Fueling Fires

Even a flaming wad of tinder or steel wool won't start much of a fire unless you can keep the flame burning. To do this, remember how fires work. First, they tend to burn upwards with the hottest part of the flame at the top. If you want something to burn, place it just above the flame, not below or to the side. Second, a fire must have a constant supply of oxygen. That means you've always got to provide "breathing space" or a draft of some kind for fresh air to work its way in and around the burning fuel. And third, you can't burn a big piece of wood with a little flame. You have to start with small and easily-combustible pieces and gradually add larger ones as the fire grows hotter.

Firemaking fuels fall into four categories. First is tinder, the light, fluffy material that catches and nourishes the first flame or spark. Next is kindling, tiny pieces of wood or twigs that range from the thickness of a matchstick to that of a pencil. Third is squaw wood, which is usually about thumb-sized to wrist-sized in thickness. And last is bulk firewood, the

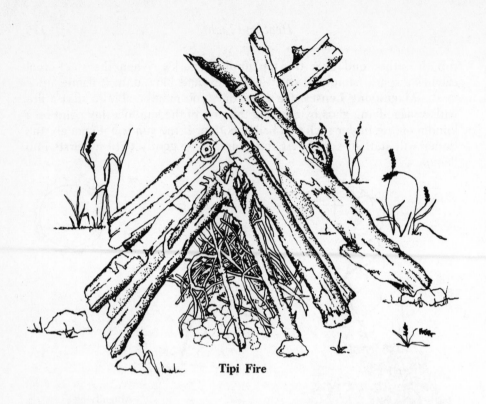

Tipi Fire

long-lasting, slow-burning logs and chunks of wood that can be almost any thickness.

These four grades of fuel can be arranged in many ways, depending on the purpose of the fire. In the wilderness I usually start by placing the tinder inside a tipi structure composed of progressively larger layers of fuel. The tipi fire is particularly good because it protects the delicate flame from wind and rain, burns hotly and smoothly, and channels the smoke upward. For ease of starting, I recommend starting with a tipi structure and then modifying the fire's shape to fit your needs once you have a good bed of coals.

If you have an open blaze outside and you want quick, hot coals, you can build a log cabin structure around the tipi fire. This is made by placing sticks or logs over each other at right angles in the manner of Lincoln logs. Taper the structure so that the hottest (highest) part of the flames will lick and quickly roast the top logs.

If you're low on fuel or want only a small, flickering fire, you can build a "star fire" after the tipi fire has produced a bed of coals. In this arrangement, the ends of three or four large pieces barely touch in the center and radiate out like the spokes of a wagon wheel. These can simply be pushed farther in as the ends are consumed.

When building fires in fireplaces, stoves, and other containers, you won't be so concerned about the shape of the fire. Your main concern will be getting the initial blaze going and maintaining the bed of coals. But regardless of where you make the fire, you still have to apply the basic principles, including proper ventilation and the right size fuel for the flame.

Conservation. Always be conservative about the amount of fuel you use. You can't be sure how long you'll have to go without power. In most cases, it's unlikely this will be more than a few days. But if you don't need the fuel today, you may need it tomorrow. Or somebody else will. Conservation is also a way of showing respect for the earth and acknowledging our dependence on the natural processes that sustain us. It is a simple way of giving thanks.

Emergency Fuel. If you run out of regular fuel and you're really up against it, anything flammable is fair game. That means everything from the backyard fence to the living room furniture. The choices get more difficult as the fuel supply dwindles. If you have qualms about burning a favorite oak desk, you may choose to sacrifice an unused portion of the house. It's rare that anyone has to take such drastic measures, but it does happen. Just remember that no material possession is worth your life.

To be on the safe side, burn only "clean" fuels. Stay away from things like charcoal, tar, and synthetics. These often produce carbon monoxide and other highly toxic gases that can cause sickness or even death when inhaled. If you have to burn a questionable fuel, make sure you're out in the open, well away from the fumes.

Heating With Hot Rocks

Other than candles, lamps, and camp stoves (which you should always use carefully and with adequate ventilation), never have an open flame in the house. But that doesn't mean you can't build a fire outside and bring the heat back in. One of the best ways to do this is to heat up rocks. Just build a roaring fire, drop a quantity of bricks or football-sized rocks or chunks of cement into it until they are red-hot, then transport them back into the house in a stainless steel bucket or big, non-coated cooking pot. Don't use aluminum, as it tends to burn through rather quickly. Also avoid any galvanized or painted containers. And always get the rocks from a high, dry area—never from a place where they may have absorbed moisture, as this can cause them to explode when heated.

Carry the bucket very carefully to avoid getting burned, perhaps running a stout pole or broomstick through the handle for two-person transport. Then place it on a noncombustible insulating platform such as a baking pan or an oven rack supported by bricks. A two-gallon bucket of

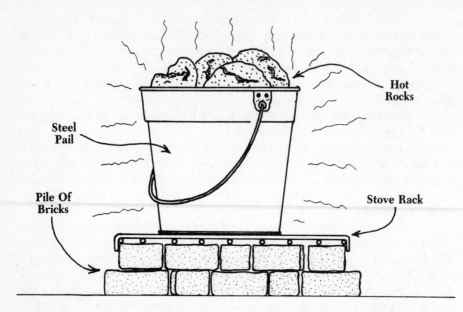

hot rocks will heat an average-sized room for hours. As long as you don't actually touch the rocks, you can get as close as you like to warm hands, feet, and other parts of the body. When the rocks have cooled off enough to touch, they can then be tucked beneath blankets to help provide a warm bed and sleeping area.

If your shelter is outside on bare ground, you can dig a trench beneath the bedding area and line it with hot rocks. Then refill the trench with dirt, allow the moisture to evaporate, and put your bedding over the top. This arrangement will keep you warm all night long.

A variation on the hot rock theme can be used to heat a large concrete bedding area. Just light a fire and fuel it so it spreads out and burns over the entire sleeping area. You can use the fire for cooking and heating during the day. Then at night when you're ready to turn in, scrape the coals away from the bedding area, wait for the concrete to cool down a little, and put your bedding right on top of the toasty concrete. If you'd rather not wait, place some form of nonflammable insulation beneath your bedding. If it's really hot, you can even use something like cinder blocks to support a "mattress" of plywood until the concrete cools down.

Hot rocks can also be used for cooking. Just plunk a small hot rock in a kettle of water and watch it boil! You can control the boil by the size of the rock. A red-hot baseball-sized rock will keep a gallon of water boiling for fifteen minutes or more. Outside, you can dig a pit in the ground and line it with hot rocks, then place the meal in a pot or cover it with aluminum foil and allow it to cook. Lacking a container, you can place the food between two thick layers of grasses before putting it on the rocks. Then fill in the rest of the pit with dirt and your food will be steam-cooked.

Makeshift Heaters and Stoves

Almost any open flame can be made more efficient by enclosing it in a metal container. Instead of quickly escaping, the heat from the flame is trapped and reflected. Then it collects and radiates through the walls of the container, casting its warmth in all directions. This is what stoves are all about. Once you have made one on your own and fired it up and huddled around it in the cold, you'll never forget how simple and wonderful an invention it is.

Basically, all wood stoves have three important elements: a combustion chamber to hold the burning fuel, a draft opening to let in fresh air, and an exhaust hole or flue for the smoke. They can be made out of anything from mass-manufactured cast iron to old oil barrels and even tin cans. It doesn't matter how primitive the stove may be; it can even multiply the heat from a candle or kerosene lamp.

Coffee-Can Stoves. Simple stoves can be made from containers as humble as coffee cans. The fuel can be anything from a candle or a kerosene lamp to a can of Sterno placed beneath the open end of the can. To create a draft, all you have to do is punch some holes around the sides of the can at both ends; then place the can open-end-down on a fireproof platform such as that created by two bricks. This way, air is sucked in through the bottom of the apparatus and feeds the flame as it flows out through the top. The heat collects and radiates slowly through the top and sides of the container.

These contraptions can be used not only as single-burner hotplates to warm food, but also as small space heaters near shelter entrances. The larger the can and the larger the flame, the more heat is produced. The heat from three candles will often be enough to boil a cup of water or heat a can of beans. With a large pot and a supply of Sterno or other "canned" fuel, you may be able to cook an entire meal. With a fire set beneath an elevated tub, you've got yourself a sizable burner for cooking all kinds of things. You can even make your own canned fuel by cutting thin strips of corrugated cardboard, rolling them up in a tuna can, and pouring paraffin over them. When the paraffin is dry, all you have to do is touch a match to the cardboard edges and you'll get a wide, hot, cooking flame.

For safety's sake, make sure the fuel source is secured in a sturdy, fireproof holder. And if you use more than one candle, keep them far enough apart so they don't melt each other. Also, whenever you're using an open flame in the house, keep someone awake and alert at all times.

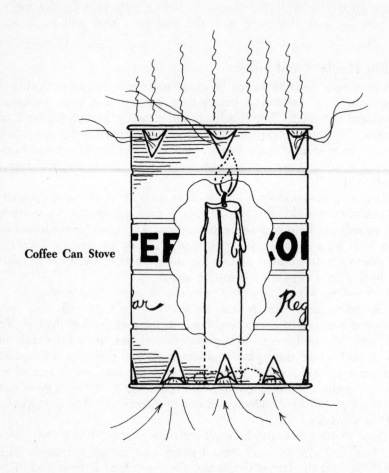

Coffee Can Stove

Medium-Sized Stoves. An unbelievably simple and effective wood-stove can be made from a five-gallon steel can such as those used for storing oil or kerosene (thoroughly cleaned, of course). If you plan it right, you can simply unscrew the cap and use that hole as an opening for the draft at the bottom. Then cut a large hole in the top or side for a stokehole (to put in the wood—not candles!) and a smaller hole in the top for the exhaust. If you're in a real hurry, just cut three sides of a stokehole and pry the "door" in and out with your fingers. If you have more time, either fashion a makeshift hinge for your side door or cut a circular stokehole in the top and use a pot lid to cover it after you get the fire going.

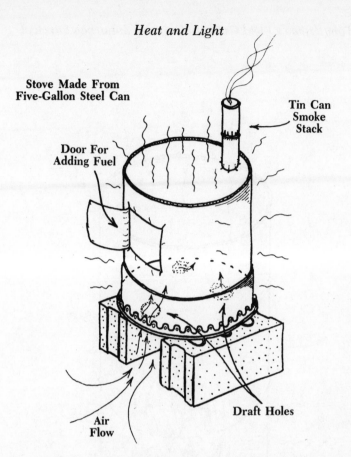

**Stove Made From
Five-Gallon Steel Can**

**Tin Can
Smoke
Stack**

**Door For
Adding Fuel**

Draft Holes

**Air
Flow**

Five-gallon cans (or larger) work fine for most emergency heating and cooking needs, but you may want to make improvements. For example, most stoves work better with stovepipes on the exhaust hole to increase the draft. These can be made out of materials as simple as a series of interlocking tin cans with the tabs folded outward on one end. As time permits, you can make larger and more complicated stoves, including those with hinged and latched doors and adjustable drafts and more sophisticated stovepipes. If your stovepipe is long enough to reach through a window or hole in the wall and you prepare a safe, non-combustible platform, you can even use your homemade stove inside.

Oil Drums and Garbage Cans. Following similar principles, you can use even larger containers for outside heating. After punching airholes near the bottom of an old steel garbage can, you can light and maintain a roaring fire right inside. The heat produced will be enough to warm many people as they gather around it. Empty oil drums also work for this purpose after their tops have been removed and they've been checked for toxic or flammable chemicals.

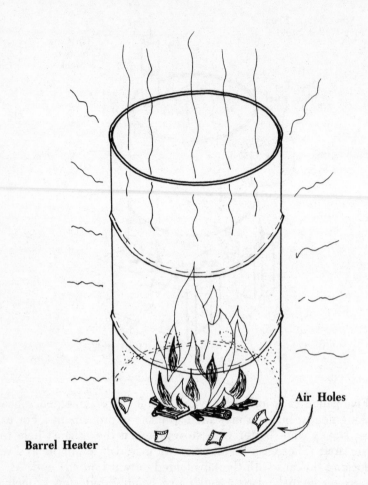

Air Holes

Barrel Heater

Such large containers can also be used in conjunction with outside shelters as makeshift "central heating" devices. Just place the can or barrel in a spot where it will reflect lots of heat. If the house foundation is still intact, put the burner at the junction of two walls. If part of the fireplace is still intact, try creating a woodstove effect by connecting the barrel with the chimney. This provides more radiant heat than a fireplace, as well as a usable cooking surface. You can also build several small shelters in a circular formation with entrances opening toward a "central heating" barrel— or a large, open shelter with the barrel in the middle and sleeping spots around the sides.

Fire and Automobiles

Automobiles offer special problems and opportunities for firemaking. It's unlikely you'll need a fire for warmth in an auto unless you're stranded and you've run out of gas in subzero temperatures without adequate insulation. If you must start a fire, though, never start it inside the car. Don't even start it near a car unless you're sure there are no leaking gas lines or combustible fumes. Always move a safe distance away and start the fire downwind from the car to prevent any sparks from blowing on or near it.

Batteries, Etc. If you don't have matches but your battery is still working, you have several alternatives. One is to use the cigarette lighter to ignite a wad of paper or other finely shredded tinder. Simply hold the glowing lighter against the tinder and blow until it catches flame. Another alternative is the battery itself. First, remove the battery and carry it to the downwind fire site. Then prepare a fire pit with a reflecting wall and the four necessary grades of fuel. Finally, attach separate wires to the negative and positive terminals of the battery, taking care not to let them touch until you're ready. When everything is set, put the tinder beside the battery and scrape the ends of the wires together. (Make sure they're well insulated except on the ends!) This will create a shower of sparks. When the sparks fall onto the tinder, gently blow them into flame.

With this method, use wires that are as thick as the ones usually attached to the battery. Ideal would be jumper cables. Lacking these, in a dire emergency you can cut short sections from the car's own battery cables. It's possible to start a fire by burning a single wire, as with flashlight batteries (see page 114), but I do not advise doing this with a twelve-volt car battery. Not only is it more cumbersome, but the added voltage increases the chances of burns and shocks.

Fuel. As for fuel, you'll have to use anything you can find. If you're in a woodsy area, you can gather tinder, kindling, and squaw wood as you would in a wilderness survival situation—from standing dead trees or from the undersides of dead branches on live trees. If you're in a very dry area, you may be able to use dry leaves, grasses, branches, or other materials taken from the ground. But in a damp area, always gather fire materials from high up where they can't absorb ground moisture. If it's extremely wet, you can give the fire an initial boost by dipping a rag into the oil chamber or treating your tinder with a little combustible grease taken from door hinges and steering rods. Never use gasoline, though; the risk of explosion is not worth it.

Burning Spare Tires. If you're in an area where there is no natural fuel and you need a fire to signal for help, you might consider lighting your spare tire. To do this, first prepare a fire pit with a reflecting wall at least ten to fifteen feet away from the car on the downwind side. If the car is not out of gas, set the fire twenty to thirty feet away, depending on the hazard. Clear the area of flammable debris. Take the tire to the fire site and deflate it by either removing the valve completely or puncturing the tire with a screwdriver or other sharp object. Don't ignite the tire if there's any air inside, as it may explode.

Cover the tire with greasy rags or other easily combustible material (not gasoline!) and light the material with an open flame. Matches, lighters, and highway flares all work admirably. Once the tire is well lit, it should burn for hours with a thick, black smoke. Because of the fumes (stay away from them), a flaming spare tire is not an ideal heating alternative, but it's an excellent signaling device that can be seen for many miles and will probably bring the State Patrol or the Forest Service into the area within minutes.

Manifold Cooking. If you've got plenty of fuel in the car, you might be interested to know that you've got a cooking stove built right into the engine. This is the manifold, the pipe on either side of the engine that leads to the exhaust. This pipe has several smaller pipes coming off it, each one leading to a combustion chamber inside the engine. Each time a piston compresses and the fuel-and-air combination inside the chamber explodes, the heat and exhaust go rushing out the manifold pipe. This pipe gets easily hot enough for cooking.

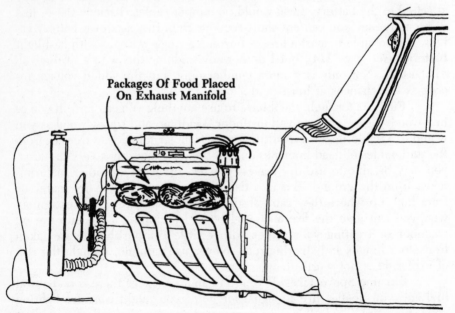

Packages Of Food Placed On Exhaust Manifold

Just how you use it depends on the manifold's size and position. But by locating it, you can figure out some interesting alternatives. If you have a can or pork and beans, for example, you can pry open the can and place it on the manifold until it starts to steam and bubble. You can do the same with a can of water. More ingenious devices can be concocted with cooking pans and other equipment. With thick aluminum foil you can wrap up a whole meal (including chicken, potatoes, and all the trimmings) and tie it to your "car cooker." One man I know has gotten so fanatic about this kind of cooking that he regularly straps a meal to his manifold at the start of a trip and stops for a bite to eat when he thinks it's done. A little eccentric, to be sure, but in a survival situation, who cares?

Fire Safety

Now, after all this talk about controlled fires, here are a few parting tips about how to avoid the uncontrolled ones and how to deal with them if they break out:

First, avoid unnecessary clutter in your home or workplace—especially things like oily rags that can start burning by spontaneous combustion. This also goes for cans of flammable or explosive liquids such as gasoline, benzene, and turpentine. Better to store and use them outside where the gases can safely escape. At the very least, use them in a well-ventilated area. And never smoke or use any flame around such substances.

Second, use your electrical appliances with care. Pay special attention to such things as irons and stoves that generate lots of heat. Turn off all electrical appliances that are not in use. Avoid short circuits by making sure all wiring is solid and well insulated. Don't overload circuits by running too many appliances on one outlet, or by running high-amp machines on low-amp circuits. Keep wiring out in the open and away from combustible materials.

Third, check your heating system to make sure it's operating smoothly. Be wary of such things as clogged chimneys and rusted or cracked furnace pipes. Keep all combustible materials away from boilers, furnaces, fireplaces, and electric lights. Finally, if you're still uncertain about the safety of your house, you may want to install a smoke alarm. These can be a real pain if they go off while you're cooking hamburgers, but they can also be lifesavers if the house starts smoking when you're asleep.

You can usually put out a small fire if you get to it soon enough. But be very careful. First make sure you know what's fueling it. If it's an oil or grease fire, don't use water or you'll only make matters worse. Shut off the fuel supply and then try to smother the fire with draperies, rugs, clothing, towels, blankets, etc. If it's an electrical fire, turn off the electricity first. Then douse the flames with a fire extinguisher, garden hose, or a bucket of water. If you can safely do so, get the burning material out of the house.

If the fire is out of control, leave the house as quickly as possible. If you see smoke billowing under a door and you think there's fire on the other side, don't open the door. Doing so will only fuel the fire with fresh oxygen. Make your exit through another door or window if possible.

If you have no choice but to work your way through a burning room, stay close to the floor. The freshest air is nearest the ground. Breathe through your nose to prevent burning your lungs. If possible, put a wet towel over your head. If you're in a building, use the fire escape or the stairs, never the elevator (which may not function, or which may open on another burning floor). Don't stop to get valuables, clothes, or other items before leaving the building. Call the fire department only after you and your family are safely outside.

5
FOOD

It's not often in our busy world that we stop to think about where our food comes from. Delivery trucks pull up to our favorite stores and restaurants with such predictable regularity that it seems nothing could interrupt their rounds. Supermarket aisles bulge with such luscious-looking displays of fruits and vegetables that it almost appears they had grown there. Meats are so neatly packaged that it seems the animal might have died without sacrifice.

Today, instead of laboriously tilling the soil and tending the herd, we push grocery carts along neatly ordered rows of packaged goods, picking our meals off the shelves more easily than apples off a tree. If we like, we can even take our food on the run, driving up to a window with a rumbling stomach one moment and driving off the next with a chicken sandwich and a chocolate sundae. Convenience is the order of the day. As long as we have money, food seems ours for the taking. The supply seems inexhaustible.

But is it? In fact, the United States has very limited food reserves. Our supermarket–restaurant–fast-food cornucopia is only the end of a long and complicated chain. Like our water and power systems, this chain includes many vital links. When we pick an avocado off the shelf, we unwittingly acknowledge not only the grocery clerk, the trucker, and the grower, but also the sun and the soil. Far removed as it may seem in its gleaming aluminum package, even a TV dinner has its roots in the earth. It is brought to us only through the efforts of hundreds of people and machines, all of which are dependent on natural processes.

In spite of our apparent security, then, any number of problems can cut off our food supply. Among others, these include floods, droughts, strikes, and even unemployment and personal illness. It's comforting to know that most food-related emergencies do not last more than a few days, and that a healthy adult can go for as much as a month or more without food. Even so, different people have different nutritional needs. Without proper nutrition, the body can weaken and become prone to diseases that may make it harder to meet more pressing needs.

For these reasons, it's wise to know how to provide emergency food. As the following pages explain, there are a variety of ways to do this, including food storage and growing and gathering your own. If you're a frugal person, you'll also be interested in knowing some ways of buying or obtaining food that will enable you to maintain your nutritional needs on a very tight budget. Finally, if you're truly destitute, you can take heart in

127

the fact that there are some unconventional but viable food sources in the city that can keep you going until you get back on your feet—even if you're flat broke and can't tell a dandelion from an artichoke.

Keep in mind as you read this chapter that it is not meant as an exhaustive study of emergency food sources, but as a broad view of what's possible. To adopt all or even some of these suggestions would take quite a bit of planning and practice for most families and might represent a major shift in life-style. So don't be overwhelmed by the possibilities. Instead, look at them realistically and decide which ones, if any, you would like to adopt. Then adopt them gradually; don't do too much at once. Most important, share with family and friends. Do further reading, take workshops, discuss alternatives, pool resources, and learn new skills and procedures together. That way your survival preparations will have a firmer foundation.

Storing Food

If you have ever watched a squirrel in the fall, you know that one of its top priorities is storing nuts and seeds for the winter. It goes about its work with amazing earnestness, stuffing seeds in cheek pouches, transporting acorns between its teeth, and caching the precious goods in places that will keep them relatively safe for the future. Sometimes the squirrel doesn't get around to eating all of its cache, or even forgets where it has left a particular meal. But its collecting and digging are deadly serious. The squirrel stores food because it instinctively knows that otherwise it will probably starve.

For most wild animals that may have to endure meager times, hunger is a pretty good reason to store food. It is also good reason for human beings. In North America, both native people and pioneers depended for centuries on what they could sock away for the winter. Even today many individuals and groups habitually store emergency supplies of food as survival insurance.

In the country, my family and I have easy access to a garden and a variety of domesticated animals if store-bought food becomes scarce. If necessary, we could even forage for our food, since we are familiar with wilderness survival skills and the nearby hills and woods abound with wild edible plants and animals. In the city, though, most people do not have access to such foods. This makes storage the most logical and reasonable alternative.

A second argument for storage is that it cuts down on food costs. Instead of buying in small quantities and at high prices every few days, you can buy most of your foodstuffs in large quantities and at low prices every few weeks and fill in around the edges. If you store, you are also more likely to keep your eye out for sales and bargain buys that you would otherwise not notice.

Finally, storing forces you to be more deliberate about what you eat. Since the first rule is that you don't store what you don't eat, you really have to think about what kinds of foods you want in your diet. Under these circumstances, you're much more likely to choose healthful foods than you would if you bought only on impulse. Having the food on hand also cuts down on last-minute trips to the grocery store, as well as the tendency many people have to rely on "junk foods."

A Two-Week Food Supply

Civil Defense authorities recommend having a two-week emergency supply of food—one that you can either use at home or take with you in an evacuation. This makes excellent sense. Such a supply would probably see you through ninety-five percent of the circumstances that might threaten your usual food supply, and would ease your entry into another community if you ever had to relocate. Also, if you didn't need the food yourself, you would be in a position to help someone who did.

In putting together such an emergency food supply, don't discount nutrition. Before you buy, consider the kinds of situations that might necessitate using this emergency food. They are likely to be very stressful and physically demanding. To prepare for them, you should include plenty of high-energy foods, as well as some lightweight, nonperishable sources of protein. Since you may also be on the move or without electricity, none of these foods should require refrigeration.

For a two-week survival situation, I would first recommend the kinds of foods you might take with you on a two-week backpacking excursion. For the least bulk and the lightest weight, you can't beat freeze-dried foods. These foods have gone through a deep-freeze process in which all the moisture is drawn off without robbing the food of its important nutrients. Weight and bulk are reduced to a fraction of the original, and the food is vacuum sealed in nitrogen for spoil-proof storage. Moreover, most freeze-dried foods contain no additives, and most of them rehydrate within a few minutes. Their only real shortcoming is their cost. (But then, one might ask, what's it worth to survive and stay healthy in an emergency?)

Other foods I would highly recommend are powdered milk, instant cocoa, dehydrated soups, beef jerky, high-energy mixes of nuts and dried fruits, dehydrated fruits and vegetables (see "Dehydrating," page 138), and ready-to-eat cereals such as granolas that have something more than air or sugar as their primary ingredient. Quick-cooking oatmeal is also a good breakfast standby, as are cream of wheat and some corn-based cereals such as hominy.

For more conventional meals, good foods to include are rice, beans, spaghetti, macaroni, and noodles. To these you might want to add some canned meats such as tuna fish, sardines, Spam, clams, and such— as well as some canned fruit juices. But keep the cans to a minimum, as you may either have to pack them on your back or abandon them, depending on the situation.

Other excellent items are peanut butter, jellies, and cheeses that can be transferred into lightweight plastic squeeze tubes or containers before storage. You should also include small containers of oil, salt, pepper, sugar, and other cooking necessities, along with enough water for drinking, cooking, and hygienic needs. (Allow at least a gallon a day per person. You can store drinking water indefinitely in gallon jugs with a half tablespoon of Clorox.)

How Much To Store? To determine how much you're going to need, sit down with a piece of paper and list the amount of each food you and your family would probably consume in a single day. (Food needs vary with age. Children and older people usually need less food than adults, but fast-growing teenagers often need more.) Include supplemental vitamins and any special foods such as baby formulas and diet foods. After you've determined a day's consumption for each food, simply multiply that amount by fourteen—or by the number of days you think you would want to eat that particular food. Fill in the gaps with other foods of a similar nature (meat, vegetable, pasta, grain, etc.) until you have a well-rounded diet for two weeks.

Finally, try living on your emergency food supply for several days (or even two weeks) and see how it works. Then amend the list in the way that seems best for you. Store the food in a cool, dry place in airtight containers. (For more specific information on keeping emergency foods, see "Storage and Rotation," page 133).

Long-Term Planning

For insurance against unemployment or other unforeseen events, you may want to keep a supply of food that will last for several months to a year or more. This kind of storage is simpler than it seems, and it can be done in a beautiful and logical way so that it fits right into your life-style.

For example, if you want a food supply that will last an entire year, you start out by buying a year's worth of food. But you buy only those foods that you and your family will actually eat on a day-to-day basis. These foods are carefully packaged, labeled, dated, and stored in neatly ordered rows. As the days go by, you draw on this supply for your regular meals. Then, at the end of each month, you replace the used food with a fresh supply and rotate the containers. This way, you're always using the oldest food first, but you never go beyond the shelf life of any given item.

You also discover very quickly how realistic your original estimates have been. If you haven't allotted enough food for a given month, that will show up before the month is over. Knowing this, you can revise your food chart to more accurately reflect your needs. It's a neat system, and you know it will work in a pinch because by the time an emergency comes around you have already honed it to a fine edge.

What Foods to Include? As with the two-week food supply, your first task is to determine what foods to store. Sit down again with a piece of paper. This time, though, divide the paper into columns, one for each month of your storage program. On the left side of the paper, list all the potential storage foods you would regularly use in your diet, as well as the shelf life or recommended replacement time for each food (see "Replacement of Stored Foods," page 135).

The simplest way of doing this is to start with the most important foods first: milk, grains, sugar, and salt. These are your staples. To give you ballpark figures, in one year an average adult would consume about 75 pounds of powdered nonfat milk, 300 pounds of cereal grains (such as oats, rice, wheat, and corn), 60 pounds of sugar, and 5 pounds of salt. Start with these, remembering the varying dietary needs of different ages and individuals. If you add 60 pounds of dried vegetables and 20 pounds of oils, you'll have a year's supply of food that will give you about 2,300 calories a day.

To this foundation I would suggest adding a good supply of dried fruits to round out the vitamin content, as well as any other nonperishable foods that you might have a craving for. As for liquids, I would include a wide variety of fruit and vegetable juices and possibly some bottled mineral water, just in case you have to go without your usual water supply for some time. And again, don't forget to include such items as baking powder, spices, condiments, and other items that will add to your taste and enjoyment.

When you've completed your list, estimate the amount of each food item you plan to use for each month of the year and write that amount in each column. (The amounts may vary with changing needs and preferences, but it's best to determine this through actual experience and amend the list as necessary.) Add the total amount of each food and write it in the final column. Then simply buy and store that amount of each food.

Best Survival Buys. Now, here's where you begin to realize the enormous payoffs of survival storage. Even if you never need your emergency food supply, you'll breathe easier knowing it's there. More tangibly, you can cut down on your shopping time and save from twenty to fifty percent on your food bill each year. How? By buying in bulk. By keeping your eyes out for sales and specials. By seeking out the best buys rather than spontaneously grabbing just what you need for tonight's dinner. By buying inexpensive but wholesome foods such as whole grains and fresh produce rather than expensive, pre-packaged pizzas and TV dinners.

If you can pool your resources with other like-minded people, you may even be able to order wholesale. And by buying a year's worth of food, you're fighting inflation. Next year, you'll still be eating some foods that were bought at this year's prices. This can be a tremendous saving—especially on foods that unpredictably double in price within a very short time.

One very useful tip is to buy your grains in fifty- or hundred-pound bags and your canned goods in cases from stores that specialize in bulk sales. In many such places, these are stacked warehouse-style. Simply pick up as many as you need, mark them with the price, and take them to the checkout stand. This way you avoid having to pay for unpacking, shelving, pricing, and display. You also get a better price because you're buying in large quantities. The items can then be unpacked at home and stored by the can or put into smaller containers.

Another money-saving approach is to buy seasonally. It's a simple case of supply and demand. Grains are usually less expensive in the fall, just after the harvest. You can get a better buy on fruits and vegetables when they're fresh off the tree or out of the ground than if they've been in storage. Also watch for supply replacements, as the price on old stock is often reduced when a new supply comes in.

Speaking of price reductions, there are lots of places you can get slightly damaged food for a pittance. Cosmetically, it doesn't look good to have the shelves stocked with mashed loaves of bread, wilted vegetables, bruised fruits, or dented cans. But these foods are often perfectly good and can be bought for a song. Sometimes they are even quietly junked without anyone knowing about it (see "Garbage," page 156). Since damaged foods aren't usually advertised (bad publicity), the trick here is to look and ask around.

Finally, you can save money and get a good nutritional boost by buying whole grains in bulk and grinding your own. All flours lose some important nutrients in processing, and they do not keep nearly as long in storage as whole grains. White flour loses almost all its nutritional value. By the time it finds its way into a loaf of bread, it's little more than thickened air. With an inexpensive home grain mill, though, you can grind your own wheat, rice, peas, soy, oats, lentils, and other basics to make high-nutrition breads, soups, cakes, and stews. With such practice, you'll be way ahead in a survival situation.

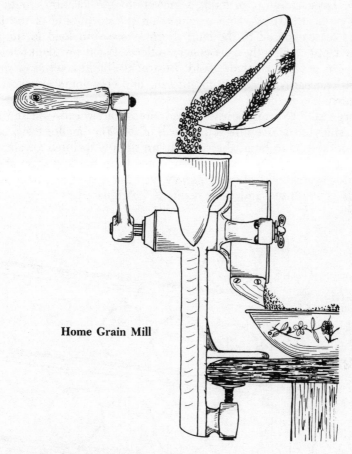

Home Grain Mill

Storage and Rotation of Foods

The enemies in the storage game are heat, moisture, light, insects, and rodents. Moisture causes rust, molds, and spoilage. Light destroys vitamins and causes rapid deterioration of foods stored in glass jars. Rodents and insects, of course, have their own survival to think about and are not about to further your plans without proper incentives (described below).

Emergency foods should be stored in airtight containers in a cool, dry, dark, and convenient place. The ideal temperature for most long-term storage foods is between 40 and 60 degrees Fahrenheit, though anything between about 35 and 70 is acceptable. Freezing temperatures may cause liquid-filled containers to burst or break their seals. Hotter temperatures will cause the food to deteriorate more rapidly.

For large amounts of food, a logical storage location would be a basement or a little-used room or closet on the north side of the house (where it's least exposed to the sun). If you store your food in the basement, don't put it directly on a concrete floor. Put it on planks or cardboard to help prevent rust and mold. Best of all, build a series of shelves where you can easily store and locate cans and containers of several different sizes.

Large storage cans can be placed almost anywhere—on the floor, on sturdy shelves, or even on top of each other. For smaller cans, one of the best methods is to build shelves that are slightly inclined (as shown in the illustration). Each time you take one can from the low side, another one rolls down to take its place. This way, you can easily keep track of how many cans you've used and what needs to be replaced.

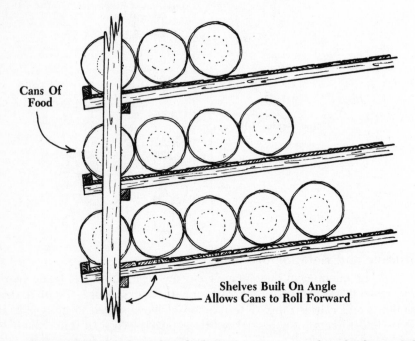

Cans Of
Food

Shelves Built On Angle
— Allows Cans to Roll Forward

Five-gallon metal or glazed plastic containers with tight-fitting lids are excellent for storage. These can be lined with large plastic bags, then filled with grains. Weekly portions of dehydrated fruits and vegetables can also be sealed in small plastic bags (the "Ziploc" type are excellent) and placed inside such containers to prevent moisture and oxygen from permeating the plastic.

When storing grains, be especially careful to avoid molds and insects. The only sure way to do this is to buy grains that contain less than ten percent moisture, to fumigate, and to store in airtight containers. One way to fumigate is as follows: Pour dry-ice crystals (about half a pound per hundred pounds of grain) into the empty container. Add the grain. Gently place the lid on top as the dry ice billows and fumes. Then seal the container tight after about two hours. (Don't seal the container too soon, or it may explode as a result of the expanding gas.) A simpler method is to place about a cup of salt in each container before sealing. This absorbs most of the moisture and will protect the grain from most molds and insects.

Replacement of Stored Foods

Following is a list of recommended replacement periods for many common storage foods. Use it to help determine your needs and to plan your survival storage program. Keep in mind that the actual shelf life varies with storage conditions such as light, temperature, humidity, and type of container. These figures, adapted for convenience into six-month replacement periods, are conservative. Many of the items listed will keep up to twice as long as the recommended replacement period. But since many of them rapidly lose their nutrients over time, it's best to rotate them. Salt and granulated sugar, if stored in metal or glass containers, can be kept indefinitely without spoilage or loss of nutrients.

(An asterisk means the replacement period is for an item stored in an airtight metal container.)

Replace Within Six Months

Flour*
Powdered Milk*
Canned Evaporated Milk
Dried Fruits*
Dry Crackers*
Condensed Soups (meat and vegetable)
Canned Yeast
Canned Berries and Cherries
Canned Citrus Juices
Peanut Butter
Canned Tomatoes
Canned Sauerkraut
Bacon Bits (Textured Vegetable Protein)
Pancake Mixes
Cake Mixes
Brown Sugar*
Ground Spices*
Herbs
Parmesan Cheese
Instant Potatoes
Instant Breakfasts

Replace Within One Year

Canned Fish	Cocoa
Canned Soups	Dry Cream Products
Dehydrated Soups*	Flavored Beverages
Dehydrated Fruits*	Baking Powder, Soda
Dehydrated Vegetables*	Bouillon Products
Ready-To-Eat Cereals*	Cornmeal
Uncooked Cereals*	Catsup and Mustard
Hydrogenated Fats	Whole Spices
Vegetable Oils	Honey
Canned Nuts	Canned Jams, Jellies
Instant Puddings	Chocolate

Replace Within 18 Months

Canned Meat	Candy, Gum, etc.
Canned Poultry	Instant Coffee, Tea, Cocoa, etc.
Canned Fruits (except citrus, berries and cherries)	Flavored Powdered Drinks
	Flavorings, Extracts (pepper, vanilla, etc.)
Canned Fruit Juices (except citrus)	Cornstarch
Canned Vegetables (except tomatoes, sauerkraut)	Syrup
	Extracts

Replace Within Two Years

Freeze-Dried Foods	Vanilla
Whole Grains (wheat, rice, oats, beans, peas, etc.)	Popcorn
	Pasta (spaghetti, macaroni, etc.)*
Flavored Beverage Powders	Coffee (unopened)*
Pepper	

If labeling and keeping track of replacement dates seems too complicated, you can simplify. Just establish two replacement periods of six months and twelve months and rotate everything within a maximum period of one year. That way your record-keeping will be easier and you'll be guaranteed safe, nutritious food. Just be sure to amend your storage chart as the months go by so it's an accurate reflection of your real needs.

Fresh Fruits and Vegetables

You can also keep fresh fruits and vegetables without refrigeration, but it takes a little more planning because they have different storage requirements. If you want to try it, you'll either have to use a refrigerator or a cool cellar or storage pit, as the recommended temperatures average quite a bit lower than for long-term storage foods. Requirements for humidity are also variable.

It's difficult to store soft fruits such as peaches and apricots for more than a month or so, even under the best conditions. You can increase the storage time by picking not-quite-ripe fruits and keeping them in a cool, dry place. Relatively hard fruits such as apples and pears can be stored through an entire fall and winter if they are kept in a moist environment (ideally a fruit storage cellar) at about 32 degrees Fahrenheit.

Likewise, very soft vegetables such as tomatoes do not keep for more than six weeks even under ideal conditions (a dry, unheated basement between 55 and 60 degrees). But many other vegetables can be stored through the fall and winter if kept at the proper temperature and humidity. Relatively hard vegetables such as turnips, rutabagas, beets, celery, cabbage, carrots, and parsnips require a moist environment—ideally a storage cellar or pit that is kept between 32 and 40 degrees. Potatoes do best in a cellar or pit that fluctuates between 45 and 48 degrees.

Softer veggies such as pumpkin, sweet potatoes, and winter squash need a dry environment between 55 and 60 degrees. On the other hand, dried beans and peas will keep for years in almost any cool, dry place between 32 and 40 degrees. Keeping these guidelines in mind, take stock of your storage space and experiment with different vegetables to see what works best for you.

Canning Fruits and Vegetables

A more reliable way to store fresh fruits and vegetables is to can them. For this process, you'll need some important equipment. First is a set of safety-tempered glass canning jars with pressure-sealing lids to keep out the air and moisture. You'll also need a heavy aluminum pressure cooker (sometimes called a "canner") with a rack and a tight-fitting lid that includes a safety valve and a pressure gauge. For tomatoes and most fruits, you can get by with a nonpressurized canner, but for meats and most vegetables the pressure cooker is the only safe way to go.

For steam canning, first sterilize the jars and lids by boiling them for a few minutes in water. Then pack them with either raw or partially cooked food and fill them to the top with boiling liquid (whatever fluid you want to preserve them in). Wipe the tops of the jars with a rag and make sure there are no residual air bubbles by running a knife around the inside of the jar.

Secure the caps tightly on the jars so they're completely sealed. Then put them on the pressure-cooker rack. Pour two to three inches of water into the bottom of the cooker and put on the lid. After the water comes to a boil, cover the vent valve to increase the pressure, and "cook" the jars and their contents according to the manufacturer's instructions. Store the jars in a cool, dry, dark place.

Boiling Water Method. If you don't have a pressure cooker, you can process only high-acid foods such as tomatoes and fruits. For this method, the jars are packed and sealed in the same way, but placed on a rack inside an open canner. The canner is filled with water until the jars are completely covered. The jars are then allowed to boil or simmer for up to half an hour or more (depending on the contents) and finally removed and allowed to cool overnight.

Canning is a somewhat risky business if you don't know what you're doing, and there are many safeguards you should take. First, be sure to learn the specific canning requirements for each food you want to preserve and follow the directions carefully. (These are usually listed along with the directions for the canner. Another good source is *Back To Basics: How to Learn and Enjoy Traditional American Skills*, by the editors of *Reader's Digest*.) Second, use only the best equipment and the best foods (fresh and not too ripe). Third, make sure the seals on the jars are tight after the cooking. (Usually the lid will be slightly depressed, indicating a vacuum inside. If you can push the lid down at all, it's probably not well sealed.) Don't take chances with questionable seals or food. Check the jars from time to time in storage, too. If they show any sign of spoilage such as molds, bulges, leaks, and the like, throw the food out.

Dehydrating Your Own Foods

An even simpler and safer process than canning is dehydration. This is the process of rapidly drawing water out of the food until it contains less than ten percent moisture. In this way, the food is left safe from the enzymes and organisms that cause spoilage, and its bulk and weight are dramatically reduced for long-term storage and transportation. Dehydrated food can be stored in about a tenth the storage space it would otherwise take, with an equally phenomenal drop in weight.

You can dehydrate almost anything—meats, vegetables, or fruits— by following a few simple directions. Basically, you cut the food into thin slices or strips that will dehydrate quickly when placed in a warm, dry, well-ventilated place. This might be in the sun, or in the oven under low heat. Best of all is to place the food on the racks or shelves of a commercial or homemade dehydrator. These little drying ovens run on little more

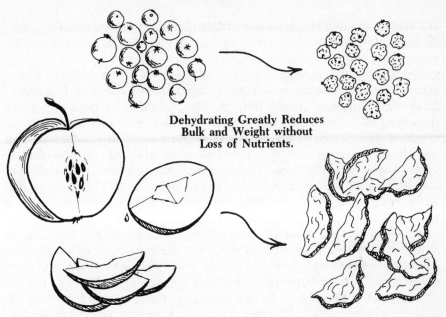

**Dehydrating Greatly Reduces
Bulk and Weight without
Loss of Nutrients.**

than the heat of a hundred-watt bulb. Even the homemade ones can easily
be made to provide the right conditions for efficient drying.

If you dry your food in the sun, it will take longer than in an oven
or dehydrator—perhaps as long as two weeks, depending on the food and
the sun. You will also have to watch and tend the food carefully. You
should be ready to bring it in during bad weather and do your best to
keep insects and animals away with a protective netting of some kind. For
oven drying, leave the door open at least a couple of inches for good ventilation (about eight inches for a gas oven), and don't let the temperature
go above 145 degrees. Excessive heat can quickly destroy vitamins and
even cook the food.

Whatever you're drying, use only firm, unblemished food. Slice it
with a sharp knife into strips no more than a quarter of an inch thick.
Larger chunks sometimes spoil before they can dry out enough. If you're
dehydrating meat, either cook it first, treat it with salt, or marinate the
strips in a salty solution such as soy sauce. If you're drying vegetables, first
steam the slices in a colander for a few minutes to half an hour, depending
on the firmness of the food. Most fruits don't need any prior treatment
unless they're going to be dried in the sun—in which case they should be
dipped in a solution of sodium bisulfite and water for two minutes and
drained well before drying. If you like, you can cut down on the oxidation
of sliced apples and bananas by dipping them in a mixture of water and

ascorbic acid (six 500 mg tablets of vitamin C per cup of water) for two minutes and draining them before drying. Orange juice also works well for this purpose.

During the dehydrating process itself, the most important procedure is to maintain the movement of warm air past the food. In a homemade or commercial dehydrator, this can be done by arranging slices loosely on well-ventilated shelves or trays. Trays made of nylon screening are ideal. The best drying temperature ranges from 95 to 105 degrees, and this should be monitored with a thermometer. Heat can be provided by electric light bulbs and controlled by a small fan or by adjusting the lid of the dehydrator. However, don't be dismayed if you don't have any of this fancy equipment. You can dehydrate foods in the open air, over a makeshift wood stove, in front of heat registers, over the hot water heater on a screen rack, in front of a south-facing window, in hot attics, in an automobile with an open window turned to the sun, or even over the hot coals from an open fire. You'll learn from experience what works and what doesn't, and how to improve your drying apparatus.

Another thing you'll learn from experience is how to tell when the food is properly dried. The general rules of thumb are the following: When cooled, meat should be leathery and stringy, not crisp or crumbly; vegetables should be hard and brittle; and fruit should be leathery and pliable. The drier the food, the longer you'll be able to store it. Properly dehydrated foods can be kept from six months to many years, depending on how they're stored.

The best storage procedure is to put small quantities of food into small, well-sealed paper or plastic bags. These in turn are put into a second set of small plastic bags and sealed again. Many of the small bags can then be put into larger opaque bags for even greater insurance against light and moisture. Large metal cans and mason jars with tight-fitting lids are also good storage containers for dehydrated foods. You can increase the shelf life of the food as much as two to three times by adding a small packet of moisture-absorbing chemicals with each large bag or can. These foods can then be taken out and conveniently eaten as snacks, dropped into soups or stews, or reconstituted in boiling water.

For more information on food drying, including some delicious recipes and detailed instructions on how to build your own dehydrator, I recommend *Dry It—You'll Like It*, by Gen MacManiman (available by writing MacManiman, Inc., P.O. Box 546, Fall City, WA 98024).

Raising Plants and Animals

Another good source of insurance, and an excellent way to supplement your food stores, is to raise your own. The "Victory Gardens" during World War II were an important source of nutrients as well as a great morale booster during times of sacrifice. Such gardens would serve similar functions in any difficult time. City gardens don't save time, and in many cases they don't even save money. But they do produce fresh, healthful, and wonderful tasting food. And working the soil, even in a small way, also provides an "earth connection" that gives a sense of well-being and understanding that is a great reward in itself.

Many people who live in the city don't have room for a traditional garden. But that shouldn't deter an enterprising gardener. In answer to the requests of green-thumbed residents, many cities have set aside unused lots for the production of "pea patches" or "people's gardens"—areas where people can stake out a small claim for a pittance and plant their own personal gardens. If you look around, you can also find patches of ground you may be able to rent or use at no cost, simply by asking the owner.

Even without a garden patch, topsoil can be brought into the house and placed in almost any kind of container. Window boxes that are traditionally used for flowers can be converted into mini vegetable gardens. Corners of rooms can be converted into greenhouses. Shelves can be fitted with flowerpots for the growing of herbs and sprouts. Lacking flowerpots, you can use buckets, baskets, cans, bowls, bottles, and old tires. Almost any room in the house, from bathroom to basement, can be put to profitable use growing something.

You can also arrange the containers so that they make best use of the available space—for example, by setting them on tiers or shelves. Many foods grow just as well inside as they do outside. The tender young leaves and blossoms of some colorful flowers are also edible—for example, violets, nasturtiums, marigolds, and pansies. And there are added advantages besides nutrition. Whether for show or for food, plants help to freshen the air and add a pleasant touch of green to the home environment.

Growing Sprouts. If you think you'd like to try some inside gardening, I suggest you start with sprouts. Sprouts are healthful, easy to grow, and a wonderful addition to sandwiches and salads. Moreover, they don't require any soil.

The main ingredients for sprouts are moisture, warmth, and darkness. You can use commercial sprouters or even glass quart jars with holes punched in the lids. If you're sprouting small seeds such as mustard, lettuce, alfalfa, or radishes, use only about a tablespoon of seeds per quart

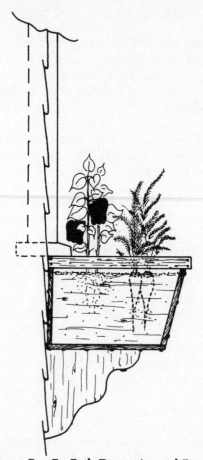

Planter Boxes Can Be Both Decorative and Practical.

container. Put the seeds in the bottom of the jar and soak them for about twelve hours. Then rinse, drain, and transfer them to a dry jar. Roll the jar so the seeds spread out and stick to the sides. Then store the jar on its side in a warm, dark place for four days or so. (This imitates conditions beneath the soil before the plant pokes up into the open air.)

During this time, rinse and drain the seeds whenever they begin to look dry. Draining is a snap if you use mason jars fitted with a patch of hardware cloth for the inner "lid." Otherwise you can turn the jar upside down into a strainer or filter of some kind. It's also a good idea to remove any hulls and unsprouted seeds and to clean the jars from time to time.

After four days in the dark, the seeds should be well on their way to germinating. At this time, you should bring them out into the light for a

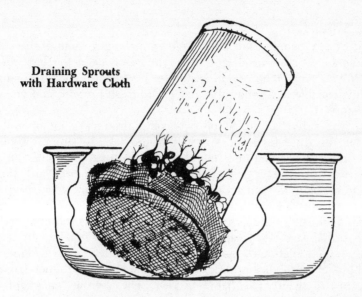

**Draining Sprouts
with Hardware Cloth**

few days so they'll absorb the rays of the sun and begin to grow little green leaves. After that, they can be air dried and stored in the refrigerator for up to a week or more, depending on their moisture content.

Bean sprouts are slightly more difficult. For the best sprouts, use a large, well-drained container. Rinse the beans in hot water and soak them for twenty-four hours in cool water. Then put about an inch of beans in the bottom of the container and pack several layers of burlap on top to keep out the light while retaining the moisture. On top of the burlap, place a three- to four-pound weight. (A bag of rocks works fine). This provides the resistance needed for the sprouts to grow firm and thick. Every few hours, pour water over the beans and watch as the weight begins to rise toward the top of the container. After about five days, wash the beans off in cold water and enjoy their delectable flavor.

Unfortunately, I cannot go more deeply into the joys and intricacies of gardening in this book, but I do want to make an important point: If you want a garden, you can have one. It's only a matter of making up your mind. What kinds of plants you grow depends on your own needs and preferences. If you're planting for survival, try a variety of vegetables under varying conditions, both in your yard and in your home, until you discover what works best. For further information, I highly recommend a trip to your local library, bookstore, or nursery. Another good source is your county cooperative extension service. There are most likely lots of experts in your area (and probably even some neighbors) who will be eager to help you get started.

Raising Animals

Most city people can't raise large animals, but some of the smaller ones could be worth considering after you've checked the laws and resources in your area. The reason is simple: If you raise your own animals, you have a reliable and renewable reserve of fresh protein, and you don't have to store it.

In the suburbs, a goat or two could produce a lot of milk and cheese for the little feed and space it would take to support them. In difficult times, the young ones could also help to supplement your meat supply. (Before you set a pair of goats grazing in your backyard, though, be sure to check with your local government to find out what the regulations are and whether a permit is necessary!)

An even better source of meat is rabbits. Rabbits require very little space or special care. They can be raised successfully in a four-by-ten-foot hutch, on a combination of inexpensive rabbit pellets and vegetable cast-offs. Rabbits are also very prolific. A single female will produce anywhere from twenty to twenty-five babies a year. These grow remarkably fast, reaching full size within about three months. Since each rabbit yields about three to four pounds of meat, they could conceivably keep your family in steaks and hamburgers indefinitely.

Depending on where you live, you might want to experiment with other animals. A single hive of bees, for example, can produce upwards of fifty pounds of honey each year. Check to see if your area has enough clover, goldenrod, sumac, willow, alfalfa, or other nectar sources to support some backyard bees. Often beekeepers will even put hives on your property in exchange for all the honey your family can eat! Depending on space, time, and legal restrictions, you might even be interested in raising a few chickens, pigs, or other more traditional farm animals. Check with your county's cooperative extension service for more information.

Whether you're raising plants or animals, you'll probably find the enterprise somewhat time consuming. But if you take the time, you and your family will gain—not just by helping to grow your own food, but through a more direct contact with the natural processes that sustain us. This is an important part of everyone's education, especially for urban children who are more cut off from the flow of nature.

Foraging for Wild Edibles

Generally I don't recommend the recreational eating of wild edibles in the city and suburbs. The negative effects of many toxins are cumulative, and there are just too many pollutants spewed into the air to make a general habit of it. On the other hand, wild edibles in and around the city can be a very viable source of food in an emergency.

All cities have some public greenery, and there is hardly a back-yard that does not produce some wild food. Dandelions, rose hips, clover, berries, plantain, grasses, and many other palatable and nourishing plants grow in urban environments—sometimes even better than they do in the wilds. If you collect them in such areas, though, be very careful. Following are some general rules that will help to assure your safety:

1. Do not gather near highways, roads, dumps, factories, railroad tracks, or other potential sources of pollution. The lead from automobile exhaust that settles on leaves is especially dangerous. Other heavy metals such as cadmium, arsenic, and mercury are also absorbed by some plants. If you plan to forage within one hundred yards of a questionable area, go upwind to reduce the possibility of collecting polluted plants.
2. Avoid all plants that grow in or near questionable water—especially water that might contain the effluent from factories. Such water may be clear yet still contain dangerous quantities of heavy metals. If the water is safe to swim in, you can usually assume the plants are OK. If you're in doubt, assume that both the water and the plants are unsafe.
3. Check with local authorities to make sure the area you're gathering in hasn't been sprayed with toxic chemicals. (This includes 2-4-D, which is widely used in urban areas. Some authorities claim it is not harmful to humans, but I have serious doubts about this.)
4. Gather only the plants you can positively identify.
5. Wash all plant parts thoroughly before eating.
6. Eat only the youngest and tenderest parts of the plant, and do not eat plant parts that are more than one season old. The older the plant, the more pollutants it may have collected.
7. Learn what parts of the plant are edible and what times they are in season.
8. Find out whether the plant can be eaten raw or whether it should be cooked first.
9. Eat a small portion at first, to see whether the plant agrees with you. If you experience any discomfort, do not eat any more.
10. Heed written warnings about specific plants. When in doubt, leave the plant alone.

(For descriptions and information on some of the most common urban wild edibles, see Appendix A, page 223. For general reference, I recommend *A Field Guide to Edible Wild Plants of Eastern and Central North America*, by Lee Peterson.

Catching Wild Animals

In desperate situations, you can also augment your food stores by catching wild or semi-wild animals. Just as cities and their environs often contain an abundance of edible plants, they also harbor hidden numbers of edible animals. In fact, many are not so hidden at all. Urban waters are often crowded with geese, ducks, frogs, and fish. Beaches sometimes contain amazing numbers of clams and other shellfish. Most urban and suburban woods abound with squirrels and other small edible rodents. Some of our most populated areas support enormous numbers of pigeons and other half-tame animals that are perfectly good to eat. And though I hesitate to mention it, even dogs and cats would be fair survival game.

Indeed, the most difficult thing about urban animals may not be catching them, but gearing your mind to think of them as food. Under normal circumstances, most of us wouldn't consider killing such animals, much less eating them. And I am not suggesting that you do so unless you are pushed to the wall. But survival makes unusual demands. What may seem repugnant under normal circumstances can become a godsend in a truly desperate situation.

It is instructive to remember that in many situations people have eaten not only the above-mentioned animals, but also mice, rats, crows, road kills, and even shoe leather. It is amazing how many things seem palatable when you're really hungry. So just remember: you can eat anything that's finned, feathered, furred, or scaled, as long as it's not diseased or spoiled and as long as it's carefully skinned, cleaned, and cooked until well done. With this frame of mind, think about your area and what it has to offer (see also "Appendix B: Common Urban Animals," page 243).

I would also urge you to think about the animals you plan to catch—in particular what it means to cause them pain or to take their lives. Living as we do in a fast food society, it is not often we stop to think about the animal sacrifices that are necessary to keep us alive and healthy. These sacrifices are gifts and should be accepted with thanks. Never should we cause an animal unnecessary pain and suffering, and never should we take a life (plant or animal) unless we plan to honor that life by making good use of it.

Finding Animals

Whether you're interested in observing or catching animals, it helps to know where to find them. All animals need an adequate supply of food and water, as well as good places to hide and raise their young. For this reason, they are most often found in "transition" areas. In the wilderness, the best transition areas are the edges of forests, meadows, lakes, and streams where smaller herbivores such as voles, mice, and rabbits feed on a variety of grasses and succulent herbs. These animals in turn attract the hawks, owls, coyotes, foxes, and other predators that feed on them.

In the city, the best transition areas are parks, greenbelts, abandoned or vacant lots, hedgerows, housing developments, backyards, median strips, and the undeveloped borders of arterials, highways, and railroad tracks. These patches of greenery are likely to harbor even larger numbers of animals if they are located near waterways.

Other productive areas tend to be located around reliable sources of garbage. In fact, many animals will abandon greenery altogether if the food is plentiful. Such animals use sewers, streets, buildings, tunnels, cars, and alleyways in much the same way that their country cousins use grasses, trees, and brush. In this respect, the city is very much like a jungle where various species of animals adapt to very different niches. The city contains "layers" of wildlife as distinct as those in a forest. Sewers and basements correspond to the subterranean level, streets and alleyways to the ground level, eaves and window sills to the understory, and rooftops to the canopy layer. Interspersed within these different layers you can find everything from rats and raccoons to pigeons and peregrine falcons.

It should also be remembered that city animals do not keep the same hours as those in the country. Though different species are still largely daytime or nighttime animals by nature, most city animals choreograph their movements to those of the people around them. For example, most suburbs are bedroom communities in which the greatest periods of human activity are late afternoon and evening. To avoid people, a lot of daytime animals tend to feed after everyone has left for work and again just before they come back. For the same reason, nocturnal suburban animals usually start their rounds quite a bit later than their wilderness counterparts.

In the city proper, many animals that in the wild would normally be active during the day tend to rest or sleep when people are about. Yet, this is not always true—especially where food is concerned. Whole populations of animals, for example, sometimes become dependent on a particular garbage pile and become most active at about the same time the food is thrown out. A raccoon I once studied in New York City lived in a rockpile on the outskirts of Central Park. In the morning, the first thing it did was go to a particular hotel's garbage area to feed on the bread that it knew had just been discarded. Then it came back and slept most of the day. But in the evening it was out again, each night hitting three of four familiar restaurant garbage areas just after dinnertime. Its circuit was the same almost every day.

As long as there is adequate cover, most city and suburban animals use the same trails and byways that humans do. For this reason, and because of the preponderance of hard surfaces in the city, animal tracks are not as distinguishable as they might be. But quite often you can find them even on walkways, marked by the trails of mud or dirt the animals have left on their ways to and from more woodsy areas. With practice, you can become quite adept at spotting telltale tracks in the soft ground of parks, gardens, and flower boxes. (For information on animal tracking, consult *Tom Brown's Field Guide to Nature Observation and Tracking.*) The city also includes a variety of good dust traps such as those found around the bases of buildings, curb edges, and untended streetcorners. If you're still in doubt about the hordes of animals that inhabit the city, check the ground around your yard or place of business the day after a snowstorm.

Stalking Animals

Stalking a truly wild animal is difficult at best. It requires a great deal of skill and patience, and in many cases it is necessary to camouflage the body and use some kind of de-scenting treatment such as smoke or wild herbs. Fortunately, you don't have to worry much about this in the city because most animals are so used to people. To most city animals, a highway full of speeding cars is hardly more noticeable than a river. And to some, a large congregation of people is as much an opportunity as it is a threat.

For most city stalking (on hard pavement or relatively flat ground), use a modified fox walk (see "Physical Fitness," page 18). That is, take short, slow, steps, coming down on the outside of the foot and rolling slowly to the inside. Wear light-soled shoes so you can really feel the terrain beneath your feet. Don't make any noises or sudden movements, and keep your eye on the animal at all times. Also keep your hands close to your sides or folded in front, and use whatever cover is close at hand (trees, bushes, grass, buildings, cars). In some cases, you won't have to use any cover at all because the animal will have no fear. But in any case, wear clothing that blends well with the landscape. If you're stalking in woods, wear mottled clothing such as plaids. If you're closer to streets and buildings, solid colors are better.

Fish and Other Aquatic Life

If you live near a waterway, find out what fish or other aquatic life it contains, and what places would be safest to do your catching, gathering, or hunting. Lots of people fish in or near cities. Some cities have public docks where you can cast out a line and pull in anything from trout and perch to salmon and red snapper. Freshwater lakes often provide crayfish in large numbers, too. And though it's not usually legal to go hunting for frogs, they would also be fair game in a survival situation. Clams and other shellfish can often be found beneath the sands of municipal beaches, and can be gathered safely as long as you check on pollution and red tides with the authorities.

STEPS IN STALKING

Lift foot high and maintain balance.

Come down on outside ball of foot.

Roll to inside ball of foot.

Lower heel and toes, then apply weight.

Under normal circumstances, you'll have access to a variety of fishing and gathering gear for such aquatic enterprises. But even in a primitive survival situation you would not be empty-handed. In very little time, you can learn to construct spears, fish traps, and even lines and lures from natural materials.

Trapping

Knowing how to trap animals is one of the handiest survival skills you'll ever learn. And it can be applied with even more effectiveness in the city than in the backwoods. One reason for this is that urban animals have far less fear of people. They're used to us. They live alongside our daily traffic and our pounding feet. They raid our garbage cans, accept our handouts, and in many cases thrive in the shadows of our lives. Though they are still wary, they are far less suspecting than their wild counterparts. If necessary, you could catch many a citified duck, pigeon, or squirrel simply by luring it close enough with bread or nuts to hit it with a club.

In the city you also have access to a wider variety of bait. Like us, most animals go for the tastiest foods they can find. Instead of painstakingly deciding whether to use alfalfa or clover leaves, as you might have to do in the wilderness, you can bait your traps with foods that most animals find irresistible. (Hint: There is hardly an animal alive that will turn down peanut butter.)

You can trap animals almost anywhere. The most promising places are parks, suburban backyards, and semi-wild spots where animals have been living partly on the castoffs of civilization. Garbage dumps harbor an unbelievable variety of animals, as do the woods around some food centers and restaurants.

Generally, look for places that offer plenty of food, cover, and water. Then watch the animal and learn its habits. Try to find out where it travels, what it eats, when it sleeps, when it's frightened, and so on. Then make a trap of the proper size and set it up with a minimum of disturbance. You won't have to be nearly as careful as you would in the wilderness, but you should try to avoid leaving human signs or scent on the trap or in the area.

Simple Box Traps. Some of the simplest and most versatile traps are the old-fashioned box traps. As their name implies, these are made out of boxes, and they trap animals live rather than killing them. One of the crudest of this type is a wooden or cardboard box that's propped upside-down with a stick attacked to a string. The bait (bread, grains, meat, etc.) is put just beneath the box and the string is raveled out to a hiding place where you watch until the animal comes by. When a bird or beast goes for the bait, you pull the string and the box falls down over the animal. A primitive box trap of this type would hardly ever fool an animal in the wilderness because it's so unnatural. But in places where boxes abound, it will often be accepted as part of the landscape. (Caution: Watch out for bites!)

Gated Box Traps. A more effective box trap is one constructed with a one-way door on horizontal hinges. This type can be made for animals of almost any size, from pigeons to bears (though I have yet to hear of someone who's actually caught a bear with it). Another advantage of this trap is that you don't have to wait around for the animal to show up.

Animals are more inclined to enter gated box traps if they can see daylight through both ends. If you have only one door, attach wide grating or grillwork to the other end. For one-way movement and easy entrance, slant the door (or doors) inward and make them from material that's heavy enough to hold the animal but not too heavy to prevent it from entering. (Remember, the animal has to actually shove the door open and slide in under it, at which point it slams shut and presumably stays shut.) Gratings and screens of varying weights and thicknesses work best for the doors.

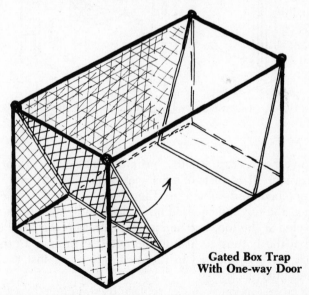

**Gated Box Trap
With One-way Door**

Depending on the size of the animal, you can make this trap from six to twelve inches square and from two to five feet long. Animals such as pigeons, squirrels, and rabbits are caught best in the smaller sizes, while fox-sized animals go for the medium-sized ones and coyote-sized animals the larger. The animals should not be able to move around much once they're caught, except to make room for others that are foolhardy enough to enter.

You can set box traps almost anywhere if they're baited. Unbaited traps are best set up like snares, ideally at the entrances to animal burrows. If you set one up in front of a burrow, be sure to get a snug fit against the entrance so the emerging animal has to go into the trap, not around it.

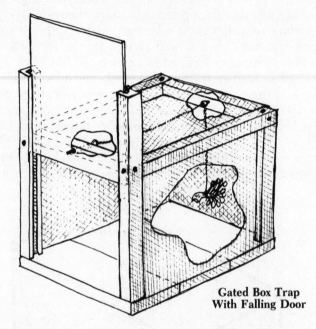

Gated Box Trap
With Falling Door

Figure-Four Trap. Another primitive trap that will work in the city is the figure four. It consists of a flat rock or log supported by three sticks that are notched and joined in the shape of a "4." The upright is dovetailed at the top and squared off in the middle on one side. The diagonal is beveled at the top, notched underneath to receive the upright, and dovetailed at the bottom to fit into the notch at the end of the bait stick; and the bait stick is notched in the center to fit against the squared-off edge of the upright.

In a city situation, you can replace the traditional rock or log deadfall with anything from a plank to a flat piece of iron. Put the end of the deadfall on the beveled part of the diagonal so that it falls free when the bait is taken. If you're on soft ground, place something hard and flat beneath the deadfall so the animal can't escape by burrowing. If necessary, pound in supporting stakes to keep the trap balanced, and "fence" in one

Figure-four Traps

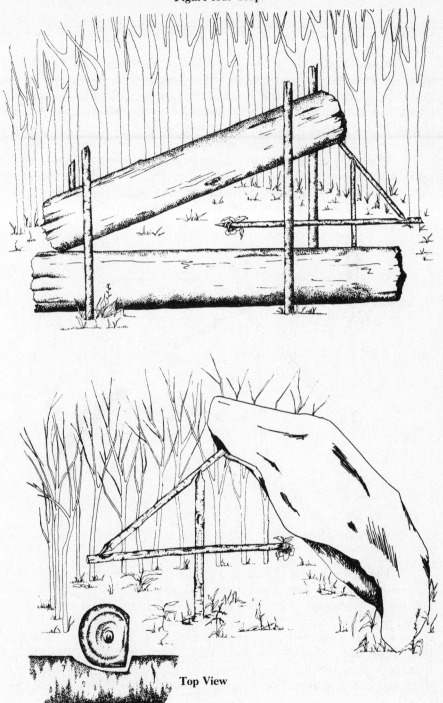

Top View

side of the trap so the animal has to pull the bait stick away from the upright.

Paiute Trap. The Paiute is much like the figure four, but with a more sensitive trigger mechanism. The upright is made exactly as before—flat on the bottom and dovetailed at the top—and the diagonal is beveled at the top and notched underneath to receive the upright. But instead of dovetailing the lower end of the diagonal, this time you tie on a fine piece of cordage. The other end of the cordage is tied to a short twig.

When you are ready to set the trap, wrap this twig once around the upright and secure it on the point of a long, thin bait stick lodged against the underside of the deadfall. Since the trigger mechanism can be tripped equally well from either direction, you don't need to wall in one side of the trap.

Paiute Deadfall

The Rolling Snare. Snares are loops of cord or wire that instantly tighten and strangle an animal when it slips its head through the noose and trips the trigger. Since the rolling snare is unbaited, it has to be set up on a known animal trail or run. You can locate these thoroughfares either by observing the animal or by looking for signs of disturbed vegetation. Trails are frequently-used animal highways, while runs are lesser-used pathways that branch off from trails to connect with feeding, bedding, and watering areas. Runs that go through rather thick foliage are the best for the rolling snare, but with a little ingenuity the snare can also be used in urban backyards and alleyways. (For example, I have set them on dumpsters using a string attached to a brick as a counterweight.)

Usually, the trigger for the rolling snare is made with two forked sticks, as shown. The long one is pushed deep into the ground, fork pointing downward, and the short one is held against it by the upward pull of a bent sapling or improvised lever and fulcrum system. The noose is tied to the small stick and suspended over the run in such a way that when the animal comes by, it pushes its head through the noose and dislodges the trigger stick. In the city, you can use many other materials for triggers, including safety pins and paper clips.

One of the best and most available materials for making snare nooses is de-insulated appliance wiring. It can be found in every home. For a noose that's suitable for rabbit-sized animals, cut a length of wire about twenty inches and separate the two strands of insulation. Peel the insulation from the wire, and you'll find that it's composed of many hair-like strands of copper. Separate ten to twelve of these strands and twist

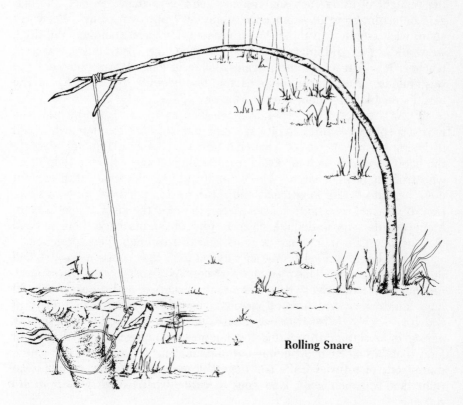

Rolling Snare

them together to form one thick wire with small loops on either end. Put one loop through the other to form the noose, and tighten it up. Use the other loop to tie on the cord that goes to the spring stick.

Variations of the rolling snare can be used to catch animals both large and small. The same system can also be used to catch animals as they come out of their burrows or when they're running up and down tree trunks. If necessary, use small sticks on either side of the run to funnel the animal into the noose.

For more details on fishing, trapping, hunting, and the cleaning and cooking of wild animal foods, consult *Tom Brown's Field Guide to Wilderness Survival*.

Unconventional Food Sources

There are many other food sources in or near the city that most people do not usually think of using. Among these are public agencies, food banks, and church organizations. For many people who are well fed, the thought of using such sources may seem repugnant. In fact, the biggest deterrent to a full stomach is sometimes our own pride. We worry about what people will think. We fret about our social standing. We think we would rather go hungry than stoop to "begging." But hunger is a great teacher. It can teach us the priceless value of food. It can point out our wastefulness. And it can help us to identify with the majority of the world's people for whom hunger is a way of life.

As a society, we generally have food to spare. Some people who have a surplus give through city agencies and churches to others who need it. Helping others is part of what civilization is all about. I do not advocate the habitual use of such food sources. People give away food to help those who truly need it—not to support a subculture of social parasites. But don't hesitate to use food banks and missions in a personal survival situation. If you feel reluctant, make a pledge to repay the favor at a later date. Many people who find themselves in difficult straits have done so, and they usually gain more than personal survival through the experience.

Garbage. A final source of survival food that needs more detailed mention is garbage. That's right—garbage. As a society, we throw away mountains of food. Every day, restaurants, bakeries, and supermarkets fill huge dumpsters with cast-off breads, vegetables, and meats, many of which are perfectly good to eat. Loaves of bread two days old or slightly damaged in shipment are rejected for hog feed. Restaurants throw out food that has been cooked but not served. The groceries of the nation dump tons of bruised fruits and vegetables every day. It does not seem right that so much good food goes to waste when so many people are starving.

I have to admit that taking food from dumpsters and garbage cans is generally frowned upon. In some places it's even illegal. But very rarely are such laws actively enforced, as long as there is real need and you don't make a nuisance of yourself. I can't help but feel that this is because even the owners can sense the injustice of keeping food from hungry people. Again, I do not suggest you become a "dumpster gourmet," but if you are truly hungry, there is no one who can tell you in good conscience not to gather food that has been thrown away.

The important thing is to make sure the food is fit to eat. There are several ways to do this. One is by familiarizing yourself with the dumpster pickup schedule. Experts suggest observing several promising dumpsters for a period of a few weeks, examining their contents and becoming familiar with the disposal schedules. By checking a couple of times a day, you soon get to know what's fresh and what's old.

Most commercial dumpsters are emptied so frequently that you won't have to worry much about spoilage. In restaurant bins, sometimes you can even find receipts along with the food that give the date and time it was sold. Try to be around when the garbage is thrown out. This helps to pin down the age of the food.

In the end, though, there is no substitute for examining the food itself. Be especially careful of foods that contain meat. Food that is wrapped is much safer than unwrapped food. Plastic bags, tin foil, paper bags, and even plastic garbage bags provide some insurance against bacteria, flies, and other beasts. Meat that's been cooked is much safer than raw meat. You be the final judge, but don't take chances. Avoid all meat that looks or smells strange in any way.

Dumpster fruit and vegetables that are wilted or partially spoiled can often be salvaged. You can cut out the bad parts of the fruits and revive the greens by placing them in cold water for about an hour. Even vegetables like zucchini and bell peppers respond well to this treatment. Others that are not too far gone can be used in soups and stews.

A final thought about dumpster gleaning: Don't do it unless you really have to. If everyone collected garbage, there wouldn't be enough to go around!

6
CRIME

When I was doing the preliminary research for this book, talking on the phone with friends in various cities, one of the first questions I asked was "What are your major concerns about urban survival?" Almost invariably, crime was at the top of the list. I was not surprised. Natural disasters take their toll, but people's fear of floods and hurricanes is nothing compared to their fear of being victimized by their fellow humans.

It is unsettling to realize that, in addition to the other dangers of urban living, we must also beware of burglars, muggers, rapists, and swindlers. Their growing presence is a sad commentary on the fragility of our social fabric. Nevertheless, crime is a fact of life. Criminals are annually responsible for billions of dollars' worth of stolen money and property, thousands of injuries, hundreds of lives, and incalculable mental anguish.

Given a threat of such epidemic proportions, it would be foolish not to intelligently prepare for it. On the other hand, crime need not be an all-consuming worry. We can reduce our chances of becoming crime statistics with very little effort. In fact, most crime prevention is common sense. Moreover, crime is not caused entirely by criminals. Criminals prosper partly because their victims make it so easy for them, because so many people are unaware and unprepared.

What Is the Threat? The first step toward crime prevention is an objective appraisal of the threat. Every environment has its dangers. If I am traveling in a wilderness area where there might be dangerous animals, I make it my business to know everything I can about them. I find out where they live, how big they are, what kind of weapons they have (teeth, claws, quills, etc.), what attracts them, what frightens them, and what to do if confronted by them. If a porcupine comes ambling across my path, I know that it has sharp quills but that is very slow and has no interest in attacking me if I leave it alone and don't get too close. The skunk has a powerful scent, and it can spray up to several yards, so I keep my distance. If I want to keep bears from ransacking my camp, I let them know I'm around and I don't tempt them by leaving food where they can easily get at it.

I don't mean to give wild animals a bad name, for they rarely have any malicious intent, but this is the same approach people should take toward criminals. Avoidance and deterrence are the keys. To prevent crime, don't go into areas where criminals are likely to be and don't attract them by carelessly displaying things they want. Do things that will make it difficult or impossible for them to take advantage of you. With this in mind, let's take a closer look at some common criminals and how to deal with them.

Burglars

Almost all burglars are men or boys, and they fall into two general categories. The first group, which includes eighty percent of all burglars, is made up of nonprofessionals. Typically these are teenagers and young men under twenty-five. (Half of all burglars are under eighteen.) They are usually quick and slight of build. They don't generally plan their jobs ahead of time, but break in whenever the time seems right: on the way home from school, while cruising in a car, or even when you leave the house for a short errand. They may burglarize friends, relatives, or strangers, most often in the same general neighborhood.

Most burglaries occur during the day or in the early evening when the occupants are away. Rarely do burglars strike after midnight. The nonprofessional burglar is almost always after money, drugs, or objects that can easily be converted into cash. (Because of this, he considers almost any home worth a try.) Above all, he wants an easy entry and exit, and under no circumstances does he want to run into people while carrying out a job.

The remaining twenty percent of the burglars are pros. These men steal for a living, and they take things that bring plenty of easy money. Unless your house contains valuable art objects, jewels, expensive stereo equipment, and the like, chances are the professional burglar won't think it's worth his trouble. To decide whether or not it is, he may spend a great amount of time "casing" an area. Through observation, he tries to familiarize himself with the flow of the neighborhood and the habits of likely prospects. He watches people coming and going. He may look through windows or get himself invited into homes and offices on some pretext so he can see what's there.

When casing or carrying out a job, professional burglars blend in with the neighborhood. They often dress like repairmen, salespeople, or movers. Sometimes they even drive large vans up to homes and move everything out in broad daylight. Though they go to more trouble than the amateurs, they are also after the easy mark, and they're just as reluctant to be confronted.

Make Your Home Appear Occupied. Since most burglars' greatest fear is encountering people, your first line of defense is to make your home look like somebody's there. You can do this in many ways. When you go out during the day, leave a radio or television on, tuned to a chatty news station. When you go out at night, leave a light or two on inside. Vary the lighted rooms so even a frequent observer or a friend wouldn't be able to tell whether you were home or not. (Lights, radio, and television can also be turned on and off by an automatic timer.) If you have a phone machine, leave a message that says you're "busy" instead of "not home," and mention that you'll be calling back shortly.

If you're going on vacation, don't advertise the fact, except to neighbors, friends, and family who can help look after your home. Discontinue the newspaper service, have the lawn mowed periodically, and have a neighbor pick up your mail and check on the house. Perhaps you can also have someone change the lights, water the plants, and shovel the driveway. Best of all, get a house sitter. If you don't have someone to look after the house, tell the police when you're leaving and when you'll return so they can pay special attention on their rounds. Leave the air conditioning and heater on (set at 90 and 40, respectively).

Simple cautions such as the above will dim the hopes of many a burglar. Others will come up to the house for a closer look. If they do, make sure they can't see in. Keep the drapes drawn. If you have a dog, give it the run of the house and teach it how to bark (most dogs do an admirable job quite naturally). Don't leave keys under the mat or in other "hiding" places, and don't leave notes on the door to friends that will confirm your absence.

Like all predators, burglars seek cover to avoid being seen during their operations. You can discourage them by trimming all foliage that obscures the view and by leaving all entries well lighted at night. If your home is particularly secluded, use a floodlight that illuminates a large area. Good lighting is a powerful deterrent to crime—so good that it's smart to keep all the entries to your home lit up all night.

Locks. If the burglar is still interested in your home, his next move is to find the easiest way in. He will probably begin by trying the doors, one by one. Make sure the knobs don't turn. If a house is locked, some burglars won't even bother with it. (Why should they, when there are plenty of others that aren't?)

On the other hand, some locks are better than others. The doors of most homes are equipped with spring locks (key-in-the-knob types) that lock automatically when the door is closed. These are very insecure, as they are made with beveled latches that can easily be jimmied (pried) or "loided" open by pushing a thin instrument such as a knife, credit card, or piece of celluloid between the latch and the doorjamb. If you have one of these locks, at least make sure it's equipped with a deadlatch, a small metal plunger that fits right beside the latch.

Much better, though, are deadbolt locks that have long, blunt latches. These have to be locked manually from the outside, but it's well worth it because of the extra time and trouble it takes to get them open. There are many kinds of deadbolt locks, and most of them are excellent. Just make sure the latch is at least an inch long with reinforced steel inside, and that the keyhole is surrounded by a tapered cylinder guard with no screws showing so it can't be wrenched or pried off the door.

Of course, strong locks on weak doors won't do much good, so make sure the doors themselves are sturdy. If they're weak or hollow, have them reinforced with three-fourth-inch plywood or sheet steel. Make sure the doorjambs are solid, too. They should be tough enough to withstand a violent kick or blow from outside, and there should be very little or no space between the jamb and the edge of the door. If there is, you can install a thin strip of metal (called "angle iron") to take up the slack. You can also buy lock-protecting devices that reinforce the door on each side of the locking mechanism. This helps to keep a new lock from being ripped out of an old door.

Garage locks are also sadly deficient in many homes. On double garage doors, a single bolt isn't enough. Both doors should be firmly bolted and locked with a padlock on a case-hardened hasp, or fastener, that is secured to the door with long stove bolts. The padlock should be of case-hardened steel and of the type that locks both at the heel and the toe. It should also have at least a nine-sixteenth-inch shackle and a key-retaining feature that makes it impossible to take the key out unless it's locked.

Manually operated garage doors of the rolling overhead kind should be equipped either with slide bolts, double cylinder deadbolt locks (the kind that lock both inside and out), or a padlock on a door trace. Better yet is to install an electronically operated garage door that lets you open and close the door without even getting out of the car. If you go this route, be sure to ask for "dual modulated" equipment with two buttons so you don't come home and find your garage door has been activated by a neighbor's (or a burglar's) remote control system that's on the same frequency. Also have it set up so a light goes on in the garage if the door is opened automatically.

Sliding glass doors can be made more secure by simply putting a length of broom handle or one-and-a-half-inch doweling in the door track to jam the movement when the door is not in use. Alternatively, you can install a protective "Charley-Bar," which does basically the same thing. With either one of these devices, a burglar will have a tough time getting in even if he does manage to jimmy the lock.

Windows that are seldom or never used (such as those in the basement) should be nailed or screwed shut permanently and covered so that nobody can see in. All the others should be locked with keyless locks. The usual locks on double-hung windows are woefully weak. A better way to secure them is to drill a sloping hole up through the top part of the bottom window frame and partway into the bottom of the top frame and insert a metal pin or nail. As long as the pin is in place, neither window can be moved up or down. When you want to open the window, all you have to do is take the pin out. For added security, install pins on both sides of the window.

Louvered windows (the kind with overlapping leaves of glass) are very poor and should be replaced with solid glass or casement windows that can be securely shut and latched from the inside. If not, they can be made more secure by installing an iron grate or grille on the outside. All windows, regardless of size or function, should be made of shatterproof, reinforced glass or some other safe, solid material. The glass on sliding doors can be reinforced with sheets of Lexan, a plastic material that is

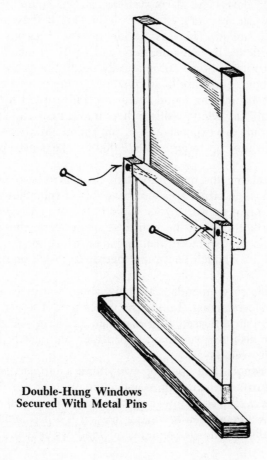

**Double-Hung Windows
Secured With Metal Pins**

three hundred times stronger than glass and lighter than aluminum. When installing these panels, use bolts that solidly connect the material to the door.

If your home is secure and well equipped with good locks, very few burglars will be able to get past its outer defenses. But outer defenses are no better than the easiest way in. For this reason, be sure to beef up hidden entries. A burglar may spend considerably more time trying to get in through a back window than a front door if he knows he'll be out of view of the neighbors. You can discourage such entries by growing holly or other thick, prickly shrubs under windows in hidden areas. And never let any tree or bush grow in such a way that it can be used as an access.

As a final precaution, get a licensed locksmith or the crime prevention unit of your local police to inspect your home. Most security checks are free, and they can greatly increase your peace of mind.

Alarms. Burglar alarms and alarm systems can't make up for inadequate locks, but they can be very effective deterrents if they are well chosen and carefully installed. There is a wide variety of alarms on the market. Some are portable, battery-operated, and easily installed. Some are loud and some are silent. Some automatically notify the police, while others alert the neighbors. Some are hand-operated, some trip on contact, and others operate when light or sound waves are interrupted by movement. Some fit on doors and window sills, others under mats and screens. Some are cheap and some are expensive. You can spend anywhere from a few dollars for a single unit up to around $25,000 for the most elaborate alarm systems.

In choosing an alarm, the most important thing is to be realistic. If you live in an isolated, high crime area and have lots of valuables such as jewels and fine art, it might be worth your while to invest in a system that protects several important areas of the house. A single alarm unit can be helpful, but no unit can protect more than one area. Most people can get along with no alarm at all, though you might decide to install one just for added peace of mind.

The only specific recommendation I have about alarms is to get a professional opinion before buying. Talk to the police first. They are much more likely to give you an unbiased appraisal than an alarm salesman. A licensed locksmith can also give you good information and install the system once you've made your decision.

Interior Deterrents. If in spite of everything a burglar gets into your home, you can further frustrate him and increase your personal security by having some well-placed interior locks. Since basement entries are quite common, it's a good idea to have a lock on the basement door. You can also install bells or other noisy items on windows or doors so that if someone does get in you will be forewarned or he may be deterred. If a burglar should get into the main part of the house while you're there, you would also be safer if you could retreat to a room equipped with a dead-bolt lock and a telephone. Nothing deters criminals faster than the realization that someone is calling the police.

On the other hand, I would not recommend keeping a safe in the home. A safe may keep the burglar away from your valuables the first time around, but it may also entice him to return at a later date and force you to open it. Much better is to keep your valuables in a bank vault or safe deposit box. Whatever you do, don't leave jewelry and other valuables in obvious places. If you keep them in your home, put them in black containers in dark, out-of-the-way places (beneath beds, chests of drawers, etc.) where they blend in and can't be seen.

Another interior deterrent that has been used successfully in recent years is to have all your valuable possessions marked in accordance with the police department's Operation Identification or the Computer Identification System. This makes it easy for the police to trace stolen articles such as stereos and television sets, and hence more difficult for the burglar to sell them. With both these systems, you can also display stickers in the windows indicating that your valuables have been marked, and this serves as an added deterrent. In addition to marking larger items in this way, it's a good idea to take photographs of your jewelry and fine silver and send copies of these to your insurance company. Also record the numbers of your credit cards, and don't leave extra copies of these lying around the house!

Guns. Never advertise the presence of firearms in your home. While it may deter some burglars to read that you are ready to use a gun in defense of your property, it can just as easily be an added enticement to a burglar who knows you're not home. Guns are both easy to steal and easy to sell, and they're rarely in just the right spot when they're needed. Furthermore, firearms in the home can be extremely dangerous—especially in the hands of an inexperienced person. They can easily be used against the person who owns them, and they are all too often used in domestic squabbles with fatal results. Also, if they are not used in accordance with the law of self-defense (that is, if you can't prove that your life was on the line), you are liable to be successfully sued by the very person who broke into your home!

Neighborhood Cooperation. There is one other proven deterrent that may prevent a burglar from even considering your home, and that's neighborhood cooperation. Part of what modern burglars (and other criminals) bank on is that you don't really know or care about your neighbors and that they don't know or care about you. This increases the chances of their breaking in and getting away unnoticed. In fact, some burglars are so good at camouflaging their intentions that they'll knock on a door and ask an unwitting neighbor to help them load up the van!

On the other hand, in neighborhoods where people keep track of each other, crime goes way down. Word travels fast in crime circles. A neighborhood that's considered "tight" will usually not be hit. Whether you like your neighbors or not, get to know them at least well enough to enhance your mutual safety. Agree to keep a lookout for strange cars that might be "casing" the area. Communicate with each other about unusual callers. Let each other know if anyone's house has been burglarized or if you've detected a prowler. If necessary, set up a "block watch" in which two or more people make regular rounds, noting unusual license plates and taking photographs of strangers who are loitering. Call on the police to help you out with this; they'll be happy to cooperate. Usually all that's involved is familiarizing yourself with your neighbors and supplying everyone with a simple map of the neighborhood that shows home and work phones.

Some communities have managed to reduce a high crime rate to almost zero, simply by developing the reputation of being alert and looking out for each other. In doing so, you may begin to see that you have more in common with your neighbors than you thought. This can even lead to new friendships and a deeper understanding of what community is all about.

Confronting a Burglar. Chances are you'll never see a burglar, because that's the way he wants it. But if you're ever confronted by one, the best course of action is to get out of the way! Most burglars want to avoid you, but if you block their escape they may well harm you. For the same reason, if you come back to a home that's been burglarized (or even suspect so), don't go inside. The burglar may still be there. Go to the nearest phone and call the police. Leave everything undisturbed until the police arrive.

If you should see a burglar at work, try to get a good description of him, including approximate age, height, weight, dress, complexion, scars, behavior, clothing, and other distinguishing features. Be alert and aware. If you don't see the burglar, maybe you can get a look at his car or jot down his license plate before he drives off. If you can't do that, listen for the sound of the engine and try to remember it. You never know what piece of evidence might complete the picture for the police and allow them to apprehend the criminal. And by all means, report the crime no matter how small it may seem. By not reporting, you only increase the chances of somebody else being victimized.

Apartment Houses. If you live in an apartment house, most of the above rules and cautions still apply. But there are added complications because your security also depends on the cooperation of other people. This makes it even more important to know your neighbors.

If possible, do this before you move in. Talk to the apartment owner and manager. Ask them about the area's crime rate and what they've done to make the building more secure. Find out who else lives in the building and whether there is a tenants' organization that is concerned about crime. Find out whether the tenants know each other, and knock on a few doors to introduce yourself.

Also, remember that the keys the owner or manager gives you may have been used by other tenants before you. Some of these people may still have their keys, and they may or may not be trustworthy. For this reason, many states have laws requiring that apartment locks be changed with each new tenant, and most of them require deadbolt locks as well. Check the laws in your state. If the landlord doesn't install new deadbolt locks before you move in, insist that it be done or do it yourself and deduct it from the rent. Many states also require one or more days' notice before a landlord can enter your apartment. Find out what the regulations are and stand up for your rights!

Automobiles. Auto burglars work almost any time of the day or night, but they too are opportunists who prey on the unsuspecting. Likewise, they don't want to be seen and they want to get in and out as soon as possible. Usually they are after money or quick-sale items, and sometimes they want the car itself.

The best insurance against this brand of thief is not to leave any valuables in your car (especially in plain sight) and to roll up the windows and lock the car every time you leave it. This may seem obvious, but it bears repeating. You can't afford to be careless. Almost all stolen cars are left unlocked, and nearly half of them have the keys in the ignition! If you present a thief with an opportunity like this, you're asking for trouble.

Another source of trouble is service stations or parking lots where the attendant asks you to leave your keys. Whether or not your car is taken, the keys can be stolen and copied (it only takes a few seconds to make key impressions in wax or soap), and your car could be broken into or stolen at a later date. If you have to leave your car keys for some reason, make sure the station owner is reputable and that he has a safe place for them. Under no circumstances leave your house keys along with the car keys.

If a burglar really wants to get into your car, there's hardly any way to keep him out. Car locks are quite easily jimmied with a variety of tools, and cars can also be hot-wired in quick order. However, you can decrease the chances of car theft with a steering column that locks automatically.

For added insurance against burglary, you might think about installing a high-pitched alarm, which sends many thieves on their way with unusual speed.

Pickpockets and Purse Snatchers

Like burglars, pickpockets and purse snatchers are usually young males. Unlike burglars, they are gregarious. They prefer crowds, and most often they prey on people in broad daylight. They rely primarily on stealth, speed, and dexterity. Rarely are they dangerous unless detained. Once again, their greatest ally is the unaware victim. They strike particularly in areas where people are preoccupied and unattached. They love the anonymity of subway stations, airports, and department stores, as well as the bustling crowds that sometimes gather for special events in or around parks, theaters, and busy streets.

Your first line of defense against these criminals is not to have what they're after. When you leave home, don't take much cash with you. If you're traveling, rely on credit cards or travelers' checks. If you do have a lot of cash, hide it in an inside pocket of your coat or stash it in the toe of a shoe.

If you're a man, it's safer to carry your wallet in an inside suit pocket or in a front pants pocket rather than a back pocket where it can more easily be seen and removed. If you're a woman, it's better to hold your purse snugly against your body with your hands over the opening than to let it dangle loosely from a strap. Avoid open, basket type handbags, and don't put your purse aside in any public place even for a moment. Sometimes purses are even snatched out of cars at stoplights when they're left out in plain view.

Wherever you go, stay alert to the possibility of theft. Especially when you're in a subway, bus, train, or other crowded place, beware of jostling and pushing that could camouflage a pickpocket's activities. Protest loudly if you're being shoved unnecessarily. At bus stops, parking lots, and other waiting places, don't open your purse and go searching through it for keys or other items. Have these things easily and quickly accessible, and reach for them inconspicuously without acting vulnerable or paranoid.

Never tempt a thief by putting your purse, wallet, or other valuables out in plain view. In dangerous areas, travel with your car windows rolled up and the doors locked. Most important, stay alert to what's happening around you. You're very unlikely to be victimized if you look awake and purposeful. From time to time, look up and assess the crowd, the situation, the area. Put yourself in the snatcher's shoes. Where would you wait? Who looks vulnerable and why? You'll learn a great deal this way and save yourself a lot of anguish.

Muggers and Rapists

I put muggers and rapists in the same category because, in spite of their differences, they have many things in common. Muggers want your money or valuables, while rapists want to sexually abuse you. But they both prefer dark, isolated spots and they are both willing to injure (and in some cases even kill) to get what they want. They attack at dusk, dawn, in the middle of the night, and at other times when few people are around. They prefer isolated spots such as underground parking lots, alleyways, laundromats, parks, bus stops, street corners, building corridors, and basements. Most rapes occur in private homes and are committed by men who are in some way acquainted with their victims.

Many muggers and rapists work alone, attacking from behind after the victim has gone by. Other times they work in pairs or in gangs, surrounding lone people like packs of wolves or systematically attacking stranded motorists. Sometimes they even fool their victims into letting them into their homes or cars, posing as salesmen, hitchhikers, and the like. Occasionally they attack in broad daylight, gambling that other people will not want to get involved (and they are usually right). Most often these criminals prey on women and older people.

Seek People and Light. If you are a woman alone after dark, consider having someone pick you up or calling for a taxi instead of waiting at a subway station or bus stop. If your car is in a parking lot, make sure the lot is well lit. Better yet, have someone escort you to the lot and make sure you're safely in your car. If you do ride a bus or train, sit close to the driver or conductor.

Whether you're a man or woman on the street at night, stay as much in the light as you can. Avoid hedgerows, dark buildings, parked cars, and other places that might provide good cover for criminals. Plan your route so that it takes you through the best lighted, most populated places. If neither the curb nor the sidewalk is safe, walk in the middle of the street. Always keep your eye out for suspicious characters and detour in plenty of time to avoid them.

Simple Deterrents. It is said that in many cities there is almost no place that's safe for a woman to walk alone at night. This may be true, and I agree that whenever possible a woman should walk in the company of other people. However, I also believe that regardless of sex you can increase your security and freedom in some very simple ways.

Most criminals, like predators in the animal world, go for the easy mark, and there is something about a confident look or walk that inspires respect and often weakens a predator's resolve. When you go out, make sure you're really awake and alert. Know where you're going and walk directly and purposefully. Don't wear clothing that attracts criminals or makes you look vulnerable. Act calm and confident. Walk with your head up and with eyes and ears well tuned to what's going on around you. If necessary, look aggressive and tough—even icy—and don't feel bad about not being nice to strangers. All these things transmit messages of strength that tend to douse most criminals' hopes.

Heightened Awareness. Concentrate on improving your awareness. Most people have what I call automatic vision. That is, when passing a place they've been before, their eyes focus automatically on the things that are most familiar. Since most people don't consciously look for new things in their environment, they miss many things that might be important to their safety. Criminals know people are habitual and half asleep. All they have to do to avoid being seen is to hide in places their victims are not used to looking.

One technique for countering this syndrome is to vary your vision. Another is a simple nature observation technique called splatter vision. It is done by periodically unfocusing the eyes and allowing your vision to "spread out" like a wide-angle lens. Though your eyes don't focus on any one thing, they can detect even slight movements over a much larger area.

If you want to get a feel for how splatter vision works, you can start right now. Wherever you are, stop and look straight ahead. Don't focus your eyes, but be aware of your entire field of vision. If you're at a desk looking toward a wall, notice the wall. But also notice the other things you can see without moving your eyes: the pictures, the books, the doorway, the lamp, and other items in your peripheral vision. When you get a chance, try this outside on a busy street corner. You should be able to see not only the objects and activities directly ahead, but also those things on the edge of your vision. Most important, notice that you can concentrate on any one of these things while remaining aware of the whole picture.

When you begin to feel comfortable with it, try splatter vision while walking down the street. Don't use it all the time; just flash in and out of it periodically. As your splatter vision improves, it will blend so imperceptibly with your focused vision that other people may begin to think you have eyes in the back of your head.

Avoidance. If your perceptions are sharp, they'll tell you when danger is near. Your next move is to avoid your would-be attacker. If you think you're being followed by someone in a car, do an about-face and walk the other way. That will force the driver to either stop or turn

around. If the driver turns around, he will then be on the other side of the
street. If you suspect someone is following you on foot, cross to the other
side of the street. If the person behind you also crosses, do something
quickly before he gets too close. Head for a well-lighted place, dump your
purse in a mailbox, or whatever seems appropriate. If you don't have any
other alternatives, run or scream. (Because of people's reluctance to get
involved, it sometimes doesn't do much good to yell "Help!" or "Rape!"
But you can often draw quite a crowd by yelling "Fire!") Act quickly, and
don't be reluctant to act for fear of embarrassment.

As you approach your home after an absence, have your keys ready
to unlock the door. If you're a woman, don't carry your keys in your purse
with your identification. It is better to put them inside your clothing in a
little pocket secured with a snap or zipper. It's also best not to leave the
door open while you're taking parcels or grocery bags to other parts of the
house.

If you live in a high crime area, stay on the safe side by not opening
the door for strangers. Have a peephole installed so you can get a good
look at whoever's there. Don't rely on chains, or "interviewers" that allow
the door to open partway. Most of these are very weak and can be broken
with a good swift kick. If you have an unexpected caller (even in uniform)
claiming to represent a particular company, ask him to show his identification. Then, if you're interested in talking, you might even want to call his
company to make sure he's not an imposter. Nobody should be able to talk
you into opening your door if you feel uneasy or suspicious about them. If
someone gets insistent or hangs around in spite of your refusals, call the
police.

Buildings. If you're a single woman living alone in an apartment
house or other large building, you may have to be especially vigilant. First
of all, don't advertise your status by putting your full name on the mailbox
or in the phone book. Use your first initial and your last name only. Second, ask the landlord to install mirrors so you can see hidden parts of the
corridors before you get to them. Don't go into the basement or laundry
room alone. And if you're headed for an upper floor, first check the elevator to make sure it's not bound for the basement first.

By the same token, don't get into an elevator with anyone you
don't feel comfortable with—or quickly get out if someone suspicious gets
in. Trust your instincts and do not hesitate or worry about being rude. If
you're uneasy about going anywhere, get an escort. These things all point
out more clearly why it's so important to know your neighbors in an apartment house, and how effective a tenants' association can be in making
your building a safer place to live.

Automobiles. Remember also to be careful in your car. If you're in a shady part of town, lock the doors and roll the windows up. Don't hitchhike or pick up strangers who ask for lifts. Do your best to avoid breakdowns by knowing how your car works and keeping it well tuned. Make sure the tires are properly inflated and that you've got plenty of gas and oil. Check the weather ahead of time to avoid being stranded in a storm.

If you do become stranded, stick with your car. Put the hood up and turn on the emergency lights. Since most highways are patrolled regularly, it's only a matter of time before the police come by. On the other hand, if you're caught in a snowstorm and the highway looks deserted, consider lying low until you're sure a police car is on the way so as not to advertise your plight to criminals. If someone comes by, don't feel bad about sending him for help without opening the door.

To avoid such predicaments, the best insurance is a citizens band (CB) radio. For as little as a hundred dollars, you can buy and have installed a simple CB with Channel Nine that will give you immediate voice contact with police, service stations, hospitals, truckers, and other concerned motorists. Not only can you radio when you're in distress, but you can call ahead to check on weather and road conditions, get up-to-date traffic reports, and even relay messages back home. If you do much traveling, a CB is a must. The cheapest ones are no more expensive than a regular car radio, and they've infinitely more useful.

Traveling. If you're planning a trip to an unfamiliar city, find out about potential problem areas. Ask a friend or travel agent for pertinent facts. Once you're in a strange place, stop at gas stations and police precincts to ask for advice and information. Remember that parts of town that may be especially attractive to tourists and visitors during the day often become high crime areas during the night. Above all, get to know where you are and what to expect. Then be aware. In any new place, look around and assess the situation. If it seems risky, leave the area.

Hotel and motel rooms are notoriously insecure, partly because the same key has been used by so many other people. One nifty device that can make your stay in such places more pleasant is a "Travelock." These little locks make it possible for you to secure not only doubtful outer doors, but bathrooms, drawers, and other enclosures.

Confrontation. If you're confronted by a mugger or rapist, above all try to remain calm and don't panic. Remember that your mind is your best defense. Quick, level thinking has gotten many a person out of a tight situation, while panic almost always leads to disaster.

What you do will depend on your own convictions about the intentions of your assailant. If you're self-assured, you may be able to dissuade your attacker by talking to him loudly and firmly. If you're afraid, you may be able to mask it and repulse your attacker by acting like a slobbering fool. But don't push such techniques too far. If the person is armed and asks for your money, by all means give it to him. Chances are he'll take it and leave you alone. Likewise, if the person is armed and assaults you sexually, it is safest not to resist. If you put up a fight, you may anger the rapist to the point where he will seriously injure you.

Most rapes are committed by men who are at least somewhat familiar with their victims. Often this very familiarity causes some women to be embarrassed, taken off guard, or shocked into defenselessness. Don't let this happen. If you are very firm with your refusals, you may be able to head off a potential attack. Whatever you do, don't arouse your attacker's anger. Scream and fight if and only if you're convinced the rapist is unarmed and unsure of himself, or if your life is on the line. And if you fight, don't be halfhearted about it. Be as vicious as you possibly can. Go for the most vulnerable areas: the eyes, groin, temple, or throat. Scratch, gouge, kick, and punch with everything you have. Seriously try to injure your attacker. Otherwise, you may only enrage him and cause more damage to yourself.

Self-Defense. Anyone whose life is threatened has tremendous reserves of energy and power. Such power can be maximized when combined with serious training in self-defense. There are many courses given in a variety of martial arts, some of which were developed by monks of the Far East who were forbidden to use weapons other than their hands and feet. Taking a course in karate, kung fu, tai-chi, tai kwon-do, aikido, judo, or jujitsu can greatly enhance your defensive abilities as well as your perception and your self-conficence—especially if the course is taught by an accomplished and dedicated instructor.

If you take such a course, stay with it long enough to become competent. Practice the techniques until they are second nature to you. But don't let your skill give you a false sense of confidence. You can't expect a few months of karate to enable you to take on a mugger with a knife or gun, or to overpower a desperate man who is twice your size.

There are also a number of mechanical devices that may help you fend off an attacker, though their effectiveness is never guaranteed. Police whistles, pocket alarms, and various repellent sprays (even hairspray) can be effective if used at the right times. Likewise, keys and other sharp objects can help you defend yourself if it comes to fighting. But these things must be "at the ready" and you must know how to use them effectively. Under no circumstances should you carry anything with you such as a gun or knife than can cause serious injury if used against you. Before you buy such things as repellent sprays, also familiarize yourself with the local laws on possession and use of concealed weapons.

Swindlers

Swindlers are basically tricksters and liars. Their main object is to gain your confidence (hence the name "con game") by selling you a line of bull, then running away with your money before you realize what's happened. Older people on fixed incomes who are worried about their health and their homes are particularly vulnerable to these ploys.

Sometimes the con game comes in the form of a mail advertisement claiming a get-rich-quick scheme. Other times someone contacts you over the phone and talks you into leaving the house, then burglarizes it while you're gone. The most common games, however, try to get you to part with your money more directly. Some swindlers systematically go through the obituary page each day, making lists of people who have recently lost loved ones, then show up at the door with items they claim the deceased has recently purchased but not paid for. Another con artist specializes in pretending to be a bank investigator, asking unsuspecting people to help solve a crime by offering some of their own money as bait for the criminal. Then there's the home repairman who has a special deal, payable in advance. And finally, there are mail frauds of all types, from phony insurance claims and miracle cures to retirement land sales and worthless stocks and bonds.

To avoid being the victim of a swindle, be suspicious of any offer that sounds too good to be true. Don't be taken in by quack cures; entrust your health only to licensed physicians and specialists. Make sure you go to a reputable company for home or car repairs. Check the references of anyone who claims to be a bank investigator or any other kind of official, no matter how convincing he may be. (Don't use the number he gives you, either—look it up yourself!) Don't sign any contract without reading the fine print. And finally, don't take your hard-earned money out of the bank for any stranger, regardless of the circumstances. If you have questions or complaints about suspected rip-off artists, consult the police or your local consumer affairs department.

Keeping Your Children Safe

Because of an increase in kidnapping in recent years, some agencies suggest fingerprinting your children. This may be some help, but there are more practical things you can do to ensure their safety. The first rule is to never leave infants, toddlers, or young children unattended. As they grow older, teach them to stay close. When they go out to play, always find out where they are going, who they will be with, and have some responsible adult nearby.

You can begin loss-proofing your children at a very early age by helping them to become more aware of their surroundings. Have them wear a "dog tag" or get them to memorize their address and learn how to find their way home. Do this by pointing out prominent landmarks and practicing route-finding with them. When driving in the car, ask them from time to time where they are and how they would get home. Make a game out of it. Ask them to show you where to turn and let them direct you. Also teach children how to get help if they're lost or in distress. Point out gas stations, police precincts, fire departments, and other places where they can get help.

If your child is lost, remember that there are many places he or she might go where an adult wouldn't go. Most children quite naturally take to wild places such as vacant lots and woodsy or watery areas. Even abandoned buildings and construction projects have a certain attraction. Know your children's likes and dislikes. Know their habits and tendencies. Also know what they are wearing so you can alert the local police with an accurate description.

Unfortunately, it's often twenty-four hours before a police department will begin looking for a lost child. For a child under ten years old, even a few hours is too long to wait. As soon as you discover the child is missing, immediately get together as many friends as you can and thoroughly search the area where he or she was last seen. Comb the streets. Call his or her name. Look in both logical and illogical places. Pass the child's description on to anyone you meet and ask them to be on the lookout. Go into nearby homes and establishments and show a picture of the child, and give each person a phone number to call. (Have someone stay at home, and keep in touch with them regularly.) Have someone drive around the area where the child was last seen, looking and asking for help. If you suspect foul play, closely observe cars and homes as well.

The more pairs of eyes you have looking, the better. For those people who aren't likely to help out of sheer benevolence, offer a reward. Don't specify an amount until the child is found, but if you suggest that it's a big one, you're likely to get the cooperation of many people who wouldn't otherwise be interested.

Keep after the authorities to do their part. Remember that in cities the police are often overtaxed and it's often the squeaky wheel that gets the oil. Be persistent but cooperative. Give the police every shred of information you can think of, even if you think it might be irrelevant. If time gets short, go to the media. Ask that an announcement be put on the local news. If necessary, offer to pay for the radio time yourself. If you spare no effort right from the start, chances are you will soon be reunited with your child unharmed.

In the long run, an assertive child who learns to think for him- or herself is going to be safer than a passive child who sees adults only as authority figures. Encourage your children to make their own decisions, but make sure they avoid potential dangers. Explain to them that although the world is a beautiful place, not all people will be nice to them and that they must be strong enough to say no to strangers who offer them rides, candy, and the like.

Sometimes they may also have to say no to those who are not strangers—for example, friends who offer them drugs or even relatives or acquaintances who want to touch them in unacceptable ways. This makes it especially important to establish a relationship of love and trust with your children and to talk openly with them about such things as peer pressure and child molesting. Never do this in a way that frightens or alienates them, and always let them know that you will give them the love and support they need to stand up for themselves. That way, your children will grow up stronger and safer, and they'll probably be your friends for life.

7
WEATHER

I once watched a hang glider circle a mountaintop, riding the wind currents like an eagle as it rose up and up. Gradually it grew smaller until I had to squint to see it at all. Then it disappeared, and it was a long time before it came into view again.

Finally, the pilot began his descent, and in time I could clearly see him preparing to land. He dangled from fabric that seemed as fragile as a moth's wing. He rode face down, hands on the control bar—pushing, pulling, leaning, twisting—hanging between ground and space in an attitude that left him as captivated as a raindrop or snowflake. Before long he sailed overhead and touched down in a nearby field.

As the pilot carried his craft back up the "runway," I ran over to ask him what it was like up there in the clouds. He sat down and reflected. He told me how it felt to launch himself over a cliff with legs churning, and what a thrill it was when the air took over. He explained what it was like to be wafted into the sky, to watch the altimeter needle, to calculate the currents, and to try to second-guess the wind. He talked about what it was like to float like an eagle and be tossed about without propellors or moorings. He also talked about what it was like to be inside a cloud—how the rising air sucked you up and sometimes threw you around and how the fog was so thick in there you sometimes couldn't tell whether you were rightside-up or upside-down until the cloud spit you out again. He also described the different kinds of clouds: what they looked like, how high they were, how they were formed, and the meanings hidden in their different shapes.

It occurred to me, as I listened to this man, that expert hang-glider pilots can read the sky like most people read roadmaps. They have an intimacy with the atmosphere like that of birds. It is an intimacy borne of survival. It brings not only greater safety, but greater joy. With this, it occurred to me that those of us who are more earthbound can also develop a greater appreciation for the atmosphere. By paying closer attention to it, we can see that it is one of the most variable and delightful aspects of nature—and one of the most important aspects of urban survival.

Wherever we live, the weather has far-reaching effects on our lives. Our homes, our clothes, and our daily activities are molded to the movements of the seasons. We all make allowances for changes in the sky. A snowstorm can bring a city to a complete standstill. A tornado can rip through a town leaving a pathway of splinters and destruction. A hurricane can rake through a city leveling trees and buildings like a high-powered fan. A deluge can leave a suburb looking like a water-soaked sponge. The weather can also affect our moods and feelings, causing everything from nervousness, apprehension, and impatience to personal doldrums and drastic shifts in productivity and reaction time.

More than any other force, the weather holds a power and fascination for us that has hardly been dimmed by technology. Even though we've harnessed the atom, we still marvel over beautiful sunsets, and we still sit in awe as bolts of lightning streak across the sky. One reason for this lasting fascination is that, in spite of our best efforts, we cannot control the weather. Like our ancient ancestors, about the best we can do is try to predict and prepare for it.

In urban areas we usually leave weather prediction to the experts. Watching satellite pictures of cloud patterns and listening to the latest forecasts is an important part of survival preparedness. But we shouldn't rely entirely on this information. For one thing, it might not be available in a survival situation. For another, it isn't always accurate. And for a third, it doesn't give us the whole picture. The picture becomes whole (and vastly more interesting) only if we make an effort to understand how the weather works.

Not long ago, I was listening to the radio when the announcer said it was time for the weather report. But the official forecast had not come in yet, and the announcer was working in an air-conditioned building that had no windows. He jokingly instructed his assistant to go out onto the roof to see if he could figure out what tomorrow's weather was going to be like.

Most of us are like that announcer—so cut off from the elements and so tied to mechanical devices that a cloud might not tell us much even if we could see it. Can animals really tell when a storm is coming? Can native peoples really "smell" rain when it's still a day away? Of course they can, and so can we. Even in the city we can train our senses to glean more from the skies, much to our own interest and benefit. Like the hang-glider pilot, the more we know, the more prepared we will be to chart a safe and enjoyable course.

A Moving Ocean of Air

In a way, we're all like crabs, scuttling along the bottom of an ocean. The "ocean" is the atmosphere—a thin film of gases, dust, and water vapor that encapsules us between black space and the edge of the earth. Ninety-nine percent of the earth's atmosphere is contained in a thin bubble of air only twenty miles thick. This ethereal shell provides the oxygen we breathe, protects us from solar radiation, and (air pollution notwithstanding) creates the fragile environment necessary to sustain all life on earth. It also creates the weather.

The basic principles of weather are quite simple. Weather is caused by moving air. Air is set in motion by the heat of the sun and the spin of the earth. As it travels the globe, air absorbs moisture from oceans, lakes, and streams in the form of water vapor. Warm air is composed of widely spaced molecules, so it can hold more water vapor than cold air. Warm air is also lighter and tends to rise, while cold air is heavier and tends to descend. As warm air rises, cold air rushes in to take its place. When warm air meets cold air, the warm air cools and contracts. As it does so, it "squeezes" its load of vapor like a saturated sponge. The vapor then condenses and falls as rain or snow. Within the atmosphere, warm and cold air are constantly shifting and battling in an attempt to reach an equilibrium. But they rarely reach a calm balance; and when they do, they don't maintain it for very long.

Global Weather Patterns. Actually, the global movement of air works on the same principles as the air moving in our own homes. A radiator, for example, heats the air and it then rises toward the ceiling. As it rises, cool air flows in along the floor to replace it. Similarly, air is heated up at the equator, then tends to rise and flow toward the poles.

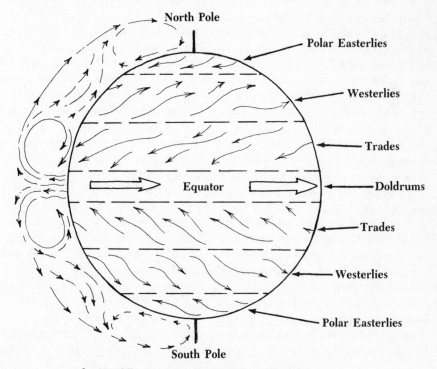

The World's Six Major Wind Belts, Created by the Heat of the Sun and the Spin of the Earth.

There it cools, descends, and flows back toward the equator again. In theory, the atmosphere works like two hemispheric conveyor belts.

If the atmosphere were stationary, this is probably the way it would work, too. But air movement is also affected by the spin of the earth. At the equator, where the earth spins eastward at about 160 miles a second, warm air rises and spins along at about the same speed, creating the effect of hardly any wind at all. This equatorial belt of air, which has becalmed many a sailor, is called the "doldrums."

As the wind rises and travels toward the north and south poles, the air is deflected by the slower speed of the earth. At about thirty degrees latitude, some of it veers off, descends, and turns back toward the equator, creating two belts of easterly winds called the "trades." At about sixty degrees latitude, the warm, pole-bound air is deflected in another direction and forms two belts of westerly winds, appropriately called "westerlies." Finally at the poles it forms two more belts of easterlies. In other words, the global weather system is composed of six huge belts of air, each one moving in the direction opposite to the one next to it.

North American weather systems are most directly affected by the "westerly" belt of air. Consequently, most major weather systems on our continent move from west to east. But there are other complications. There are no fixed boundaries between these air belts. Sometimes they mix and collide, causing turbulences that go off in different directions. Moreover, the earth's surface is not regular. Some is water and some is land, and the land is contoured in vastly different ways. Oceans, mountains, deserts, and other topographical features all affect the movement, temperature, and humidity of the air. So does the rising and setting of the sun. The result is a constantly changing cauldron of atmospheric activity.

But even on a grand scale, there is a pattern to this activity. For example, the weather pattern over North America is determined by seven major air masses (see map, page 179). Each of these masses forms in a "source area"—a place where the air stands still long enough to pick up the character of the surrounding seascape or countryside. Some of these are low pressure systems (warm air) and some are high pressure systems (cool air). The Polar Pacific mass picks up cool moisture over the North Pacific and often dumps it in the lowlands and mountains of the Pacific Northwest. The Polar Canadian air mass carries cold air southeast across Canada and the northern U.S., bringing cool, dry winds in summer and wet, biting cold in the winter. The Polar Atlantic mass usually spins southeast toward Europe, but it sometimes blankets the Atlantic states with cool, moist air in summer and heavy snows in winter. The Tropical Pacific mass carries some of the warm, humid character of the South Pacific Ocean northward toward California, while the Tropical Continental mass forms over sunny

Mexico and transfers its heat to the Gulf states as it travels toward the northeast. The Tropical Gulf and Tropical Atlantic masses both contain warm, moist air and tend to travel northeastward after reaching the mainland. These bring hot summers (sometimes with thunderstorms and tornadoes) and mild winters with lots of rainfall.

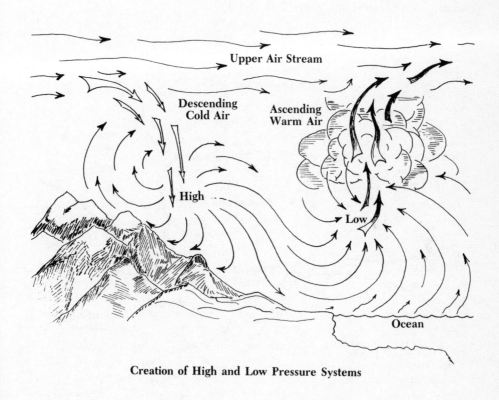

Creation of High and Low Pressure Systems

If you can locate your area on the map below, a brief study of these air masses will give you an idea of where most of your weather comes from and why your area experiences the climate it does. However, keep in mind that these air masses also change character as they move. They may cross a coastline, rise and cool as they work their way over the land, drop their moisture on a mountain range, descend over a hot desert, pick up more moisture from lakes and streams, billow upward to form thunderheads, and descend to fill valleys with dew and fog. One air mass may create more than a hundred storms as it floats and flows across the continent (see illustrations pages 184 and 185).

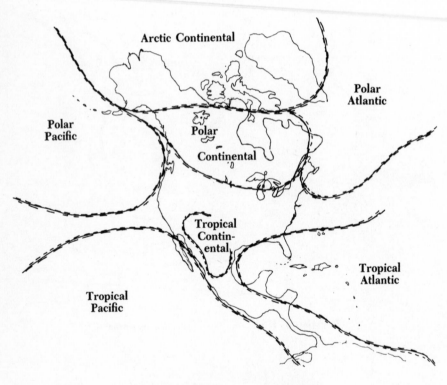

NORTH AMERICAN AIR MASSES

Two or more air masses may also bump into each other. And where they meet (commonly at boundaries called "fronts"), they often create a lot of turbulence. Usually, when a cold front meets a warm front, warm air rises and cold air wedges in beneath it. If the cold air rushes in from two or more directions, it may start spinning. And before long, it may form a cyclone—a cloud-filled merry-go-round measuring up to a thousand miles across. On satellite weather pictures, cyclones look a little like huge pinwheels. They are circular masses of warm, moist, light air (often called "lows," or low pressure systems) spinning slowly within masses of cool, dry heavy air (often called "highs," or high pressure systems). The battle between these two different air masses brings most of our everyday storms (see illustrations, page 186).

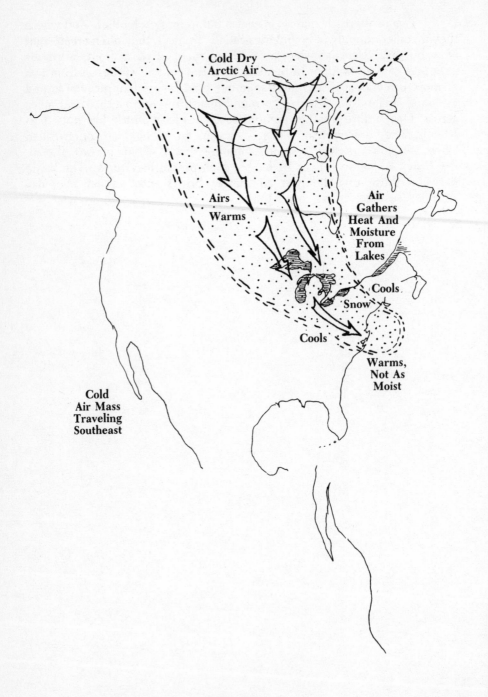

Cold Dry
Arctic Air

Air
Gathers
Heat And
Moisture
From
Lakes

Airs
Warms

Cools

Snow

Cools

Warms,
Not As
Moist

Cold
Air Mass
Traveling
Southeast

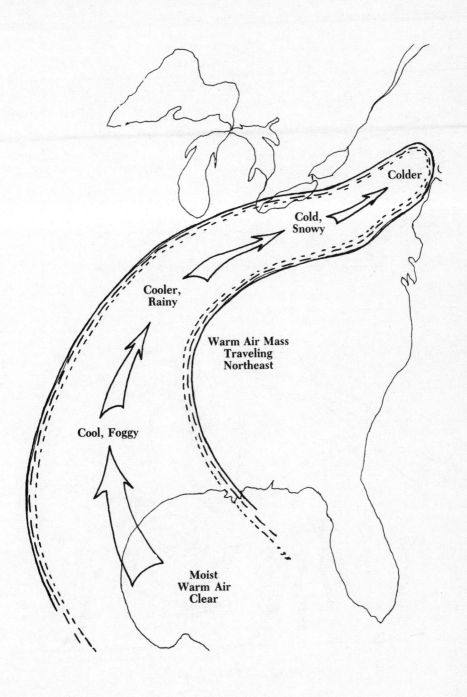

Colder

Cold,
Snowy

Cooler,
Rainy

Warm Air Mass
Traveling
Northeast

Cool, Foggy

Moist
Warm Air
Clear

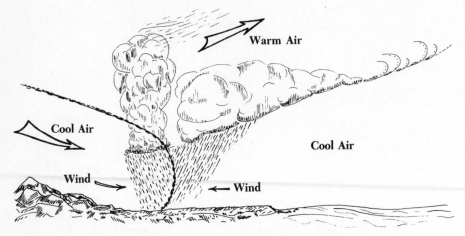

Meeting of Cold and Warm Fronts Creates Turbulence.

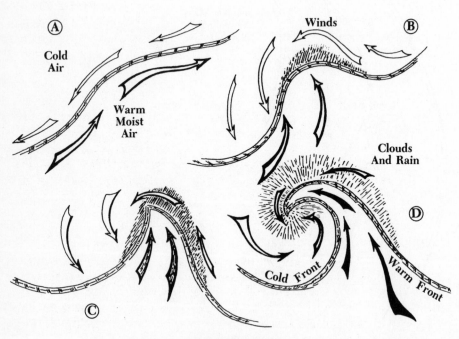

Creation of A Cyclone

Another kind of pinwheel, formed more violently, is a hurricane. Hurricanes are quite a bit smaller—only 100 to 150 miles wide—but much more concentrated. They also have a central "eye" where winds are calm or nonexistent. These pancake-shaped collections of thunderheads usually travel at a mere ten to fifteen miles an hour, but the winds that whirl inside them reach velocities between eighty and 150 miles an hour. The more powerful hurricanes can destroy almost anything in their path. At sea they whip up enormous waves that toss ships around like corks. On shore they rake through towns and cities, flooding streets, uprooting trees, and crushing buildings.

Hurricanes in the northern hemisphere are formed in tropical seas. They spin counterclockwise and travel in a northerly direction. Most of them take shape in late summer or fall and primarily affect the Gulf states. Fortunately, hurricanes are easily recognized on satellite photographs and travel slowly enough to allow people at least some time to prepare for them. (For information on hurricane safety, see "Hurricanes," page 208.)

Tornadoes are much smaller and shorter lived than hurricanes, but they are also less predictable and even more devastating. They consist of a long "spout" of wind dangling like an elephant's trunk from the bottom of a thick, dark thundercloud. Inside the spout, the wind roars around like a corkscrew at velocities up to three hundred miles an hour. Almost anything in the "twister's" path is doomed to destruction. Autos are thrown off highways, trees yanked from the earth, buildings demolished, and tons of debris and garbage sucked into the sky as through the hose of a giant vacuum cleaner.

Most tornadoes are formed in the summertime from the movements of warm, moist Tropical Gulf air flowing northeastward over the central plains. For this reason, they almost always show up east of the Rockies (most frequently in Iowa, Missouri, and Kansas). They travel east or northeast at twenty to sixty miles per hour. They may last anywhere from half an hour to several hours and travel up to three hundred miles before spinning themselves out. (For information on tornado safety, see "Tornadoes," page 214.)

Common Weather Phenomena

Violent storms are always exciting, but usually we experience more mundane weather phenomena such as rain and snow that have their origins in the clouds. Clouds are collections of condensed water vapor that reflect the light of the sun. These are formed when the air becomes so saturated with water vapor that it forces the vapor into tiny liquid spheres. Initially, each of these droplets forms around a nucleus of dust, and each droplet is so light that it floats on air. (If you look carefully, you can see these airborne water worlds sailing about in a cloud of fog.)

If the droplets stay small and low to the ground, they may form a cloud of fog or mist. If they are higher and grow larger, they may form a rain cloud. Rain is produced when microscopic water droplets grow heavier than air and begin to fall. On their way down, they hit other droplets and grow larger. By the time they become full-fledged raindrops, they have often grown to more than two thousand times their original size.

Contrary to popular opinion, raindrops are not spherical on one end and pointed on the other, but round with slightly flat bottoms. They plummet to earth more like tangerines than teardrops. There they seep into the ground, work their way through cracks and crevices, sculpt the landscape, mix with minerals, and add their fuels to the vital processes of life.

Dew is a form of earthbound rain. It is formed on calm, cloudless nights when moisture-laden air condenses on contact with cold surfaces such as blades of grass and spiders' webs. Frost is formed by a similar process when the temperature drops below freezing.

Similarly, snow is airborne vapor that has condensed in the form of ice crystals. Like frost, it is formed only in subfreezing temperatures, but usually at high altitudes. As long as the air stays below freezing, the crystals maintain their characteristic icy structure, which is almost always a variation on a few basic patterns. Solid, needle-like crystals form high up where the clouds are cold and dry, while six-pointed, lacy ones form lower down. Despite their similarities in shape, snowflake variations are so endless that out of the countless billions that have fallen, it's unlikely that any two have ever been exactly alike.

Unlike snowflakes, hailstones resemble frozen raindrops. Hail is formed in thunderclouds when raindrops are repeatedly swept up and down through the freezing zone of the cloud. Each time they go through this cycle, a new layer of frozen rain is added to their outer coat, leaving them a little thicker. The larger the hailstone, the more times it's been through the deep freeze. To give you an idea of what this yo-yo routine can produce if it keeps up long enough, the largest hailstone on record fell in Kansas in 1970. It measured eight inches in diameter and weighed one-and-a-half pounds.

Even more remarkable is lightning. Lightning is the most abundant and natural form of electricity. Though it can be frightening and cause a great deal of damage, it is also an important part of nature's scheme and deserves our appreciation. For example, lightning helps to create the atmospheric nitrogen that's necessary for plant growth. Even more fundamentally, it may have helped to create life itself by forming amino acids in the primordial seas.

SNOWFLAKE PATTERNS

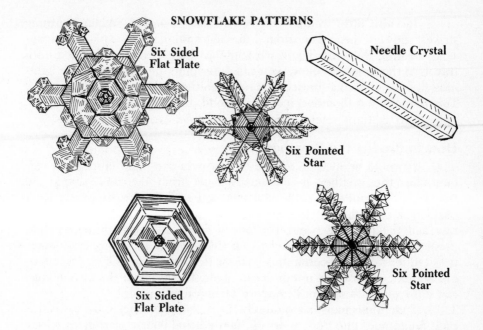

Six Sided
Flat Plate

Needle Crystal

Six Pointed
Star

Six Sided
Flat Plate

Six Pointed
Star

Initially, lightning is generated by the movements of air and water in a thundercloud (see "Cumulonimbus," page 193). As warm air rushes upward, the lower part of the cloud develops a negative electrical charge and the upper part develops a positive charge. The ground is also positively charged. In between, the air acts as an electrical insulator, tending to keep the charges separate.

When the charge differential (or voltage) becomes great enough, a thin, invisible stream of electrons (called a "leader") forces its way through the air at about 240 miles per second. When this routefinder reaches the ground, its path is instantly retraced by a much larger and faster bolt that blasts upward at more than 60,000 miles per second. This bolt may be followed by several more that flash so quickly they all seem to be part of a single bolt. Typically, a lightning bolt measures from one to six inches in diameter and from two hundred feet to twenty miles long.

Regardless of where it strikes, lightning almost always travels the path of least resistance. Usually that path is the shortest possible route between negative and positive charges: cloud to cloud, cloud to rooftop, cloud to tree, or even cloud to airplane. At the moment they strike, most lightning bolts create a channel that's superheated to about fifteen thousand degrees Centigrade, or two-and-a-half times the surface temperature of the sun. It's little wonder they start so many fires.

It's also little wonder they cause such a racket. When lightning strikes, the superheated air around the bolt undergoes an explosive expansion, creating the sonic boom we know as thunder. Since thunder itself travels at the speed of sound, you can determine the distance of the lightning flash by counting the seconds between the flash and the thunderclap. This is roughly a thousand feet per second, or about five seconds to the mile. (For lightning safety tips, see "Lightning," page 210.)

How to Predict the Weather

It would be nice to be able to rely with one-hundred-percent certainty on the weather predictions we get from the newspapers and television. But quite often they turn out to be wrong. Friday's newspaper predicts fair weather for the weekend and it rains. The weatherman says rain and the next day we get a foot of snow. In recent years weather predictors have gotten themselves off the hook by reporting percentage possibilities instead of certainties—and with good reason. Given the amazing number of variables in our ocean of air, that is about the best anyone can do, even with the most modern technical equipment.

Sometimes moist air suddenly turns cold and drops snow instead of rain. Sometimes one front veers off its predicted course or collides with a second front that changes the character of both. An endless variety of things can happen to air masses to alter weather predictions, and in a very short period of time. That's why it's a good idea to supplement weather predictions with our own observations.

Watching the Wind. Sometimes we can tell a lot about the weather by watching the wind. Though it is a gross generalization, west winds (those blowing from the west) in most parts of the country bring fair weather, while east winds bring rain. If the wind blows from the south it most often means heat and showers, while north winds most often mean clear, cold weather ahead.

To determine wind direction, hold a wet finger in the air and wait till you feel one side getting cold. That side is the direction the wind is blowing from. You can also detect wind direction by watching the way steam and smoke travel, or by watching the sway of trees.

Windspeed is also a weather indicator, especially if it is accompanied by clouds (see "Watching Clouds," page 191). The faster the wind, the faster the weather is changing. In perfectly calm air, smoke rises vertically. Up to three miles per hour, wind causes a subtle drift of smoke. At five miles per hour, you can feel wind on your face. At ten miles per hour, you can see leaves and twigs moving. At twenty miles per hour, small trees begin to sway and flags start to ripple. At thirty miles per hour, you can see large branches swaying and begin to hear power lines whistling and flags beating. At forty miles per hour, whole trees are swaying, flags are completely extended, twigs and branches begin breaking from trees, and it becomes difficult to walk. At fifty miles per hour, you'd better get inside and batten down the hatches.

Other Signs. There are many other signs that foretell changes in the weather, and some of them are characterized by familiar rhymes. For example, "A stormy day will betide sound traveling far and wide." The basis for this rhyme is that sound carries better in moist air than in dry air. If sound carries especially well, it could mean rain is on the way.

Another sign is given by air pressure. Air pressure is nothing more than the weight, or density, of the air molecules in a given area. Warm, moist air weighs less, so when a warm front comes in, it creates an area of low pressure. Dry, cool air weighs more, so a cold front usually creates an area of high pressure. High atmospheric pressure makes the mercury in a barometer rise higher, while low pressure allows it to drop lower. If the dial goes up, it usually means good weather ahead; if it goes down, it usually means bad weather.

Even without a barometer, you can sensitize yourself to pressure changes in the atmosphere. There's an old saying, "If smoke goes high, no rain comes by; if smoke hangs low, watch out for a blow." The cool, dry air of high pressure systems allows smoke to drift upwards, while low pressure systems keep smoke particles heavily laden with moisture. For the same reason, low-flying insects are also a clue to bad weather.

So is sky color. You've no doubt heard the saying, "Red at night, sailor's delight; red in the morning, sailors take warning." The red sky is created by the sun's rays filtering through dry, dusty air. Since weather tends to travel from west to east, if the dust is to the east (as in the morning), it often means that dry air is being pushed out by wet air coming in from the west. If the dust is to the west, it usually means the air to the west is dry and will bring clear weather the next morning.

Finally, you can even learn to forecast bad weather by becoming more aware of your own aches and pains. Old injuries and ailments tend to flare up when bad weather is brewing. This is caused by atmospheric conditions—especially low pressure and cold, damp air—that affect muscles and joints.

Watching Clouds

When all is said and done, the best natural weather predictors are clouds. These airy puffballs come in many shapes and sizes, and they form at many different altitudes. If they are watched carefully—not just their forms, but how they change—they can be very good atmospheric indicators. Following are the most common cloud forms and the hints they give us about how the weather is changing.

Cirrus clouds (also called "feather clouds" or "mare's tails" because of their thin, wispy appearance) are the highest clouds. The bottoms of these clouds form at 25,000 to 35,000 feet, or about five to seven miles up. At this altitude, the air is extremely cold, so cirrus clouds are composed entirely of ice crystals. They are the first sign of an approaching low pressure system. They may thicken, or they may disappear. If they thicken, they usually mean bad weather within twenty-four hours.

Cirrostratus. When cirrus clouds thicken, they form cirrostratus clouds. These tend to spread out in thin, milky veils (usually from 18,000 to 30,000 feet up) and are marked with many streaks and blotches. They often leave the sky looking like a tangled web. If this web begins to blot out the sun, it's likely a storm is approaching. You can make sure by keeping an eye on the characteristic halo they leave around the sun. If the halo grows smaller (thicker clouds), bad weather is on the way. If it grows larger (thinner clouds), the weather may clear up.

Cirrocumulus clouds, as their name suggests, are halfway between wispy cirrus and woolly cumulus clouds. They form high up, from 18,000 to 25,000 feet, and their icy needles form into flaky rows that give the sky a pattern much like that of the markings on a mackerel fish; hence the term, "mackerel skies." These clouds are almost always accompanied by other high-altitude clouds such as cirrus and cirrostratus and help to indicate an incoming low pressure system and possibly stormy weather.

Altocumulus, or "sheep" clouds, look much like cirrocumulus but are more clumpy than wispy. They are medium altitude clouds, forming from 6000 to 21,000 feet up, and most of them contain water instead of ice. Tower- or castle-shaped altocumulus clouds usually mean rain within eight hours.

Altostratus. If a storm is imminent, cirrostratus clouds will usually turn into altostratus, or "curtain," clouds. These clouds form at about 10,500 to 18,000 feet and create the impression of a thick, formless haze that almost or completely blots out the sun or the moon. In the winter these often mean snow, since their upper parts are high enough for vapor to condense into freezing needles. At other times of the year, they bring a light, steady rain.

Stratus clouds are like flat gray sheets or layers spread uniformly across the sky. They form at 2000 feet or less and are of the same thickness throughout (anywhere from 50 to 1000 feet). These clouds can mean many things, but most often they are not threatening. In the early morning, they are usually nothing but fog that burns off as the day grows warmer. If they form later in the day or at night they may bring a light rain or drizzle, but never heavy storms. Watch them, though, as they can also develop into full-fledged rain clouds.

Nimbostratus clouds ("nimbo" means rain) are the most common rainmakers. These often develop from altostratus clouds. They are thick layers of gray that float low to the ground (from 100 to 3000 feet) with no definable shape, but often with thin, gray wisps hanging like torn sheets from their undersides. These clouds completely blot out the sun and are an almost certain sign that rain or snow will fall within four to five hours. If they form in the winter, you should be ready for a deluge that may last eight hours or more.

Cumulus clouds are the common white "woolly" piles we see floating through the skies on fair days. These form from 1500 to 6500 feet up and range from less than a thousand feet to nearly a mile in thickness. They are formed during the day wherever vapor rises high enough to cool and condense, and they usually disappear at night when warm air cools and descends again. However, they should not be taken lightly. An average-sized cumulus cloud can contain as much as a thousand tons of water, and if the cloud grows larger, watch out! It may become a thundercloud (see "Cumulonimbus clouds," below).

Stratocumulus clouds should be watched even more closely, as they often precede thunderclouds. These form from cumulus clouds anywhere from 1500 to 6500 feet up and may look like patchy, layered puffballs or even irregularly twisted croissants. If you see them, consider the situation. In the evening they might just be heralding the setting sun. If they're gray with lots of billows and a blustery wind, they may mean an impending storm—anything from a light rain or snow to a full-fledged thundershower.

Cumulonimbus clouds are the famed thunderheads, the most dynamic and dangerous of the cloud family. These start out as cumulus clouds with flat bases at 2000 to 5000 feet. From here they billow upward, forming high piles of white cumulus with flat tops until they look like enormous, windblown cauliflowers. At a distance they appear brilliant white, but as they cut off the light, they grow dark and very threatening. They can bring anything from rain and hail to thunder and lightning. East of the Rockies they can even spin themselves into tornadoes. These clouds should not be taken lightly under any circumstances. They often hold more than half a million tons of water.

City Weather

In many ways, urban and suburban environments create their own weather, and this must also be taken into account in any personal predictions. For example, concrete and asphalt tend to reflect lots of heat, which in turn warms the air and creates more wind. We've all experienced the "canyon" effect of winds rushing between tall buildings. Walls create currents and eddies that can be quite devastating as winds increase, but they can also provide protective enclaves during inclement weather.

During the day, acres of concrete, brick, and asphalt absorb and radiate a great deal of heat, leaving the city warmer than the surrounding countryside. Factories and cars also add their heat, as well as their wastes. In quiet, rainless weather, clouds of pollution trap the sun's rays, creating a "greenhouse effect." This blanket of atmospheric garbage helps to keep cities warmer, but it also creates more health hazards. Sulfur dioxide mixes with rain to form a low grade sulfuric acid that eats away at everything it comes in contact with—including air-breathing lungs.

Air Pollution. Many daily newspapers publish an air pollution index along with the weather report, intended to advise citizens of the level of junk that's likely to be floating around on any given day. When soot, smoke, and sulfurous fumes reach a certain level, the index shows an alert and people are advised to stay indoors and to refrain from heavy physical activity until the cloud has passed.

It often strikes me as ironic that different cities have very different levels of "acceptable" pollution. Predictably, the worse the pollution in a given city, the higher the acceptable level tends to be. It is sad to think that we can no longer enjoy fresh air or water as our ancestors did, and that we are literally poisoning ourselves with our industrial and automotive wastes. This is one of the prices we pay for our modern conveniences.

However, it does not make good survival sense to be too fatalistic about these things. Like any survival threat, we should always be alert to air quality and take the necessary steps to insure our health. This is most important at times of the year (early fall and spring in most areas) when temperature inversions trap clouds of pollution for days at a time. If you live in such an area and you have breath-related health problems, I would strongly recommend moving to a healthier environment. If this is not possible, use a mask or other air-filtering device during the worst pollution periods.

Other Local Factors. Wherever you choose to live, keep in mind that other local factors can also affect the weather. For example, woodlands cut down on windspeed and help to cool off the air at ground level during the warm summer months. Bodies of water create a cooling effect in summer and a slight warming effect in winter, moderating the area's dominant weather trends. Coastal cities tend to receive cool sea breezes during the day and relatively warm winds at night.

Remember also that altitude greatly affects the weather. The higher you go, the colder it will be. Generally, you can expect a three-degree drop in temperature for every thousand feet of elevation gain. In valley bottoms, nights are chillier because of cold air descending, while ridgetops are often buffeted by high winds. Middle ground is the best place to be.

Although you can't change the weather, you can choose where to live. Whether you choose the city or the country, make it a place that is well suited to your physical and psychological needs. Decide what kind of climate you want and what kind of weather risks you're willing to take. In doing so, do not discount the airborne bacteria, viruses, and pollens that cause colds, flu, and respiratory ailments such as asthma. (One of the most useful books in this respect is Robert Shakman's *Where You Live May Be Hazardous To Your Health.*) By all means, pick a healthy environment and keep an eye on the weather. That way, you'll probably be ready for anything the atmosphere brings your way.

8
DISASTERS

Fragile and beautiful as it is, the earth's atmosphere is ever changing and uncontrollable. It can wreak devastating destruction on cities through storms, floods, hurricanes, blizzards, tornadoes, lightning, heat, and cold. In the face of such power we sometimes seem as helpless as ants. Nor is the earth's crust always a stable and hospitable homeland, as evidenced by frequent shiftings and rumblings that manifest themselves in the form of earthquakes, tidal waves, and volcanic eruptions. As if wild nature were not hazard enough, the world is made more precarious still by human nature. Like the earth itself, the human species is also young and evolving. We, too, are unstable and unpredictable, and our fate is by no means certain. Until about forty years ago, the danger of our own destructive power was limited. Now, with the proliferation of nuclear and biological weapons, there is literally no limit to the death and destruction we can cause ourselves and the planet.

Such potential disasters give us something to think about. The forces of nature, over which we have no control, are a challenge both to our survival and our humility. Since we can do nothing about them, they give us only something to prepare for and to cope with. Manmade disasters, on the other hand, give us this and more. They offer us the challenge to avert them.

Each of the sections below deals with a different kind of emergency or disaster. Since it is important to understand the forces we're dealing with, each section begins with a brief explanation of the force and its effects and potential hazards. This is followed by directions on how to best prepare for or avoid the disaster—or if avoidance is not possible, how to cope with it. You'll find that many directions apply to two or more different situations. This is not meant to bore you, but to instill the important points even more firmly in your mind. There are common themes in survival situations. The more you think about them, the more quickly they will come back to you when you need them.

A final word before we go on: As usual, preparation is the best insurance. But preparation will do you infinitely more good if it's done early. By the time you hear an official warning, it's already panic time. People flock to stores and gas stations in droves, trying desperately to store up their resources, and in no time the emergency supplies are gone. Within hours after major storm warnings, many grocery stores are stripped bare of perishables such as milk and eggs, and you can't find a sheet of plywood, a candle, or a can of Sterno to save your life. If by some lucky chance you can find what you're after, you'll most likely have to pay many times what it's really worth. It's even worse the day after a disaster, when the unprepared flock to emergency suppliers intent on getting the necessities at almost any cost—including violence.

Stay immune to the panic syndrome. Prepare early. Buy everything you need six months in advance, not six hours. Rehearse emergency procedures for various disasters with your family so that you can face almost any situation with calm confidence. Make sure everyone knows just where to go and what to do. Brainstorm with each other, asking "What If?" questions: What if you're caught at school in a tornado? What if an earthquake hits when you're walking down the sidewalk? What if you're at the beach house when you get word of an approaching tidal wave? What would you need? What would you do? How would you save yourself? Develop your survival abilities and reflexes by asking such questions frequently. Make a game out of it, each family member coming up with new and different survival problems to be solved in the fastest and safest way possible.

Blizzards (See also "Weather," page 177)

Of all the ravages of winter, blizzards are potentially the worst. Technically, blizzards are cold, heavy snowstorms with winds in excess of thirty-five miles per hour and temperatures below twenty degrees Fahrenheit. Severe blizzards are characterized by winds in excess of forty-five miles per hour and temperatures less than ten degrees Fahrenheit.

However, nature does not make such neat distinctions, and most of the information that applies to blizzards applies equally to winter storms of less severity. Such storms include (1) heavy snows, which means four or more inches of snow in a twelve-hour period, or six or more inches in a twenty-four hour period; (2) snow flurries, characterized by small amounts of snow falling at irregular intervals; (3) snow squalls, short storms with lots of snow and gusty winds; (4) ice storms, in which rain freezes when it hits the ground and may even get thick enough to knock down trees and telephone wires; and (5) sleet, which is basically a "deluge" of frozen raindrops.

What Are the Hazards? The dangers of winter storms vary with their intensity. Blizzards are extremely dangerous because they combine high winds with lots of snow and extreme cold. To most of us, this means low visibility, immobilization, and a high potential for hypothermia and frostbite. Anyone caught unprepared in a blizzard (and somewhat less so in other winter storms) is extremely vulnerable. Even wind and cold without snow should be enough to give you a healthy respect for winter storms. The effect of cold is multiplied quickly as winds increase. At ten degrees Fahrenheit in a twenty-mile-an-hour wind, you can get frostbite within one minute. Whatever the storm, there is always danger of traffic accidents or being stranded on the highways. Even after the storm has passed, there is a serious danger from overexertion in the effort to dig out.

Stay Tuned. The first rule for an impending winter storm (as for most potential disasters) is to stay tuned to your radio (Civil Defense is 640 or 1240 on your dial) or television. Listen carefully to know the kind of storm that's predicted, where it's most likely to do damage, and how to prepare for it. Act as quickly as possible on the recommendations of local officials, but don't rely on their predictions. If anything, assume the storm will be worse than anticipated.

Stay Put. Don't go outside in a blizzard unless absolutely necessary, and if so, only for short periods to perform essential tasks. Even with lesser storms, the best advice is to stick close to home and make sure you have the essentials to last it out. Do like the animals do. Make sure your shelter is well insulated and well stocked with survival necessities. In a blizzard, these include emergency heating equipment and fuel, emergency food and water, first-aid equipment, firefighting equipment, and a battery-powered radio with extra batteries. If necessary, consolidate your living quarters into a single room for added warmth (see "Shelter," page 41), and be sure to batten down the hatches and make important phone calls before the wind-and-snow combination causes power outages.

If you're a long way from home, don't try to get home until after the storm has passed. Take shelter in a hotel, motel, public building, or other safe place until the storm has passed and it's safe to travel. You may not feel as comfortable in a strange place, but at least you'll be warm and safe.

Emergency Travel. Travel during a winter storm of any kind is risky, and travel during a blizzard is insane. If you must drive during a winter storm (and any time you're driving on ice or snow), go as safely as possible. Make sure your car is in good working order—well tuned, filled with gas and oil, and equipped with chains or snow tires. Make sure the car is also well stocked with the necessary winter supplies. These include (not necessarily in order or importance) a blanket or sleeping bag, food and water (better yet, hot drinks in a thermos), jumper cables, snow shovel, extra warm clothes (including mittens, heavy coat, and warm woolen hat), first-aid kit, firestarters, flashlight, knife, axe, windshield scraper, road maps, and compass. For added safety, it wouldn't hurt to throw in a sack of sand and a tow chain.

Don't travel alone; take another competent person with you. Best of all, travel in the company of another car so that if one vehicle gets stuck, you'll have the other to fall back on. Travel only in the daylight and on major highways, and plan the shortest and easiest route to your destination. Keep your radio tuned to the weather and don't take chances.

To get started on ice or snow, first clear a path for several feet in front of the wheels, either by shoveling or by driving back and forth in the parking space. Keep the wheels pointed straight and accelerate very gradually in second gear or "drive." If the wheels spin and begin digging a ditch, get out and put some kind of traction material (such as sand or salt) in front of the wheels.

Drive defensively, allowing approximately four to six times the distance you would allow between you and the next car under dry conditions. Make sure you get up enough speed so that you don't get stuck on hills, but always stay alert for signs of trouble. Be ready to turn, change lanes, and perform other movements long in advance of reaching the critical area. And be ready to maneuver around stalled vehicles without having to brake.

Stay on the lookout for icy or slippery surfaces. Remember that some parts of the road such as bridges and overpasses freeze more quickly than others, and that stopping distances on different kinds of ice and snow can vary greatly. Use the brake as little as possible. When you brake, do so with a gentle pumping action to prevent the wheels from locking and skidding. If your rear wheels go into a skid, put your foot on the clutch or shift to neutral and turn the car smoothly in the direction of the skid until it straightens out. In a front-wheel skid, de-clutch or shift to neutral and wait for the wheels to grip the road without turning the steering wheel. Then put the car in gear again and accelerate slowly. In any driving maneuver, always turn the steering wheel smoothly and gently, never with quick or jerky motions.

If you get stuck in a snowstorm, don't panic. Stay with your car and make it as comfortable as you can (see "Car Shelters," page 59) until the storm has passed. Be sure to provide some means of signaling (a bright-colored cloth on the end of an antenna, for example) so rescue crews can find you if the snow gets too deep. Don't leave the car unless you're absolutely sure you can get to safety. The added snow on the automobile will actually help to insulate you against wind and cold, providing a ready-made "auto-igloo." Your main job will be to keep the leeward window open a crack to provide oxygen, and to avoid carbon monoxide poisoning. Run the engine only when necessary. Don't get snow in the car, and keep the radiator and exhaust pipe free of snow.

If the car becomes completely buried with snow, don't run the engine at all, and be sure to provide a vent for fresh air. Avoid going to sleep in a snow-stranded car. Exercise moderately by rubbing hands and limbs and moving around inside the car. If you feel a little claustrophobic, remind yourself that this is exactly how the animals survive inside their warm burrows while snowstorms are raging. If you can keep calm and relax like a snowshoe rabbit, chances are you'll come through just fine. If you have an emergency supply of food and drink, you can probably even enjoy yourself. Above all, maintain a positive attitude.

If you're caught in a snowstorm without an automobile and can't reach safety, you're in a pickle. But you still might be able to survive by burrowing into a snowbank. Snow has tremendous insulating qualities—particularly if you can keep most of your body away from direct contact with it. Adequate footwear and warm woolen clothes beneath a good protective shell can save your life in situations like this, if you have the patience to wait out the storm and endure a little discomfort. (Just ask the fox, which sometimes waits out snowstorms by huddling in a ball with its long bushy tail wrapped around it and letting the snow cover it over.) Such emergency bivouacs can be enlarged as time and energy permit.

Don't Overexert Yourself. Just because the storm is over doesn't

mean there's no more danger. A blanket of snow can present serious hazards even on a hot day. A surprising percentage of the deaths that occur
during and after winter storms result from overexertion—people slogging
through deep snow, digging out cars, and shoveling sidewalks. Most often
these tragedies occur with older people who put too much strain on their
hearts. But it can happen with younger people, too, because cold weather
puts an added strain on the body to begin with.

Don't add to the strain with any sudden or prolonged exertion. If
you walk somewhere after the storm, go slowly and with plenty of warm
clothes. If you're shoveling a driveway or sidewalk, pace yourself. Take
frequent breaks. Refresh yourself with high-energy food and hot drinks.
Easy does it!

Earthquakes

We still can't predict just where and when earthquakes are going to
occur, but we've learned a lot about them in recent years. We know, for
example, that they are caused by the cracking, shifting, and buckling of
the earth's crust. This crust is like a thin, brittle shell—a broken shell,
actually—floating on a sea of hot molten plastic. The pieces of the shell
are massive "plates," sometimes carrying whole continents and oceans on
their backs. These plates in turn ride the molten depths, shifting, buckling, scraping, and bumping into each other on their ponderously slow
journeys. It is now generally accepted, for example, that the continents
were once a single supercontinent that broke apart hundreds of millions of
years ago and whose pieces have been drifting ever since. If you look at a
globe, you can see that North and South America could fit quite nicely
against the coastlines of Europe and Africa. It's also well established that
these continents are moving away from each other at the rate of a few
inches per year.

An area where two plates tend to collide, pull apart, or scrape
against each other is called a fault. One of the most famous faults is the
San Andreas, a tremendous crack in California where the Pacific Plate
scrapes alongside the North American Plate. At such weak points in the
earth's crust, seismic pressure builds up and is finally released in the form
of an earthquake. It's a little like putting gradual pressure on a sheet of
ice. You don't see the effects at first, but when the pressure becomes great
enough, the ice suddenly breaks. And when it breaks, it sends out a series
of shocks, or vibrations. The waves from these vibrations can be devastating when they reach the surface.

The severity of the surface waves is what determines the destructive power of the earthquake. Every year the globe is subjected to several

million earthquakes. Only about seven hundred of these (rated at 5.5 or more on the Richter scale) are powerful enough to cause much damage to human settlements. But occasionally the earth shivers quite violently—especially along well-established fault lines and where mountains are being pushed up as a result of plate collision.

What Are the Hazards? The dangers of earthquakes are many. The major ones include landslides, tidal waves, collapsing walls, falling objects, broken glass, downed power lines, and fires. Quakes often cause major power outages and destruction of water and sewer systems. They can also destroy highways and transportation systems, which may make it more difficult for rescue and relief workers to come to your aid.

What to Do. With this in mind, find out whether you're in a high risk area. If so, make sure you have enough food, water, first-aid supplies, and emergency cooking equipment for at least several days. Check to see that your home is structurally sound. Reduce fire hazards by bolting down gas appliances. Find out where to turn off the gas, electricity, and water at a moment's notice. Take a look around the house with an eye to reducing the hazard of falling objects. Put loose and heavy things down low, and pick areas in every room that would be relatively safe from falling objects. Have a battery-powered portable radio handy, and make a plan that you could carry out instantly in any situation.

Most large earthquakes are heralded by such things as swaying lamps, rumbling ground, and rushing wind. They come on so fast that you may be pitching and stumbling before you realize what's happened. At that point, keep calm and remember your plan. Most quake injuries occur when people are hit by falling objects as they try to get in and out of buildings. Stay where you are. If you're inside, take refuge by or under a stable structure such as an inside wall, an inside doorway, or a sturdy table. Pick a place where you'll also be protected from falling objects such as brick or plaster, and where there's no danger of shattering glass.

If you're in a tall building, find refuge under a sturdy piece of furniture, in a doorway, or against an inside wall. Don't use the elevator. If you're caught in a crowded building such as a theater or department store, find shelter where you are. Don't rush for the exit or you may be injured by others who have the same idea.

If you're outside, stay there. Try to find an open place away from buildings, overhead wires, and other hazards. If you're in a moving car, stop and stay put. The car will shake, rattle, and roll, but in most cases it will provide good protection. When the quake is over, proceed with caution. Be on the lookout for landslides, cracked or weakened roadways, collapsed overpasses, and downed utility wires.

Don't move about until you're sure the quake is over. If the house or building is severely damaged, leave it as soon as possible. If it's OK, quickly check for fires, leaky gas lines, and short circuits. Keep in mind the possibility of aftershocks. Don't light matches or smoke cigarettes, and don't take flames of any kind (including lanterns) into a building. Use battery-powered flashlights for exploration. If you suspect a hazard, turn off the gas and the electricity. Then check the water and drainage systems for leaks. If you encounter cracked pipes, turn off the water.

Be sure to wear shoes around broken glass, and don't eat from containers that may have picked up glass splinters. Refrain from using your water until you get the official word that it's safe. If municipal pipes have cracked, there may be sewage mixed in with it. Also check your home for structural damage, taking special care around chimneys and walls where loosened objects may be ready to topple. Do all this with extreme care, and completely avoid any seriously damaged buildings.

Finally, stay in a safe place until you're sure it's OK to be out and about. The famous naturalist John Muir was once so excited by a Yosemite earthquake that he rushed toward a churning rockslide and hopped gleefully among the rolling boulders before the dust had settled. But Muir had nine lives. Don't go sightseeing. Instead, tune in your radio or television to find out the location and extent of the damage and plan your movement accordingly. If the damage is severe, local officials may need your help. Be ready to give it.

Fire (See also "Fire Safety," page 125)

Floods

Technically, a flood occurs when water rises above the level where property can be damaged without earthworks or other protection. To the average resident of a flood-ravaged city or suburb, what this often means in simple terms is water, water everywhere. Water in the streets, water in the basement, water on the highways, water in the yard. It also means stranded cars, short circuits, undermined roadways, mud-lined boulevards, polluted water and food supplies, and in severe cases complete inundation of communities, requiring emergency evacuation and relocation.

Floods have many causes, both natural and manmade. One of the most common is seasonal rains that cause rivers to swell. Another is an unusually heavy snowpack that's exposed to a sudden springtime thaw. Flooding can accompany major storms such as hurricanes, as well as landslides, earthquakes, and avalanches that block off the regular flow of streams. Unwise decisions can also contribute to floods—such as the over-grazing and timber cutting that denude large areas of water-absorbent vegetation, poor planning or operation of manmade dams, and landfills in wetlands. Whatever the reason, the result is the same: too much water in the wrong place at the wrong time.

What To Do. First of all, be aware of the flood hazards of your area. If you live near a watershed, check its history. Is it prone to flooding in regular cycles? How far above the usual floodline is your property? What would you need to do to protect it, and where would you go to reach safety? Do you live downstream from a dam? How reliable is the dam? Is it built on an earthquake fault? (Don't laugh—some of them are!) Also keep track of the weather—specifically the snowfall and runoff in nearby watersheds. And pay attention to flood warnings issued over radio and television.

If you're living in a flood-prone city or suburb, sock away emergency food, water, cooking, lighting, and medical supplies and have them ready to put in the car. Keep the car gassed up and ready to go, and have extra batteries on hand for your portable radio. Also keep emergency waterproofing supplies at the ready—including sandbags, plywood, lumber, and plastic sheeting.

If you receive an urgent flood warning, as in a flash flood, leave for higher ground immediately. If you still have some time, spend it gathering supplies and shoring up valuables. Transfer furniture and other items to the top floors. Turn off gas, power, and water lines, and/or disconnect appliances. Above all, make sure you can get to higher ground in time to avoid the floodwaters.

If floodwaters threaten your property, follow the advice of local officials about whether to stay or retreat. If you stay, shore up your property as best you can with sandbags and other earthworks. However, don't build such walls around your house, as the floodwaters may seep beneath the foundation, causing pressures that may weaken or even lift it out of the ground. Ironically, it's better to let the basement be flooded, or even to flood it yourself, to equalize the water pressure on both sides of the walls. If you have to leave your house and car, try to lock all doors and windows before you go.

If you're caught in a flood, don't walk through flowing water that's any higher than your knees unless your life depends on it. Don't drive on flooded roads or highways, and don't drive through pools of water until you have determined that the deepest part is no higher than the middle of the car's wheels. Drive very slowly to avoid sloshing water onto the engine. If the car stops, get out immediately and move to higher ground. Don't waste time trying to start or save the car, as rising floodwaters can buoy it up and carry it downstream for quite a distance. Many people die because they forget that their lives are more important than their possessions.

If, in spite of all caution, you're trapped in the house with waters rising dangerously, don't panic. Go to the upper floor and take with you anything that will float. An inflatable raft is ideal. Life jackets are a good second. If you live in a flood-prone area, it's a good idea to keep a life jacket on hand for each member of the family. If not, you can use other items as makeshift rafts, including wooden tabletops, styrofoam mattresses and pillows, empty fuel cans, and even spare tires.

In such a situation, don't leave the building until it's absolutely necessary. More than likely, the water will begin to recede before it reaches the rooftop, or you'll be plucked out of the house by a rescue crew. If not, don't despair. As long as you're holding onto something that floats, you'll have a good chance of reaching safety under your own power.

Cleaning Up. When the flood is over, there may be a great deal of cleaning up to do. Before entering a flood-ravaged home, report broken utility lines to the fire department or police. Make sure the gas and electricity have been turned off from the outside and check to see that the house is structurally safe. If doors are swollen shut or blocked with mud and debris, enter through a window or other opening. Don't use matches. If you detect any suspicious smells, let the house air out before entering.

Once inside, be on the lookout for weakened ceiling plaster, weak walls, floors, and foundations, broken glass, protruding nails, and other hazards. Using a flashlight—not a flame—do a complete damage inventory, and knock loose plaster down before it falls. Do a thorough job of defusing all structural hazards before you move back in. Report all damage to your insurance company.

Remove water and mud from the house as soon as possible. You can get rid of basement odors and disinfect at the same time by sprinkling bleaching powder on the wet floor and sweeping it away after it's dry. But the bleach is poisonous and caustic, so heed all cautions on the container, provide plenty of ventilation, and keep children away from it.

Water is a great conductor of electricity, so be especially careful when getting ready to turn the power back on. Have the wiring system checked by an electrician to make sure it's safe. Never stand in water or wet places when reactivating the power to your house. Always wear rubber boots and rubber gloves when flipping switches for the first time. If there's dampness in the main box, you can even electrocute yourself while changing a fuse (see "Electricity," page 87).

Carefully check and clean your home's heating system, taking special care to see that flues and passages are free of mud that could cause a boiler to burst or fill the house with carbon monoxide by cutting down on the draft. If you have an oil-heating system, call in an expert to service the burner before igniting the fuel. Whenever you're in doubt about the safety of a heating system, electric motor, chimney, or other vital housing accessory, have it checked by a specialist. Don't take chances.

Don't take chances with food or water, either. Throw out all food that's come into contact with floodwaters, and avoid drinking tap water until it's been declared safe by the health department. Meanwhile, treat all drinking water by filtering and boiling it for ten to twenty minutes and/or by adding the appropriate amounts of chlorine or iodine (see "Treating Water," page 83).

Heat Waves

We usually think of heat as a threat only on arid deserts, not in cities and suburbs. But as the summer sun makes its rounds, it creates conditions in many urban areas that lead to a surprising number of deaths. In fact, statistics show that heat waves are responsible for more deaths (about 175 a year) than earthquakes, floods, hurricanes, or tornadoes. Only lightning and winter storms take a greater toll.

Knowledge and common sense are the best ways of dealing with heat waves. Excessive heat and humidity tend especially to affect the very young, the very old, and those with heart problems. Men are more prone to heat problems than women because they sweat more. Sweating causes loss of vital salts that help to hold moisture; the more salt the body loses, the faster the water loss and the quicker dehydration sets in.

The main things to remember during a heat wave are to keep cool and quiet. If you're in heat wave country, install air conditioning and plant shade trees. Provide a sprinkling system or some other source of cool water that you can refresh yourself with. Pay attention to weather reports.

When a heat wave hits, stay out of the sun as much as possible—especially during the first few days. Let your body adjust gradually, and don't get sunburned. Drink lots of liquids, and include moderate amounts of salt in your diet. If you sweat a lot, consider taking salt tablets to boost your body's water retention. Wear lightweight, light-colored clothing, and don't spend any more time in the car than necessary. Be especially careful not to leave any person or pet in a parked car in the heat. Also be aware of the signs of heat stroke and heat exhaustion and know how to give first aid for them. Especially if you have heart problems, call a physician if you begin to feel faint or nauseous or if your skin gets overly hot, clammy, red, or dry.

Hurricanes

A hurricane is a violent cyclonic storm with winds in excess of seventy-four miles per hour. At the center, or "eye" of the hurricane, winds are often calm and skies clear. But the eye is deceptive. Around it spiral forces of terrible destruction.

Hurricane destruction is caused not only by high winds that uproot trees and knock down buildings and utility wires, but also by enormous masses of wind-driven water that cause widespread and devastating floods. Some of this water comes in the form of rain, but hurricanes can also blow water right out of its channels and reservoirs as the storm rushes through an area. These "storm surges" and their resultant floods and pounding waves cause most of the hurricane's destruction and fatalities.

Anytime from June through November, hurricanes are a possibility along the Atlantic and Gulf coasts. If you live in these areas, I would suggest you learn as much as you can about hurricanes and their potential effects. I would also urge you to take the same precautions you might for a winter storm or flood. That is, keep your automobile gassed up and in good working order. Have on hand a mobile emergency supply of food, water, first-aid equipment, a battery-powered radio, and vital tools. And pay particular attention to weather reports during the hurricane season.

Fortunately, hurricanes are very visible, move quite slowly, and their movements are somewhat predictable. This leaves some time for warning, but not much. If the National Weather Service says a "hurricane watch" is underway, this means they're tracking a storm that could eventually (but will not necessarily) threaten our coastline within twenty-four hours. This is to caution people to wake up and get ready. If a "hurricane warning" is issued for a particular area, that means the storm is expected to hit within twenty-four hours. Sometimes there is only a twelve-hour gale warning. Along with it, you'll probably get small-craft warnings, gale warnings, various estimates of the potential force and damage of the storm, and suggested emergency procedures.

Whichever message is broadcast, use the remaining hours wisely. Stay tuned to your radio (640 or 1240) or television for changing information and instructions. Secure all moveable items both inside and outside. Move valuables up to the top floors in case of flood. Board up the windows to protect them from wind pressure and flying objects. And keep your eye out for flooding, which can occur even before the hurricane has reached land.

If you've received a hurricane warning and you live in a low-lying area or mobile home, leave for inland shelter as soon as possible. (Arrange this with relatives and friends long in advance.) If your home is sturdy and on high ground, stay there unless you're told to evacuate. Store plenty of fresh drinking water in gallon jugs and fill sinks and bathtubs with auxiliary water. Stay inside during the entire storm, and don't be fooled by the "eye." Within minutes the wind might be blowing just as strongly from the opposite direction.

If you get the word to evacuate, treat the situation just as you would a flood (see "Floods," page 204). Transfer emergency supplies to your car (gassed up and ready to go, of course). Turn off gas, electricity, and water if you're told to. And leave early enough so that you can get to safety. Most often you'll be told where to go and given safest routes to follow. Follow these routes to the prescribed destinations. Don't fool yourself into thinking you'll be OK somewhere else. Many people have died because they decided not to heed official instructions.

As with floods, drive carefully and slowly, avoiding downed wires, debris, and deep areas. Stay away from coastal and low-lying roads, and be on the lookout for storm surges and flash floods. Stay in the shelter area until the storm has passed completely and you get the OK to return home. Once you get back, be particularly cautious about gas and electricity around your home. Report damaged water, sewer, gas, and electrical lines to local authorities, and be on the lookout for spoiled food and contaminated water. (For more specifics on cautions and cleanup procedures, see "Floods," page 204.)

Landslides

Landslides are sliding, slumping, or shifting of the earth caused by gravity acting on a weakened section of the landscape. This can be caused by many things, including earthquakes, erosion, construction, heavy rains, glaciers, or a combination of factors.

Different circumstances produce different kinds of slides. For example, the gradual wearing away of the earth may cause landslides that are composed entirely of dry material, as in rockslides and earth avalanches that are triggered up high and tumble down a mountainside. Lots of rain in an area that's been denuded of water-absorbent vegetation can seep into the earth and turn it to mush that flows like tons of thick pudding. Earthquakes in unstable areas can cause one layer of land to slide on top of another, or even to sink as though into a liquid.

It's difficult to predict just where a slide is going to occur, but there are certain signs to watch for. Most slides tend to occur on slopes of between five and thirty-five degrees. Sliding is also more prevalent in areas where there's lots of rain—especially in hillside areas where housing developments or other constructions have destroyed protective vegetation.

Certain areas such as cliff edges, ravines, and unstable soils are also more susceptible to slides.

Foresight is the best insurance against landslides. Obviously, it's wise not to buy or build a home in an area that's prone to sliding or slumping. If you already live in such an area, or if you've fallen in love with a home there, check for cracks in basement floors or walls. Look around the neighborhood. Check sidewalks, walls, and other homes and establishments for signs of instability. Check hillsides for oozing water. Look for tilted trees and telephone poles. If you're still in doubt, get a geologist or other expert to check for you. And if there's danger, think about moving. At the very least, install a special drainage system to reduce the water content of the soil during heavy rains.

Once a landslide starts, there's not much you can do but get out of the way. And there isn't much time to move. Most often you have only seconds to save yourself, and there is certainly no time to think about salvaging precious possessions. Don't run downhill; that's where the landslide is going. Run laterally as fast as you can in the direction that will take you most quickly to safety. Alert officials of any broken gas, telephone, or water lines. And don't go back to the slide area until it's been declared safe.

Lightning

Thunderstorms rumble all over the world, spreading their electrifying effects twenty-four hours a day. The earth is hit by lightning approximately one hundred times every second. Given this frequency, it is little wonder it causes so much damage. Every year in the United States alone, lightning kills up to three hundred people and seriously injures about another six hundred. As an atmospheric hazard, the lightning bolt doesn't get the publicity of a hurricane or a tornado because its effects are so spotty and localized. But the casualties it causes (higher than for either hurricanes or tornadoes) indicate that it deserves at least as much understanding and respect.

As explained previously, lightning is created by positive and negative charges that build up in clouds and on the ground during a storm. When the charge differential becomes great enough, a gigantic spark jumps through the air. Typically powered by more than a hundred million volts and superheated to fifteen thousand degrees Centigrade, lightning causes fatal shocks (eighty percent of the victims are men involved in outdoor sports activities) and starts three-fourths of our forest fires.

Statistically, some areas of the country are more prone to lightning than others. In particular, the Gulf Coast and major river valleys such as the Hudson and the Mississippi are high risk areas. So are major mountain ranges such as the Colorado Rockies. In urban and suburban areas, lightning causes most deaths at outdoor gatherings such as golf matches, football games, and picnics. But statistics don't paint the real picture, because you can be vulnerable to lightning almost anywhere—even in your home.

What To Do. The best way to avoid a lightning strike is to be able to recognize a thunderstorm and realize its potential dangers. Fortunately, there's no mistaking such a storm. It is almost always foreshadowed by a dramatic-looking thunderhead (see "Cumulonimbus," page 193). Though it may develop slowly and imperceptibly, you will most often hear the rumble of thunder that follows a lightning flash when it is still quite far away.

If you are in the path of the storm, take shelter while there's still plenty of time. Most homes are excellent shelters, since their walls and ceilings provide lots of insulation. In fact, many houses and buildings are equipped with lightning rods that channel the electricity harmlessly between earth and sky. (It's a good idea to have one installed if you live in lightning country.) But even inside, stay away from open doors and windows, metal pipes, and other electrical conductors such as sinks and stoves. Unplug electrical appliances, or at least refrain from using them during the storm. Especially avoid making telephone calls, as lightning can enter the house through the phone wires. Don't go outside until the storm is over.

If you're in a car that you can close up completely, stay there. The wheels and upholstery will effectively insulate you between the ground and the sky, which is exactly where you want to be. If you're inside a boat on open water, get to shore as quickly as possible. Water is an excellent conductor of electricity. Avoid it whenever possible, and under no circumstances stand in it.

Most of all, remember that lightning takes the easy way. This is commonly the shortest distance between the cloud and the ground. It usually strikes the highest object it can find. If you're outside, take shelter down low and away from isolated objects such as trees and poles. If you're on an open hillside, run to the bottom and kneel under a clump of low bushes. If you're on the flat in the open and a strike seems imminent (when your skin tingles and your hair stands on end), don't lie down. Hunker on your haunches and hold your knees. If you're wearing rubber-soled shoes or have some insulating material under your feet, so much the better. The less body contact you have with the ground, the safer you'll be.

Finally, stay away from all metal objects. Drop your golf clubs. Abandon your bicycle. Stash your umbrella. Get away from bridges and metal railings. (Don't stand under a bridge, either, because when lightning hits, it often "splashes" and spreads like water.) Look around to make sure there's nothing nearby that could serve as an easy channel for electricity. Stay alert and enjoy the celestial display from a safe spot.

If someone is hit by lightning, go to that person's aid immediately. You cannot get a shock by touching a lightning victim. He or she will probably be unconscious and badly burned, but you may be able to save a life by acting quickly. Call for help (specifically, an ambulance) as loudly as you can. Using standard first-aid procedures, check immediately for breathing and heartbeat. If you detect none, and you have the necessary training, administer mouth-to-mouth resuscitation and/or cardiopulmonary resuscitation until an aid car comes.

Tidal Waves

Actually, the term tidal wave is a misnomer, since these giant breakers have nothing to do with the tides. The proper term is "tsunami" —pronounced "soo-na-mee." This is the Japanese word for "harbor wave," which is exactly where so-called "tidal waves" do most of their damage. With this disclaimer, we will continue to call them tidal waves.

Tidal waves are formed by disturbances in the earth's crust underlying the ocean. One of the most common causes is earthquakes. When tremors rumble beneath the sea, they create waves that travel to the surface and to distant shores. Often they slosh back and forth across the sea two or three times, like echoes bouncing off walls, before the water smooths out again.

Most tidal waves are only a couple of feet high when they start out, but they travel at speeds up to six hundred miles per hour on the high seas. As they approach land, the waves usually slow down to less than forty miles an hour in shallow water. The energy of the wave then becomes concentrated in its height. A breaking tidal wave may crest out at more than a hundred feet high and pack more energy than the most powerful hydrogen bomb.

Tidal waves cause unbelievable destruction. Big ones have flattened whole towns and wiped out thousands of people. What makes them even more destructive is that they usually come in twos, threes, and fours, the last wave often being the most devastating. The time interval between these waves is several minutes or more, and the breakers are so large that the ocean seems to be receding long before they hit. Secondary disasters can include anything from landslides to floods and fires.

Because of their destructive potential, the National Weather Service keeps a constant lookout for tidal waves. If there's even a possibility of danger the Weather Service issues a "tsunami watch" as an alert. When a wave has been confirmed, there follows a "tsunami warning," which includes the wave's estimated time of arrival at any one of fifty or so ocean ports. What the Weather Service can't say is just how big the wave will be when it hits those ports. Because of geological and other factors, wave size and power varies greatly in different locations.

What To Do. Be prepared for the worst. If you live in a coastal area (particularly one that's experienced tidal waves before), consider the location of your home. According to the Coast and Geodetic Survey, if your home is less than a hundred feet above sea level, it could be damaged or destroyed by a locally generated tidal wave. If it's less than fifty feet above sea level, it could be destroyed by a wave that begins more than a thousand miles away.

Tidal waves can hit in any coastal area. The Pacific Coast is especially vulnerable. If you live in a hot spot, prepare much as you would for a hurricane or flood. Have an emergency supply of food, water, and medications on hand. Have a battery-powered radio that you can take with you. Keep your car gassed up and ready to go. Know the best escape routes to higher ground. And rehearse what you would do in the event of a tsunami warning.

If you feel an earthquake, consider the possibility of a tidal wave. It usually takes a quake of magnitude 7.5 or greater on the Richter scale to produce a giant breaker, but the quake you feel may be of distant origin and actually much larger than you think. Tune in for information on potential tidal waves. If specific instructions are given, follow them.

If you have several hours to evacuate, treat the situation as you would a hurricane or a flood. Do what you can to protect your home. This may include a quick shutting and boarding up of windows and doors, tying down loose objects outside or bringing them inside, and stowing valuable possessions on the highest floor. If you have time, turn off the electricity and the main gas and water lines before you leave. If you aren't sure how much time you have, leave immediately for higher ground. Don't go down to the beach to watch for the wave. A tidal wave is impressive and exciting, but by the time you can see it, it is usually to late to get away.

Remember also that tidal waves usually come in groups of several or more, and they are often widely spaced. Stay away from the coast until you're sure all the waves have passed. When you get back (after getting the all-clear signal on your radio), be aware of downed electrical wires, broken gas lines, and other hazards. (For information on cleanup procedures after a tidal wave, see "Floods," page 204.)

Tornadoes

Tornadoes are short-lived but devastating storms consisting of long, dark funnels of wind roaring at velocities up to three hundred miles per hour. These "twisters" are formed at the bottoms of thunderclouds, where cold air rushes in from two or more directions to take the place of rapidly rising warm air.

Though the probability of a tornado hitting a specific area is very low and its destructive path is quite limited (averaging about an eighth of a mile wide and rarely more than ten miles long), the destruction within that path is almost total. Buildings are blown up, people and animals are thrown through the air like rag dolls, power lines and pipes are snapped and twisted like spaghetti, and glass splinters rocket through the air like deadly missiles. Tornadoes should never be underestimated. They can mow down or suck up almost everything in their path.

Twisters have occurred in every state in the union, but they most frequently occur east of the Rockies—especially the Gulf, Plains, Midwest, and Southeast Atlantic states. Over half of them occur between April and June. The season starts in February in the Central Gulf states, when warm, wet winds from the coast begin to collide with cold air coming down from the north. In March and April, as warm air penetrates farther north and east, tornadoes occur mostly in the Southeast Atlantic states. In May and June they occur with greatest frequency in the southern Plains states, shifting northward toward the Great Lakes in June. Especially in these areas, tornadoes may occur almost anywhere. They can show up singly or there may be several within close proximity.

What To Do. If you live in a high-risk area, your best insurance is to build a concrete- or steel-reinforced storm shelter and to be wary during the tornado season. Tornadoes usually come from the south or southwest—except when they're associated with hurricanes, in which case they usually approach from the east. Look for them especially on warm afternoons. If you spot a funnel-shaped cloud in the distance, call the police or other local authority immediately and tune in by radio or television.

Don't use the telephone to get information during the storm. Normally, you'll hear about tornado dangers from the authorities if you stay tuned to the weather each day. If there's a possibility of tornado danger, the Weather Service will issue a "tornado watch." If a twister has actually been spotted, you'll hear a "tornado warning."

If the twister is headed your way and you have time, turn off gas, water, and electrical power. To reduce the danger of explosion if the tornado passes directly overhead, open windows and doors on the lee side (usually the northeast) of the approaching storm. Most important, take cover in some form of solid shelter. If you don't have a ready-made storm shelter, grab your battery-operated radio and take refuge in the southwest corner of the basement. (Since most tornadoes move from southwest to northeast, this is the place that's least likely to suffer falling debris if the house is torn apart.) If you have no basement, sit in a small closet or bathroom in the central part of the house, or under a heavy piece of furniture away from outside doors, windows, and walls. This will present the least hazard from falling walls, plaster, and other debris. If you have time, protect yourself further with mattresses and pillows.

Avoid taking shelter beneath weakly supported roofs such as those in most gyms and auditoriums. Stay away from windows where you might be hit by flying shards of glass and other debris. If you're in an office building, take shelter in an interior hallway on the lowest floor. Use protective materials such as heavy furniture and mattresses wherever you can find them. If an approaching tornado catches you in bed in the middle of the night (identified by an unmistakable roar), crawl under the bed. Any protective action is better than none.

If you're in a trailer or mobile home, get out and take shelter somewhere else. Twisters make short work of these contraptions. Sometimes they even lift them not-so-merrily into the air before dumping them like a heap of trash. Plan in advance where you'll go, perhaps arranging with friends who have a secure basement or storm shelter.

If you're in a car, you may be able to get to safety by driving at right angles to the tornado's path. But don't count on it. If you're not sure where to go, quickly get out of the car and take shelter in a sturdy building. Never try to last out a tornado in an automobile. If you're caught in the open, dive into a ravine or ditch and lie flat with your arms over your head until the twister has passed.

After a tornado, take the same precautions you would for most other disasters. Watch out for downed electrical wires. Don't go into a building until you're sure it's structurally sound. Don't explore damaged buildings with matches, lanterns, or any other kind of open flame. Use flashlights only and don't smoke until you're positive there's no danger of gas explosions. Check all utilities (especially gas and electricity) with great caution. If you doubt their safety, turn them off or leave the building and let an expert handle the problem.

Nuclear Attack

Now to conclude with a brief look at an overwhelming subject. Today the world bristles with more than fifty thousand nuclear weapons, most of them aimed at large population centers. The potential effects of detonating these bombs are beyond anything we are equipped to imagine. No one can say how many would survive a full scale nuclear attack, or if warning and preparation would do anything to improve our prospects. No natural disaster can compare with the devastation that might be wrought, both to ourselves and to all other creatures on the globe. It is even possible that all life on earth would be extinguished.

The lack of absolutes in the nuclear dilemma is almost as unsettling as the threat itself and the wide variety of opinions and feelings this uncertainty generates is bewildering and confusing. To be honest, I have agonized over this section. I have asked myself over and over again, "What can I possibly say about a survival situation like this? What practical advice can I give about preparation and survival for a world in which life, if it persists at all, may be so barbaric that those left alive would wish themselves dead?"

The answers are few, and they have not come easily. I have nothing to say about fallout shelters or relocation plans. I have nothing to say about the physical effects of radiation. What I can offer is this: The outcome of any survival situation is determined partly by our willingness to recognize the threat for what it is; to listen to the warning voice and to do something before it is too late. That voice is speaking to us right now. We can all hear it if we listen. Like a cancer, it lies just below the surface, gnawing at all our hopes and dreams and darkening all our endeavors. We are, at this moment, facing the most monumental survival situation of all time.

Often I hear people ask, "What can I do? How can I possibly affect an issue of such enormous magnitude and complexity?" My answer is that already we affect it—each of us—in much the same way that a single bird affects a huge flock. Many times on the beach I have watched flocks of sandpipers scuttling along the tideline, probing for tidbits exposed by the waves. Almost as one they race along the beach in a little cloud, goose-stepping from one spot to another, running with the ebb and flow of the wind and waves. As they probe with their beaks and peep to one another, they stitch ephemeral tapestries in the sand. When one bird finds a good feeding spot, the others crowd around. When one is frightened, the whole flock explodes in a burst of beating wings.

Once airborne, the sandpipers' togetherness is even more amazing. Hundreds of them race across the sky, heading off with a concerted flutter of wings. Then, in a fraction of a second, as if on some sudden impulse, the flock veers away. A hundred white bellies flash in the sun, and the symphony of movement now takes another direction.

What communication keeps these birds together? What determines the destiny of the flock? It is something beyond their dancing legs and flashing wings. They are bound by a collective consciousness, by an intangible affinity for one another that holds them together as surely as a hive of bees. Each bird makes a difference; each helps to determine the flock's direction by contributing to the spirit that moves through all of them.

In some ways, humanity is a flock, too. We rush through our lives, searching and probing for meaning and happiness. We trace fleeting footsteps on sidewalks and highways. We call out, connect with, and affect each other. We, too, are tied in subtle but powerful ways. Like sandpipers, each one of us transmits the current of our being to the universe, and in doing so, helps to determine the direction and flow of humanity.

What can one person do to prevent nuclear war? First, remember your humanity. Your heart will tell you what to do. Listen to it. Pay attention to the quality of your thoughts. Throw out cynicism and negativity. Open your mind to the possibility of peace. Create a vision of the kind of world you want; then work to make it a reality.

The more we learn as we listen to our inner voices, the better equipped we will be to help our foreign policymakers move toward constructive solutions for a safer world. There is no shortcut through the nuclear maze. It will require all the maturity and patience we can muster. But no enterprise is more worth the effort, because the challenge is nothing less than to save the world.

CONCLUSION:
ENJOYING THE CITY

Urban survival is a "heavy" subject in many ways. But the city is also a fascinating place, and it would be a shame not to acknowledge the positive and joyful things about it. Most people choose to live in cities not just because of their convenience and comfort, but also because they offer such a wide range of opportunity and experience. Since the art of survival in its broadest sense is learning to make the most of any environment, I would like to conclude with a few words about enjoying the city and suburbs.

I can barely begin to suggest the possibilities for getting more out of city life. However, it is safe to say that most people do not get nearly as much out of it as they could. Part of the problem is that most people quickly become numb to a new environment. We can see this with the tourists, who at first gawk and exclaim in excitement over a new place and then gradually become used to it. Before long, they look at the same things over and over and finally follow the same routine day after day. Before long, they're stuck in ruts like everybody else.

We all get into ruts. But sometimes the ruts are so deep we can't see over the sides. That's when it's time to break the monotony by doing something unique or by looking at things in a fresh way. If we can learn to see the city anew—to approach it as a tourist again—we can discover new horizons in our own backyards.

I mean this literally. One of the things I suggest to my nature observation students is that they go out into their backyards and closely observe a single square foot of ground for fifteen minutes. The reactions I get to this exercise are as revealing as they are exciting. Seen through new eyes (or better yet, through a magnifying glass), a small area that at first appeared to be nothing but a patch of ground becomes a fascinating jungle. Most yards are crawling with spiders and potato bugs, sparkling with dewdrops, and gleaming with green foliage. The key is to see freshly, to vary the vision, and to look at old and familiar things in new and unusual ways.

This can be done in any environment, but the more familiar the place, the more conscious and deliberate you have to be. For example, if you find yourself taking the same route home each day, take a different path. You'll see a hundred different things. Even at home and at work there are ways of refreshing your vision. Notice things you haven't seen before. Look at things from new angles. Pay closer attention to other people—not just how they walk and what they say and wear, but who they are on a deeper level. Some people do not really know their own spouses, though they have lived with them for years. There is always more to experience and share if we look more deeply.

The same is true of the city in general. The city becomes a prison only when people limit their vision. If you live in a large city, go to a local library or bookstore and get a guidebook to that city. Read the book as a tourist might read it. Try things you've never done before. Go places you've never been. If you prefer, explore the city on your own. Hop in a car and drive to a new place. Better yet, get on a bus or bicycle or take to your feet and really notice the area you're passing through. Slow down, relax, enjoy. Look at your city like Alice in Wonderland. Talk to other people. Find out how they see the city and what's important to them.

One of the most distinguishing features of cities is that they are always changing. The urban landscape is hardly the same from one day to the next. Old buildings fall and new ones rise like trees in a forest. Have you ever stopped to watch a construction project? It's fascinating to see how a skyscraper goes up from day to day, as steel girders are moved about on cranes like giant erector sets and concrete is poured into giant molds. Construction workers sometimes appear no bigger than fleas, and it's easy to marvel at their industry and the organization of the overall plan.

Even the flow of traffic along a freeway is fascinating if you can see it freshly. Sometimes when I'm in a city (and often in the wilderness, too), I pretend I'm an explorer from another planet. The world takes on aspects of wonder and mystery it can never have when seen only out of habit. From an habitual point of view, the stream of cars flowing along a highway generates anxious thoughts: noise, danger, pollution, speed, and the eternal rush of the city. From a detached point of view, though, it becomes a miraculous scene, and I can't help but wonder at the metallic "monsters" and the ingenuity of the animals that have produced them. I feel the same way when sitting in an airplane suspended miles above the ground, or when watching a jet nose its way into the sky.

One of the reasons I feel these things is that, no matter how far removed from nature I may be, I always remember the connection. The truth is, we are never far from nature. Every tree-lined boulevard, every pond, and every leaf and blade of grass feeds our spirits with fresh, renewing energy. That's why parks are so important to a community's well-being. Even the weeds that poke up through the middle of sidewalks and abandoned roadways are reminders that nature is waiting in the wings. We are just as dependent on greenery as the grasshopper and the firefly.

There are many ways of cultivating our awareness of nature, and there is much to be gained by doing so. One thing we can do is not hide so much from the weather. We can look up more often into the sky and let the wind brush across our faces. We can feel the rain and snow and really experience the thunder and lightning for the grand show that it is.

We can also cultivate a garden. Have you ever eaten a truly fresh tomato? Do you know what it smells and feels like when it's just been picked? When you bite into it, you can almost feel the earth and smell the sunshine in it. But you don't have to have your own garden. Many cities have public markets. These spots are festivals of sight and smell. At most of them, fruits, meats, and vegetables are brought in fresh each day from outlying farms. Many times a short drive will take you to such farms. There, for a small price, you can probably pick your own.

Another way to feel a connection with nature is through our pets. Dogs, cats, fish, and birds enliven many urban and suburban homes. Their meaning in our lives becomes even greater if we provide well for them and conscientiously treat them as the unique and wonderful beings that they are.

Similarly, wild and semi-wild animals abound in city parks and refuges. We can invite many birds and animals to our homes with well-placed feeding stations. Don't be under the mistaken impression that the only forms of wildlife in the city are rats and pigeons. In fact, many wild animals you might not expect to find in the city probably live right under your nose (see "Appendix B: Urban Animals," page 243). All you have to do is slow down and watch.

Often a wildlife photographer need go no farther than a half-wild city park to get closeups of some very unusual and captivating creatures. Getting to know and appreciate such animals is not only fun, but important. It hones our observation skills, brings us closer to the wilderness of the mind, and ultimately helps to give us a better perspective about ourselves and our place on the planet.

And what is that place? It seems to me that one of the greatest reasons we are here is simply to share our beings with one another. City living is often seen as rather anonymous, and it certainly can be. With all the urban conveniences, people appear not to need each other as much as they do in the country. Certainly they don't need each other as much as people in primitive societies. At times, in fact, urban communities seem to be glued together less through geography than through automobiles and telephone wires.

But this is not a true picture of the city situation. We are all communal animals, and whether or not we realize it, we are tied to each other through powerful bonds we only dimly recognize. In times of social stress the strands of dependence become more visible, and we band together to cooperate for our common good. But we need to feel the echoes of our humanity on a day-to-day level, too. Our interdependence is based not just on meat and potatoes, but also on fulfillment and self-esteem. We need each other. Each of us is like an individual cell in the great body of humanity, and each personality makes a difference in its overall health and well-being.

There is an old saying, "Many a live wire would be dead without connections. Plug in!" That's good advice for the urban dweller. The city is rich with opportunities for the expression of energies and the expansion of personal horizons. Art, history, education, politics, recreation—whatever your interests, there is a place to get more deeply involved.

Most people, of course, find themselves involved enough with their own families and businesses. The challenges of raising children in the city are great, but so are the opportunities. Nowhere can young people be exposed to a wider variety of life-styles. Nowhere do they have a wider range of choices and possibilities for personal growth. If parents are curious and courageous, children will also be more apt to push through the boundaries of the familiar and get more out of city living. If adults approach life with optimism and good cheer, most likely their children will do the same.

Perhaps when you have your own survival taken care of, you'll feel the urge to reach out to a wider community. If you're inclined toward community service, you can start right in your own neighborhood. From crime reduction to clean air and water, the city is a cauldron of common needs and problems. And whatever the need, your contribution will make a difference.

Many people are reluctant to get involved because they think they are powerless. They feel their effort will go to waste or that their hopes won't be realized. Millions of people even think their vote doesn't count. If not theirs, then whose? We're all in this together. No matter what we do (or don't do), we can't avoid affecting the world. Each city is tied to all others. The world is a network of nations and wildlands whose interdependence can no longer be ignored.

This is all the more reason for us to have faith in our creativity. We all have hidden powers if only we will tap them. The great challenge of the cities is to push beyond mere survival to become all that we can be. Over and over we read about people who have made outstanding contributions to society; people whose courageous example inspired others to unusual action; people whose conviction and energy made the world a better place to live in. Nothing is impossible if we seek our own vision and apply ourselves to the task. We are all important in the grand scheme of things, and we all have unique gifts to give. That is what makes survival worthwhile and gives life its fullest expression.

APPENDIX A:
COMMON URBAN EDIBLES

Following are descriptions and illustrations of some of the most common wild edibles found in urban areas throughout the United States and Canada. Most of these plants were chosen not just for their abundance in the typical waste grounds and disturbed soils of cities, but also because they are relatively easy to identify, easy to distinguish from poisonous species, and among the least likely to absorb pollutants. (Even so, gather and eat them with caution. See "Foraging for Wild Edibles," page 144.)

Keep in mind that wooded and semi-wooded areas in cities and suburbs will commonly contain not only most of these plants, but a wealth of others not mentioned here. For further information on wild edibles and their uses, consult *Tom Brown's Field Guide to Wilderness Survival*.

AMARANTH
Amaranthus spp.
Amaranth family
Leaves: Late spring to early fall
Seeds: Late summer to late fall

Description: Stout, weedlike, annual herb, 6 inches to 6 feet tall. Stems rough, hairy, freely branching. Leaves usually 3 to 6 inches long, alternate, toothless, rough and veiny, ovate to lanceolate. Undersides of young and lower leaves purple. Flowers in green axillary clusters up to 2½ inches long. Seeds abundant, shiny black, in chaffy bracts at the ends of stems and branches. Roots red. **Habitat:** Waste ground and disturbed soils, including construction sites, fringes of hedgerows, yards, and parks; usually in direct sunlight. **Range:** Throughout U.S.A. and Canada, except alpine and desert areas.

Food: Young leaves can be eaten raw; mature leaves are boiled as potherbs; seeds can be parched and ground into flour or boiled into cereal. **Warning:** Amaranth sometimes accumulates high levels of nitrates and can cause discomfort if eaten in large quantities. **Medicine:** Tea from the leaves is effective for diarrhea and excessive menstruation.

BLACKBERRIES
Rubus spp.
Rose family
Young shoots: Spring
Leaves: Summer
Berries: Summer

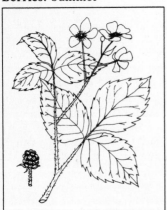

Description: Thorny or prickly shrubs, often vinelike, 1 to 6 feet high. Genus includes blackberries, raspberries, and dewberries (including salmonberries). Stems usually green or red. Blackberry stems angular; raspberries round-stemmed, dewberries with low, trailing stems. Leaves 2 to 10 inches long, compound, with 3 to 7 leaflets. Flowers 5-petaled, white (occasionally reddish), conspicuous. Berries juicy, red, black, or salmon-colored. **Habitat:** Open woods and thickets, often found in vacant lots and undeveloped city parks. **Range:** Throughout U.S.A. and Canada.

Food: All berries and young shoots can be eaten raw. The dried leaves make a nourishing tea.

BURDOCK
Arctium spp.
Sunflower family
Stems: Spring to summer
Leaves: Spring (first year only)
Roots: Summer (first year only)

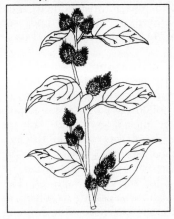

Description: Large, brushy, biennial herb, 1 to 5 feet tall. Stems coarse, stiff, many-branched. Leaves ovate (lower ones heart-shaped), toothless, densely hairy beneath, with wavy edges. First-year leaves in rosettes, second-year leaves alternate. Flowers red to purple, composite, on spiny seed-pods. Seeds in roundish clusters, with many-hooked spurs. **Habitat:** Waste ground and disturbed soils, including roadways, construction sites, and cracks; in direct sunlight. **Range:** Throughout Canada and U.S.A., except extreme south and southwest.

Food: Stems and roots are peeled and boiled as vegetables. Leaves should be boiled in several changes of water. Seeds can be dampened and grown as sprouts.

CATNIP
Nepeta cataria
Mint family
Leaves: Early spring

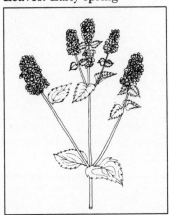

Description: Aromatic herb, up to 3 feet tall. Stems square, erect, branching, covered with dense whitish hairs. Leaves 2½ inches long, opposite, arrowhead-shaped, coarsely toothed, covered with whitish hairs—especially on lower surfaces. Flowers ½ inch long, two-lipped corollas, pale pine, spotted with bright purple; borne in dense whorls near top of stem. Fruits 4-sided nutlets. **Habitat:** Roadsides and waste ground, including cracks, sidewalk seams, and construction sites. **Range:** Throughout U.S.A. and Canada.

Food: Dried leaves make a soothing tea; but the aroma is very volatile, so the plant itself should not be boiled.

CATTAIL
Typha spp.
Cattail family
Young shoots: Spring
Flower heads: Late spring
Pollen heads: Summer
Sprouts: Summer to winter
Rootstocks: All year

Description: A reedlike plant easily identified by its swordlike leaves, long, stiff stalks, and sausage-shaped seed heads. Sometimes reaches a height of 9 feet. In spring, two green flower heads form at the top of the stalk—the male above and the female below. Male flowers become a golden pollen mass, while female flowers eventually transform themselves into the characteristic downy seed head. **Habitat:** Swamps, marshes, and wet ground. **Range:** Throughout U.S.A. and Canada.

Food: In early spring, young shoots and stalks can be peeled and eaten raw or boiled. In late spring, green flower heads can be husked and boiled. In early summer, pollen heads can be picked and eaten raw, or dried into flour. From late summer through winter, horn-shaped sprouts growing from the rootstocks at the base of the plant can be eaten raw or boiled for a few minutes. The rootstocks can also be crushed, dissolved in cold water, and made into flour after draining and drying. **Medicine:** Ripe cattail flowers can be mashed and used as a salve for cuts and burns. The sticky juice between the leaves makes an excellent styptic, antiseptic, and anaesthetic. It will even numb an aching tooth if you rub it on the gums.

CHICKWEED
Stellaria media
Pink family
Stems: All year
Leaves: All year

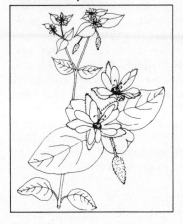

Description: Low-growing annual or winter annual, 3 to 8 inches tall, with trailing stem to 16 inches. Stem loosely ascending, finely-haired, many-branched. Leaves to 1 inch long, opposite, ovate, pointed at the tip. Flowers with 5 small bilobed white petals, each deeply cleft. **Habitat:** Woodlands, thickets, meadows, fields, waste ground, and disturbed soils. **Range:** Throughout U.S.A. and Canada.

Food: Tender stems and leaves can be eaten raw. Tougher stems and leaves should be boiled for a few minutes. **Medicine:** The leaves can be mashed into a poultice to treat burns and rashes.

CHICORY
Cichorium intybus
Sunflower family
Leaves: Early spring or fall
Roots: Early spring

Description: Perennial herb, 1 to 4 feet tall. Stem naked with rigid, angular branches. Leaves 3 to 6 inches long with lobed or toothed edges, radiating from base like those of dandelion; stem leaves often small and clasping. Flowers in disks, 1½ to 2 inches across, deep blue to white, attached directly to stem; petals square-tipped with cleft ends. Flowers close in afternoon or when overcast. Taproot white and fleshy. **Habitat:** Waste areas, fields, meadows. **Range:** Throughout U.S.A. and Canada.

Food: White, subterranean parts of young leaves can be eaten raw in salads. Greens should be boiled 5 to 10 minutes before eating. Roast the roots until dark brown and brittle, then ground them into a coffee substitute. (Add about 1½ teaspoonfuls per cup of water.)

CLOVERS
Trifolium spp.
Pea family
Leaves: Spring to summer
Seeds: Spring to summer
Roots: Fall to winter

Description: Low-growing herb, 2. to 24 inches long. Leaflets 3, finely-toothed, round, ovate, or heart-shaped, ½ inch to 2 inches long. Flowers in dense heads, ½ to 1 inch long; petals pea-like, white, yellow, or pink. **Habitat:** Disturbed soils, dry woods and fields, construction sites. **Range:** Throughout U.S.A. and Canada.

Food: Young leaves can be eaten raw, while older leaves should be boiled. Flowers can be boiled, steeped as a tea, or fried in fat. Seed heads are dried and ground into flour, while roots are scraped and boiled like vegetables. **Warning:** Raw clover leaves eaten in large quantities may cause indigestion. Double boiling recommended especially for clovers gathered in urban areas.

DANDELION
Taraxacum officinale
Sunflower family
Leaves: Early spring
Roots: Fall to early spring
Flower buds: Early spring

Description: Common herb, 1 to 18 inches tall. Stems weak and hollow, with milky white sap. Leaves basal, 3 to 15 inches long, with sharp, deep, irregular lobes. Flower heads 1½ inches across, composed of many yellow ray flowers. Taproot with yellow skin. Fruiting mass a silky, downy head composed of seeds with long white bristles. **Habitat:** Waste ground and disturbed soils in full sunlight. Especially prolific in gardens and yards. **Range:** Throughout most of U.S.A. and Canada.

Food: Young leaves can be eaten raw. Older leaves and buds should be boiled before eating. Roots are dried, roasted, and ground into a coffee substitute. Flowers make tasty fritters when dipped and fried in batter. **Medicine:** All edible parts are especially good for blood circulation.

DOCK
Rumex crispus
Buckwheat family
Leaves: Spring to summer
Seeds: Summer to winter

Description: Stout herb, 1 to 4 feet tall. Stem erect and many-branched. Leaves 6 to 10 inches long, oblong to lanceolate, growing mostly from bases in rosettes; thick and coarse, with wavy edges. Flowers very small, reddish or greenish, in slender clusters at tops of stems. Fruits borne in whorls on upper part of stem, dark reddish-brown when ripe, 3-sided, each side-winged. Taproot red-yellow, up to 12 inches long. **Habitat:** Waste ground and disturbed soils, including lawns, fields, and roadsides. **Range:** Throughout U.S.A. and Canada.

Food: All species of dock are edible. The young leaves can be eaten raw, but older leaves should be boiled in several changes of water to reduce the bitter taste. Seeds can be dried, threshed, and ground into flour. **Warning:** Do not eat the roots, due to their high tannic acid content. **Medicine:** Roots can be mashed into a poultice to treat skin rashes and itches.

GOLDENROD
Solidago odora
Sunflower family
Leaves: Early summer to fall
Flowers: Summer to early
  fall

Description: Smooth, licorice-scented annual, 2 to 5 feet tall. Leaves 1 to 4 inches long, lanceolate, smooth, toothless, with parallel veins. Flowers in tiny yellow heads about 1/16 inch long, borne in cylindrical clusters on one side of plant. Seeds in downy heads. **Habitat:** Dry, open areas well exposed to the sun. **Range:** Throughout central and eastern U.S.A.

Food: Young leaves near flowers can be boiled and eaten as a potherb. Small leaves and flowers can be dried or used fresh to make anise-flavored tea. Seeds can be crushed and added to stews for thickening.

GRASSES
Graminiae spp.
Grass family
All parts edible

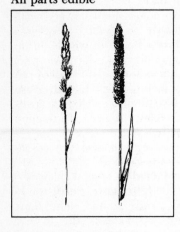

Food: Almost all bladed grasses are edible, from stems and leaves to roots and seeds. Young shoots up to about 6 inches tall can usually be eaten raw. Most mature grasses are quite fibrous and difficult to digest, so it's best to chew them thoroughly and spit them out after swallowing the juices. Alternatively, steep the green or dried leaves into a refreshing tea.

Grass seeds are very rich in protein. These can be eaten raw, roasted, and ground into flour, or boiled into mush. **Warning:** The seeds of a few grasses are toxic if eaten raw. For this reason, I recommend roasting the seeds of unfamiliar grasses before eating. Also make sure the seeds are either green or brown. Purple or blackish seeds may indicate the presence of a toxic fungus.

GREENBRIERS
Smilax spp.
Lily family
Shoots: Spring to summer
Leaves: Spring to summer
Roots: All year
Tendrils: Spring to summer

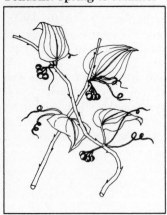

Description: Vine, 3 to 9 feet long. Stems prickly, woody, and freely branching. Leaves to 5 inches long, leathery, parallel-veined, round, oval, fiddle-shaped, or oblong. Berries bluish-black, in tight little clusters. Roots thick and knobby to long and slender. **Habitat:** Swamps, bottomlands; sandy, fertile soils. **Range:** Throughout central and eastern U.S.A. and Canada.

Food: Young shoots, leaves, and tendrils can be eaten raw or boiled as vegetables. Rootstocks can be dried and ground into flour. The flour mixed with water makes a refreshing cold drink and is also a good thickener for soups and stews.

HEMLOCK TREES
Tsuga spp.
Pine family
Inner bark: Spring
Needles: All year

Description: Tall, straight, evergreen trees, 100 to 150 feet tall; trunks 2 to 3 feet in diameter. Top branches drooping, especially in young trees. Bark thick, dark brown to reddish brown, with flat scales. Needles often unequal in length, ¼ to ¾ inch long, yellow-green to blue-green, white below, set in two rows on either side of stem. Cones hanging, oval, ¾ to 1¼ inches long. **Habitat:** Hilly or dry, rocky woods and parks (eastern species); wet, shady woodlands and parks (western species). **Range:** Throughout U.S.A. and Canada.

Food: The inner bark can be dried and ground into flour. The green needles, diced and steeped, make a tea that is very high in vitamin C. **Warning:** Do not confuse the hemlock tree with toxic herbaceous plants of the same name.

LAMB'S QUARTERS
(Pigweed)
Chenopodium album
Goosefoot family
Leaves: Summer
Seeds: Fall to early winter

Description: Succulent herb, 1 to 6 feet tall. Stems straight, many-branched, often red-streaked, slightly grooved when mature. Leaves alternate; lower leaves toothed, triangular or diamond-shaped; upper leaves narrow and bluish-green with mealy white scales. Flowers very small, without petals or stalks, in greenish or reddish clusters. Seeds black and very small. **Habitat:** Waste ground and disturbed soils. **Range:** Throughout U.S.A. and Canada.

Food: Young leaves can be eaten raw. Young shoots and older leaves can be boiled as potherbs or vegetables. Seeds can be boiled or ground into flour. **Warning:** Lamb's-quarters resembles Mexican tea, whose aromatic leaves are edible only when dried.

MAPLE TREES
Acer spp.
Maple family
Sap: Early spring
Seedlings: Early spring
Inner bark: Spring
Seeds: Fall

Description: Trees of variable shape and height, from 5 to 60 feet tall. Trunks oppositely branched. Leaves opposite, fan-shaped, with 3 or more pointed lobes. Seeds winged and double. **Habitat:** Damp woodlands and loamy soils, frequently planted in city parks and along roadways. **Range:** Northern U.S.A. and Canada.

Food: The sap can be used as tea water or boiled down into syrup. Young seedlings can be washed and eaten raw. Older seeds can be husked and boiled till tender. Inner bark can be dried and ground into flour. **Warning:** Do not mistake maples for viburnums.

NETTLES
Urtica spp.
Nettle family
Shoots: Spring
Leaves: Summer
Roots: All year

Description: Erect, leafy herbs, 2 to 6 feet tall. Stems unbranched, square, covered with fine stinging hairs. Leaves 2 to 4 inches long, oblong to ovate, coarsely toothed, deeply veined, with stinging hairs on undersides. **Habitat:** Damp, shaded areas, stream banks, rich thickets, swamps; often found in undeveloped city parks. **Range:** Throughout U.S.A. and Canada.

Food: Young shoots and leaves can be eaten after boiling or steaming only 2 to 3 minutes to rid the plant of its toxic qualities. The leaves, either fresh or dried, make a tasty tea. Roots can be boiled to make a base for soups or stews. **Warning:** Do not gather with bare hands. The fine, hollow hairs contain formic acid, which raises stinging welts on contact with the skin. As an antidote, crush and rub on leaves from the jewelweed or another plant containing large amounts of tannic acid. **Medicine:** Tender nettle tops can be brewed as a tea for relief from rheumatism.

OAK TREES
Quercus spp.
Acorns: Fall

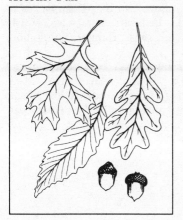

Oak trees are common in most parts of the country. Even when green, all acorns are edible and very nutritious if properly prepared. Just a handful of these tasty nuts has as much nutritional value as a pound of hamburger. Acorns from the white oak and the pin oak can be eaten raw. All others either have to be leached in running water for several hours or boiled in several changes of water to get rid of their bitter taste. Don't throw the water out, though, since it makes a powerful antiseptic for skin diseases, cuts, sore throats, and toothaches (gargle only, please).

PINE TREES
Pinus spp.
Nuts: Fall
Needles: All year

Description: The pines are tall, multi-branched trees with scaly bark and sharp evergreen needles arranged in bundles of two to five. The female cone is a large, egg-shaped structure with many scales. Under each scale are two winged seeds.

Food: You can eat several different parts of any pine tree. Chop and boil the needles into a tea that contains more vitamin C than fresh-squeezed oranges. (Dice them as finely as you can and let them steep for five minutes in boiling water.) In spring, the male pollen anthers can also be eaten and are very high in protein. And the seeds from the mature cones are as great a delight to a survivalist as to a squirrel. If you're desperate, you can even eat the tree's inner bark.

PINEAPPLE-WEED
Matricaria matricarioides
Sunflower family
Flowers: Summer to early
    fall

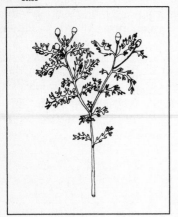

Description: Low-growing, inconspicuous herb, 4 to 8 inches tall. Stems smooth with fine ribbing. Leaves opposite, lacy. Flowers greenish-yellow, with pineapple odor when bruised. **Habitat:** Roadsides, waste places, disturbed soils. **Range:** Throughout northern U.S.A.

Food: Flowers can be steeped in hot water to make a pineapple-flavored tea. **Medicine:** A tea made from the dried leaves acts as a diuretic and antiseptic in the urinary passages.

PLANTAIN
Plantago spp.
Plantain family
Leaves: Early spring
Seeds: Summer

Description: Low-growing herbs, annual or perennial, 6 to 18 inches tall. Stems erect. Leaves in basal rosettes, 4 to 12 inches long, prominently veined, ovate, elliptic, or lanceolate. Flowers minute, greenish-white, in dense spikes on leafless stems. Fruit a small capsule with 2 or more small black seeds. **Habitat:** Waste ground and disturbed soils, including most city habitats. **Range:** Throughout U.S.A. and Canada.

Food: Young leaves can be boiled and eaten as a potherb. Seeds can be dried and ground into flour or dried, boiled, and served as a hot cereal. **Medicine:** Crushed leaves are a powerful remedy for minor wounds, stings, bruises, and sprains. Seeds are high in the B vitamins. Take 1 or 2 pods daily as an insect repellent.

ROSES
Rosa spp.
Rose family
Petals: Summer
Fruit: Late summer to early winter

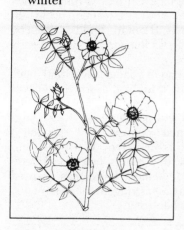

Description: Thorny shrubs, 1 to 15 feet tall. Stems prickly, often growing in clusters. Leaves variable, pinnately compound, with ovate to elliptical, finely-toothed leaflets. Flowers white, pink, or red with 5 petals. Rose hips orange-red with 5 calyx lobes at end. **Habitat:** Borders of fields and woodlands, thickets, streamsides, springs, moist soils; commonly planted in city gardens, parks, and along highways. **Range:** Throughout U.S.A. and Canada.

Food: Flower petals can be eaten right off the bush, added to salads, or steeped as a tea. The pulpy rind of the rose hips can be eaten raw. The entire hip, either fresh or dried, can be steeped to make a tea that is very rich in vitamin C. **Medicine:** Fresh petals can be moistened and used to protect minor cuts. When dry, they form a scab-like bandage.

SALAL
Gaultheria shallon
Gaultheria ovatifolia
Heath family
Berries: Fall

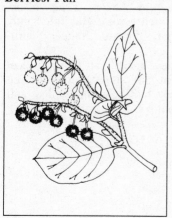

Description: Perennial shrub often forming dense, low thickets 1 to 8 feet high. Stems many-branched, strong, flexible, hairy. Leaves leathery, evergreen, round to heart-shaped, finely toothed, glossy green above, pale beneath. Flowers urn-shaped, pinkish to white, nodding in long slender clusters. Berries purple to black, thick-skinned, hairy, mealy, about ⅓ inch in diameter. (*G. ovatifolia* similar to *G. shallon* except that plants are only 2 to 6 inches high, mainly prostrate, and with red fruit.) **Habitat:** Prefers moist soils in humid areas; often found in parks and other semi-wild urban areas; sometimes used as a ground cover. **Range:** West Coast of U.S.A. and Canada.

Food: Berries can be eaten raw, boiled, or dried and pressed into cakes for storage. **Medicine:** Leaves can be chewed and used as a poultice to treat burns and sores, or brewed as a tea for diarrhea and coughs.

SASSAFRAS
Sassafras albidum
Laurel family
Leaves: Spring to summer
Roots: All year

Description: Shrub or tree, 2 to 50 feet tall. Bark reddish-brown. Stems green, often branched, sometimes hairy. Leaves 2 to 9 inches long, toothless, ovate or lobed. Flowers greenish-yellow, ¼ inch across, 6-parted calyx in long clusters. Fruits ½ inch long, dark blue, fleshy, 1-seeded, ovoid, on thick red stems. **Habitat:** Fields, thickets, edges of woodlands. **Range:** Throughout eastern U.S.A.

Food: Tender young leaves and buds can be eaten raw if nibbled sparingly. Leaves can also be dried and used for thickening soups, or dried and powdered as a seasoning. The root bark makes an excellent tea. Boil it until the water is light red. **Warning:** Contains a chemical that causes cancer in laboratory animals. **Medicine:** The tea can be used as a mouthwash and astringent for minor cuts, poison ivy, and bee stings.

SAW PALMETTO
Serenoa repens
Palm family
Fruit: Fall
Terminal bud: All year

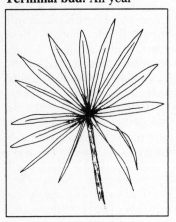

Description: Shrublike palm, 3 to 7 feet tall. Stems usually thick and low to ground. Leaf stalks long, with short sharp spines. Leaves 1 to 3 feet wide, stiff, fanlike, segmented into many pointed blades. Flowers white, in fragrant clusters. Fruits black, oblong, up to 1 inch across. **Habitat:** Sandy soils, prairies, pine forests. **Range:** Southeastern U.S.A.

Food: The "hearts" at bases of leaf stalks can be cut out and eaten raw. The bases of terminal buds can be boiled and eaten like vegetables.

SHEEP SORREL
Rumex acetosella
Buckwheat family
Leaves: Spring and summer

Description: Vigorous perennial herb, 6 to 12 inches tall. Leaves ¾ to 2 inches long, arrowhead-shaped. Flowers very small, reddish or greenish, in branching spikelets on upper half of stems. Fruits seedlike, shiny, golden brown. Rootstocks slender reddish runners. **Habitat:** Open sites and waste places. **Range:** Throughout U.S.A. and Canada.

Food: Leaves can be eaten sparingly in salads, boiled as potherbs, or steeped as a tea that is rich in vitamin C. **Medicine:** Taken as a tea, the leaves can help to stop internal bleeding and soothe sore throats. Crushed and applied as a poultice, they can help to cure skin diseases and slow external bleeding from minor wounds. **Warning:** May cause stomach cramps if eaten in large quantities.

SPICEBUSH
Lindera benzoin
Laurel family
Leaves: Spring to summer
Berries: Late summer to early fall
Twigs and bark: All year

Description: Shrub, 5 to 15 feet tall. Stems slender, brittle, spicy-scented. Bark smooth. Leaves 2 to 6 inches long, dark green, oblong, toothless, aromatic, with prominent veins on lower surfaces. Flowers very small, yellowish, clustered, appearing before leaves in spring. Berries reddish, oval, ¼ to ⅜ inch in diameter, aromatic, oily, with one large seed. **Habitat:** Damp woods, streamsides, swamps; also found occasionally in shadows of buildings, near housing or industrial developments. **Range:** Eastern U.S.A. and Canada.

Food: Young leaves, twigs, and bark can be steeped in hot water to make an especially healthful winter tea. Berries can be dried and powdered as a general seasoning. **Warning:** Do not eat berries whole. Use only as a seasoning.

SPRUCE TREES
Picea spp.
Pine family
Inner bark: Spring
Young shoots: Spring
Needles: All year

Description: Thick-crowned, steeple-shaped evergreen trees with drooping branches, 50 to 90 feet tall. Bark silvery-gray or brownish, with long deciduous scales. Needles 1 inch long, evergreen, 4-sided, sharp-pointed, stiff, borne in spirals around twigs. Woody bases remain on twigs after needles are removed. Seed cones about 2½ inches long, cylindrical, brown, drooping, woody, with pale brown papery scales. **Habitat:** Well-drained uplands to boggy soils in cool to cold areas. **Range:** Throughout most of U.S.A. and Canada.

Food: Inner bark can be peeled, dried, and ground into flour. Young shoots can be boiled and eaten as vegetables. Green needles can be boiled into a tea that is rich in vitamin C. **Medicine:** Crushed needles can be applied as a poultice for skin rashes. The tea can be used as a mouthwash to treat sores.

SUMAC
Rhus spp.
Cashew family
Berries: Summer

Description: Small shrub to small tree, 3 to 30 feet tall. Stems upright, mostly branched above. Staghorn sumac, *(Rhus typhina)* has velvety branches. Leaves 2 to 4 inches long, feather-like, compound, with many pairs of finely toothed leaflets. Dwarf Sumac *(Rhus copallina)* has winged leaf stalks and toothless leaves. Flowers small, greenish, in dense terminal clusters up to 6 inches long. Fruits red, small, hairy, clustered to form a conelike structure. **Habitat:** Poor soils, old fields, dry hillsides. **Range:** Throughout U.S.A. and Canada.

Food: Berries can be bruised and soaked in cold water to make an acid-tasting but refreshing drink. They can also be dried and stored. **Warning:** Poison sumac *(Rhus vernix)* causes severe dermatitis on contact. It has white berries and toothless leaves and is found mostly in swamps and bogs. **Medicine:** A strong, hot tea from the fresh or dried red berries makes an effective gargle for sore throats.

SWEETFERN
Comtonia peregrina
Bayberry family
Leaves: Late spring to early fall
Nutlets: Summer to fall

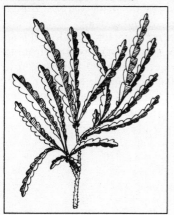

Description: A woody, many-branched shrub. Stems slender, grayish, 1 to 5 feet high, usually with hairy twigs, aromatic when crushed. Leaves fernlike, gray-green, 3 to 6 inches long. Fruits green, burr-like, round, bristly, up to 1 inch long; contain hard, glossy, olive-brown nutlets, ⅛ to ¼ inch long. **Habitat:** Sterile pasture lands, sandy soils, open woodlands. **Range:** Throughout most of eastern U.S.A. and Canada.

Food: Leaves can be steeped as a tea. Nutlets can be eaten raw. **Medicine:** Crushed leaves can be applied externally as a poison ivy remedy and insect repellent. Tea from leaves and twigs is an effective treatment for diarrhea.

THISTLE
Cirsium spp.
Sunflower family
Leaves: Spring to early summer
Stalks: Summer (before bloom)
Roots: Spring to fall

Description: Biennial herbs, 1 to 6 feet tall. Stems straight, branches or unbranched, with or without spines. Leaves 5 to 10 inches long, alternate, spiny, lanceolate, with wavy edges. Flower heads 1 to 1½ inches wide, single or many per plant, with white to purple disk flowers. Taproots fleshy or stringy, on horizontal rootstocks. **Habitat:** Meadows, pastures, waste soils. **Range:** Throughout U.S.A. and Canada.

Food: Young leaves and stems can be eaten raw or boiled after the spines are removed. Older stems and roots can be peeled and boiled as vegetables. If the stalks are too stringy, chew them and spit out the fiber.

VIOLETS
Viola spp.
Violet family
Leaves: Spring
Flowers: Spring to early
  summer.

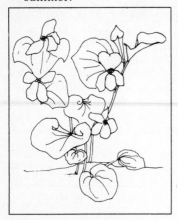

Description: Dainty, low-growing herbs, 3 to 10 inches tall. Stems thin. Leaves 1 to 4 inches long, ovate, with heart-shaped bases. Flowers blue, violet, yellow, or white, 5-petaled; lowest petal thickly veined, others usually bearded. **Habitat:** Wet meadows, damp woodlands, semi-shaded areas. **Range:** Throughout U.S.A. and Canada.

Food: Most species edible, though some yellow species may act as a mild purgative. Young tender leaves and flowers can be eaten raw, added to soups or stews, or dried and steeped as a tea. **Medicine:** Leaves and flowers are both very rich in vitamin C.

WATERCRESS
Nasturtium officinale
Mustard family
Young leaves: All year
Stems: All year

Description: Creeping perennial herb, 4 to 10 inches tall. Stems fleshy, smooth, sometimes form dense mats in water or mud. Leaves pinnately compound, with 3 to 9 oval leaflets, the terminal leaflet the largest. Flowers very small, white, borne in elongate clusters. Seed pods ½ to 1 inch long, slightly upcurving. **Habitat:** Streams, springs. **Range:** Throughout U.S.A. and Canada.

Food: Raw leaves and stems are excellent in salads. **Warning:** When gathering, make certain the water in which the plant grows is not polluted. **Medicine:** Very high in vitamins A and C, watercress is an effective remedy for scurvy.

WILD ONIONS
Allium spp.
Lily family
Leaves: Spring
Bulblets: Summer
Bulbs: All year

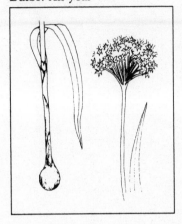

Description: Erect-growing herbs, 6 to 24 inches tall. Leaves 4 to 18 inches long, slender, quill-like, tubular or nearly flat. Flowers in umbels at ends of stems, with 3 petals and 3 petal-like sepals. Bulbs oblong, up to ½ inch in diameter, often in clusters, with onion odor. **Habitat:** Fields, open slopes, rocky soils. **Range:** Throughout U.S.A. and southern Canada.

Food: Bulbs and leaves can be eaten raw or boiled. Bulbs can also be used as a seasoning. **Medicine:** Juice from the bulbs serves as an antiseptic.

APPENDIX B:
COMMON URBAN ANIMALS

Many people are under the mistaken impression that there are hardly any animals to be found in the city besides rats, mice, cats, and dogs. I want to dispel that notion. The following is a partial list of some of the more common mammals that can be found either in or on the outskirts of many major cities. I include these here not so much for survival purposes as for a brief introduction to some of the many fascinating wild denizens that share the shadows and fringes of civilization with us.

For more information on these and other animals, I recommend a trip to your local bookstore or library. The appearances and wildnerness life-styles of most of the mammals discussed below are described in *Tom Brown's Field Guide to Nature Observation and Tracking*.

Bats

Though bats are typically country animals, they can also be found in cities. There, they hole up under eaves and in attics of buildings during the day and come out on warm nights to sweep the skies for insects. They should not be feared, since they are usually harmless and do a lot of good by keeping insects in check. You can often see them around street lights, where moths and other insects gather in their winged frenzy. I remember once seeing several bats hovering around the lights at the entrance to the Lincoln Tunnel in New York. It was especially reassuring to see these little wilderness representatives in an area of unrelieved traffic and concrete.

Black Bear *(Ursus americanus)*

Rear

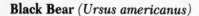

Front

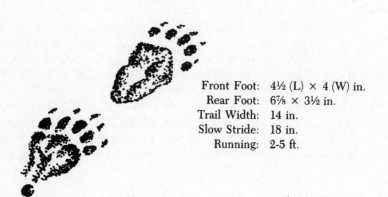

Front Foot:	4½ (L) × 4 (W) in.
Rear Foot:	6⅞ × 3½ in.
Trail Width:	14 in.
Slow Stride:	18 in.
Running:	2-5 ft.

Bears

The members of the bruin family don't like well-populated places, but you're likely to see them or their leavings on the outskirts of some cities—notably those in wilder areas of the country such as Alaska. Having omnivorous appetites, especially just after they come out of hibernation, they are often attracted to the delicacies offered in garbage dumps.

Coyote *(Canis latrans)*

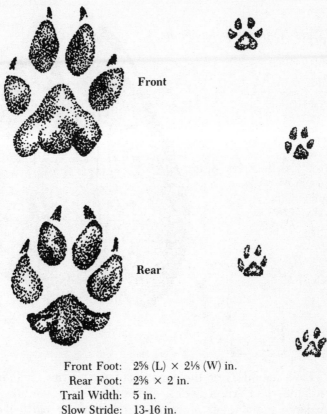

Front

Rear

Front Foot:	2⅝ (L) × 2⅛ (W) in.
Rear Foot:	2⅜ × 2 in.
Trail Width:	5 in.
Slow Stride:	13-16 in.
Running:	16-50 in.

Coyotes

Though often persecuted, the coyote has been amazingly successful at adapting to human societies. In some areas it seems to have expanded its range and slips in and out of many cities with as much stealth and dispatch as it does in wilder country. City residents should appreciate the coyote as an effective and natural check on rodent populations.

Mule Deer *(Odocoileus hemionus)*

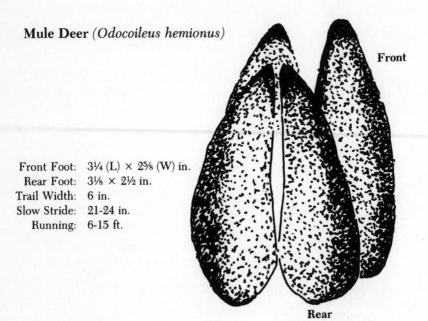

Front

Front Foot: 3¼ (L) × 2⅝ (W) in.
Rear Foot: 3⅛ × 2½ in.
Trail Width: 6 in.
Slow Stride: 21-24 in.
Running: 6-15 ft.

Rear

Deer

I have seen deer on the outskirts of many cities, including Philadelphia, Atlanta, and Minneapolis. Sometimes they venture surprisingly close to large populations of people, and they are particularly adept at hiding along highways—sometimes right on the median strip. Crafty and extremely good at camouflage, they habitually sleep during the day and come out in the evening to feed, just as human activity begins to slow down. Look for them at the fringes of forests and fields. When driving along a highway, try to get your vision to penetrate the edge of the woods. If you spot a deer from a car, you can often use the vehicle as a blind from which to view it at closer range.

Red Fox *(Vulpes fulva)*

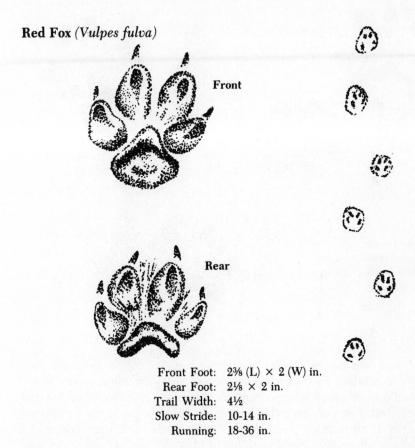

Front

Rear

Front Foot:	2⅜ (L) × 2 (W) in.
Rear Foot:	2⅛ × 2 in.
Trail Width:	4½
Slow Stride:	10-14 in.
Running:	18-36 in.

Foxes

Generally, the gray fox prefers seclusion and brushy areas. But the red fox can often be found in recently developed areas. Suburbs that are still surrounded by woods are likely possibilities. Foxes are sometimes spotted in city parks, too, where they can appear quite tame.

White-footed Mouse *(Peromyscus spp.)*

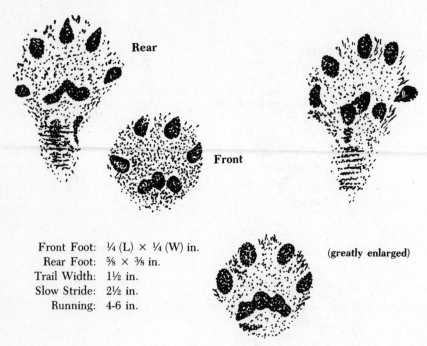

Rear

Front

(greatly enlarged)

Front Foot: ¼ (L) × ¼ (W) in.
Rear Foot: ⅝ × ⅜ in.
Trail Width: 1½ in.
Slow Stride: 2½ in.
Running: 4-6 in.

Mice

There are lots of species of mice in the city. Aside from the common house mouse, I've seen harvest mice, jumping mice, white-footed mice, and several other species. Superficially, most mice look pretty much the same, but if you observe them carefully you'll begin to see interesting differences in appearance and activity that distinguish each species. If you're really observant, you'll even begin to notice the personality characteristics that set one individual apart from another.

Moles

Moles are familiar tenants in outlying residential areas, suburbs, parks, and golf courses. They eat insects, worms, and other tiny life, and they can cause minor eruptions of dirt on even the best of manicured lawns. This can be frustrating to the homeowner who takes pride in a well-manicured lawn. On the other hand, you can learn a lot from moles and their mounds. In the fall, for example, their diggings often forecast cold weather.

Moose (*Alces alces*)

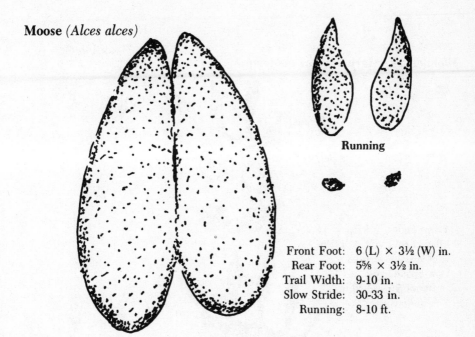

Running

Front Foot: 6 (L) × 3½ (W) in.
Rear Foot: 5⅝ × 3½ in.
Trail Width: 9-10 in.
Slow Stride: 30-33 in.
Running: 8-10 ft.

Moose

These unusually large and ungainly members of the deer family have been known to walk right down the streets of Bangor, Maine and Fairbanks, Alaska. But outside of the relatively wild lands of the far north, an urban siting of this animal would be highly unusual.

Shrews

Shrews are tiny, mice-like carnivores that live in most meadow areas, whether city, suburb, or wilderness. In urban areas, they eat primarily garbage and the wide variety of insects that feed on it. They also eat mice babies.

Woodchuck, Marmot *(Marmota spp.)*

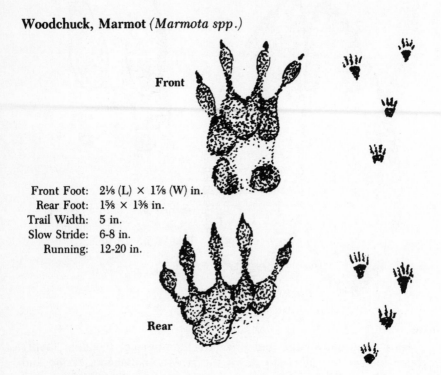

Front

Front Foot: 2⅛ (L) × 1⅞ (W) in.
Rear Foot: 1⅝ × 1⅜ in.
Trail Width: 5 in.
Slow Stride: 6-8 in.
Running: 12-20 in.

Rear

Woodchucks

Often called groundhogs, these animals can be found on the outskirts of many cities—usually near disturbed grounds and farmlands
where there aren't too many dogs or people. Some city parks are also well
known for their collections of woodchucks. I've even seen a few of their
dens in New York's Central Park. Since the park is virtually inacessible to
the outside (unless they've been brought in by automobile), it is likely
they have been there for generations—possibly since before the Declaration of Independence!

Blacktail Jackrabbit *(Lepus californicus)*

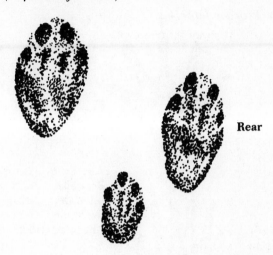

Rear

Front

Front Foot:	1½ (L) × 1⅛ (W) in.
Rear Foot:	2⅝ × 2 in.
Trail Width:	7½ in.
Slow Stride:	9-12 in.
Running:	5-12 ft. (max. 15 ft.)

Rabbits

Many kinds of rabbits can be found in city environs if you look in the right places. The most common are the cottontails, which like thick brush or rocky cover in heavily wooded parks, spacious gardens, and along the fringes of roadways. Jackrabbits seem to enjoy the median strips of grass right alongside airport runways. Where rabbits reach great numbers, keep your eyes open for predators. You're almost sure to see hawks, owls, coyotes, and sometimes even foxes.

Raccoon *(Procyon lotor)*

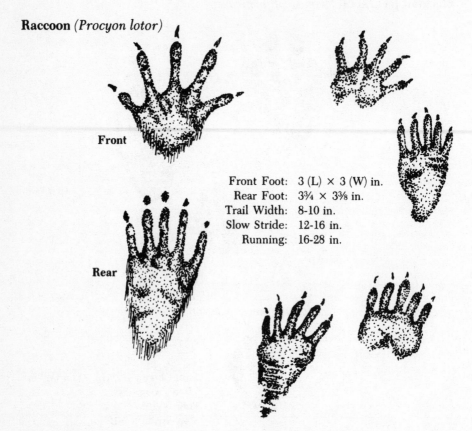

Front

Rear

Front Foot:	3 (L) × 3 (W) in.
Rear Foot:	3¾ × 3⅜ in.
Trail Width:	8-10 in.
Slow Stride:	12-16 in.
Running:	16-28 in.

Raccoons

These masked bandits are prolific in almost every city across the country, with the exception of hot, arid places. They are as sly as weasels and feed quietly on the castoffs of civilization. People usually think of raccoons as being rather clumsy and lumbering, but they are quite fast and very good at escaping detection. Following streams and other waterways, they work their way right into the heart of major cities. There they hole up under buildings and in bushes and trees and eat anything from garbage to crayfish.

Norway Rat *(Rattus norvegicus)*

Walking gait

Front

Rear

Front Foot:	⅝ (L) × ¾ (W) in.
Rear Foot:	⅞ × ⅞ in.
Trail Width:	3⅛ in.
Slow Stride:	2½-5 in.
Running:	5-8 in.

Rats

Aside from the Norway rat, the ubiquitous and little-loved rodent of sewers, garbage dumps, and abandoned buildings, you may also spot the gentler bushy-tailed woodrat (or packrat) and the eastern woodrat in some cities. Muskrats can also be found in many waterway environments within cities and suburbs. Almost any sizable and semi-secluded body of water where cattails and pond lilies grow is a likely place to look for them.

Spotted Skunk *(Spilogale putorius)*

Front Foot: ⅞ (L) × 1 (W) in.
Rear Foot: 1⅛ × 1¼ in.
Trail Width: 6 in.
Slow Stride: 4-6 in.
Running: 8-12 in.

Skunks

Skunks are also scavengers that enjoy human garbage, but their success is more limited than that of the raccoon. This is just as well, as it's not usually a good idea to seek them out. If your dog comes back from a woodsy foray smelling like a skunk, though, don't be surprised. And beware when driving down the highway during the evening hours, as skunks can't run very fast.

Gray Squirrel (*Sciurus carolinensis*)

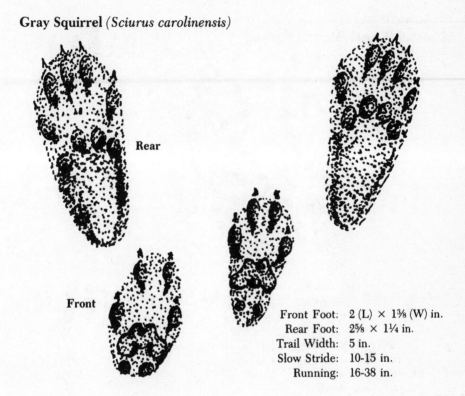

Rear

Front

Front Foot:	2 (L) × 1⅜ (W) in.
Rear Foot:	2⅝ × 1¼ in.
Trail Width:	5 in.
Slow Stride:	10-15 in.
Running:	16-38 in.

Squirrels

There are many species of squirrels and chipmunks in urban areas. Most of them live off nuts and fruits and the castoffs of civilization. The eastern gray squirrel is beautifully adapted to most urban parks and suburbs, where it can be seen bounding across lawns, scuttling up tree trunks, and wandering leafy skyways. The red squirrel, too, is a fairly common resident of city parks. This fiery ball of fur is unmistakable with its high-pitched, scolding chatter and boundless energy.

Red and gray squirrels can be found in some of the most congested parts of the city, as long as they have plenty of upper treework for movement and protection. Ground squirrels tend to be less accepting of human society but can often be found on the fringes of some cities. Likewise are the chipmunks, which tend to prefer rural fenceposts, brushpiles, and burrows.

Longtail Weasel *(Mustela frenata)*

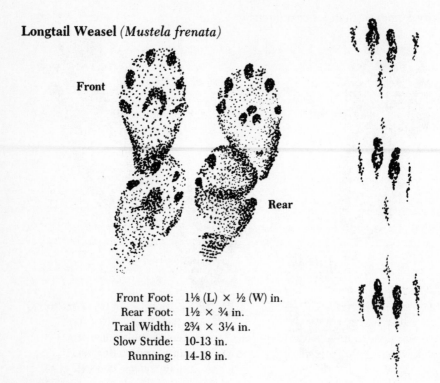

Front

Rear

Front Foot:	1⅛ (L) × ½ (W) in.
Rear Foot:	1½ × ¾ in.
Trail Width:	2¾ × 3¼ in.
Slow Stride:	10-13 in.
Running:	14-18 in.

Weasels

These sleek little bolts of lightning are the most vicious and deadly predators in the wilderness. Though few people are aware of it, they have also brought their teeth and claws into the city, where they seem to have adjusted very well. I have seen weasels in well-populated areas of New York, Chicago, and other cities—most often carrying mice or other luckless creatures in their mouths. In Seattle I spotted one out in front of a movie theater, waiting in the shadow of the curb for the crowd to go in so it could move back to its den in the sewer. Though vicious, weasels are as important as street sweepers, since they help control the populations of mice and rats.

APPENDIX C:
SURVIVAL SUPPLIES

Home Survival

Radio (battery-powered)
Flashlights (with spare batteries)
Lanterns (with extra fuel)
Knife
Candles (long-burning type)
Cigarette lighter or matches
Steel wool (00, for tinder)
Water supplies
   Commercial water filter
   Deflatable gallon jugs
   Extra treated water
   Coffee filters or gauze pads
   Clorox or purification tablets
   Eyedropper
   Solar-still equipment
      Clear plastic sheeting
      Surgical tubing (six feet)
      Container for drinking
Food and cooking supplies
   Extra food
   Can opener
   Camp stove (with extra fuel)
   Sterno
   Cooking utensils
   Aluminum foil
   Eating utensils
   Multiple vitamins
Medicines
First-aid kit and instructions

Extra clothing
Extra blankets
Bedding materials
Fire-fighting equipment
Writing materials
Shovel
Broom
Axe
Crowbar
Rubber hose (for siphoning, etc.)
Half-inch rope (minimum 25 feet)
Toolbox items
   Wire
   Hammer
   Pliers
   Screwdriver
   Adjustable wrench
   Nails, screws, and tacks
   Strong nylon cord (fifty feet)
Toilet items
   Emergency toilet (watertight
   container with snug cover)
   Toilet paper
   Disinfectant
   Plastic garbage bags
   Toothbrushes and toothpaste

Car Survival Kit

Survival guide
Citizens Band (CB) radio with
Channel 9
Durable plastic tool box
  Knife
  Cigarette lighter or matches
  Compass
  Flashlight (with extra batteries)
  Flares (half dozen)
  Electrical tape
  Electrical wiring
  Adjustable wrench
  Screwdriver
  Hammer
Water needs
  Commercial water filter
  Gallon container
  Solar-still apparatus
  Coffee filters
  Water purifiers
First-aid kit

Sterno
Plastic garbage bags
Space blanket
Extra clothes
  Wool hat
  Wool socks
  Wool sweater
  Poncho
  Waterproof boots
Canned food
Can opener
Spoon
Steel container
Towel (for windshield)
Windshield scraper
Jack
Spare tire
Chains

Carry Anywhere Kit

The following survival items can be packed in a duffel bag and taken anywhere on short notice:

Survival guide
Pocketknife
Cigarette lighter or matches
Strong nylon cord (fifty feet)
Commercial water filter
Coffee filters
Solar-still items
  Clear plastic sheeting

Surgical tubing (six feet)
  Drinking container
Monofilament fishline (fifty feet)
Fish hooks
Plastic garbage bag
Wool sweater or sleeping bag
First-aid kit and instructions

INDEX

As you know from reading this book, sharing the wilderness with Tom Brown, Jr., is a unique experience. His books and his world-famous survival school have brought a new vision to thousands. If you would like to go farther and discover more, please write for more information to:

The Tracker

Tom Brown, Tracker, Inc.
P.O. Box 927
Waretown, N.J. 08758
(609) 242-0350
www.trackerschool.com

**Tracking, Nature, Wilderness
Survival School
City Survival Classes**

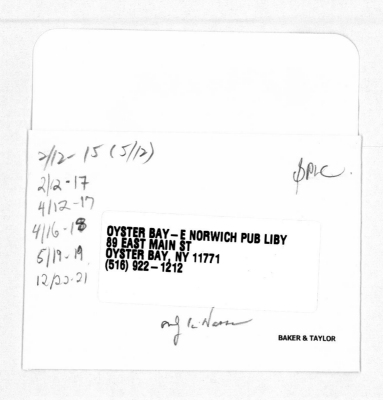

MAY 0 1 2012